Swords in Col

Including other Edged Weapons

ROBERT WILKINSON-LATHAM
Special photography by John Searle Austin
Colour drawings by Peter Sarson and Tony Bryan

BLANDFORD PRESS
Poole   ·   Dorset

First published in 1977
by Blandford Press Ltd,
Link House, West Street, Poole,
Dorset BH15 1LL

Copyright © Blandford Press 1977

ISBN 0 7137 0818 2

All rights reserved. No part of this book may be reproduced or transmitted in any form or by any means, electronic or mechanical, including photocopying, recording or by any information storage and retrieval system, without permission in writing from the Publisher.

For Edward

Typeset in 11 on 12 point Bembo by
Woolaston Parker Ltd, Leicester, England
Printed by Fletcher & Son Ltd, Norwich
Bound by Richard Clay (Chaucer Press) Ltd
Bungay, Suffolk

SWORDS IN COLOUR
Including other Edged Weapons

By the same author

Infantry Uniforms, Including Artillery and Other Supporting Troops of Britain and the Commonwealth, 1742–1855
(with Christopher Wilkinson-Latham)

Infantry Uniforms, Book 2, Including Artillery and Other Supporting Corps, of Britain and the Commonwealth, 1855–1939
(with Christopher Wilkinson-Latham)

Cavalry Uniforms of Britain and the Commonwealth,
Including Other Mounted Troops
(with Christopher Wilkinson-Latham)

Contents

Acknowledgements	7
1 Introduction and Early History	9
2 The Military Sword	25
i) Britain	26
ii) France, Belgium and Netherlands	33
iii) Prussia, Germany and Austria	39
iv) Russia and Asia	44
v) Siam, China and Japan	49
vi) India	53
vii) Denmark, Sweden and Norway	54
viii) United States and South America	65
3 Scottish Weapons	72
4 Staff Weapons and Lances	83
5 Dirks, Knives and Daggers	89
6 Bayonets	99
7 Native Weapons	128
The Plates	145
Plate Descriptions	209
Edged Weapon Collections	223
Index	225

Acknowledgements

I would like to thank the following whose helpfulness and kindness with illustrations or information greatly aided me in the writing of this book. Firstly thanks to Michael Collins and Dennis Lipscombe of Wilkinson Sword Ltd, who gave myself and John Searle Austin unlimited access to the numerous swords and patterns in their care and allowed us to disrupt the museum and pattern room for the photographic sessions. John Searle Austin deserves special thanks for his superb and artistic photography of many of the plates and Peter Sarson and Tony Bryan also deserve praise for their superb drawings of a number of the plates in colour and black and white. Other collectors and friends kindly disrupted their own collections to supply either weapons or actual plates and I would like to thank especially Peter White and Herman Mauerer for their help and encouragement.

Valuable information and assistance in supplying plates was given by Christopher Wilkinson-Latham; Robert W Fisch, Curator, West Point Museum; W. A. Thorburn, Keeper, Scottish United Services Museum; Dr. Hanns-Ulrich Haedeke, Deutches Klingenmuseum, Solingen; and W. Hofrat, Heeresgeschichtliches Museum, Vienna. I would also like to thank Lynda Jackson who patiently typed and re-typed the drafts and final manuscript.

Lastly, I must thank my father whose deep knowledge and experience of edged weapons of the world was always unstintingly at my disposal whenever called upon.

Robert Wilkinson-Latham
Brighton, 1977

Illustration credits

The author and publishers would like to thank the following for supplying illustrations:
Wilkinson Sword Ltd, London; Wilkinson-Latham Collection; Peter White; Herman Mauerer; John Oliver; National Maritime Museum, Greenwich; Scottish United Services Museum, Edinburgh; Deutches Klingenmuseum, Solingen; J. A. L. Franks Ltd, Brighton; West Point Museum, New York and Jack Blake;

Details for drawing the colour plates were supplied by the following:
Musée de l'Armée, Paris; Musée Royale de l'Armée et d'Histoire Militaire, Brussels; Musée de l'Emperi, Salon-de-Provence; The Wallace Collection, London; HM Tower of London Armouries, London; National Maritime Museum, Greenwich; Wilkinson Sword Ltd, London; Tøjhusmuseet, Copenhagen; Kungl. Armemuseum, Stockholm; and The Mollo Collection.

1 Introduction and Early History

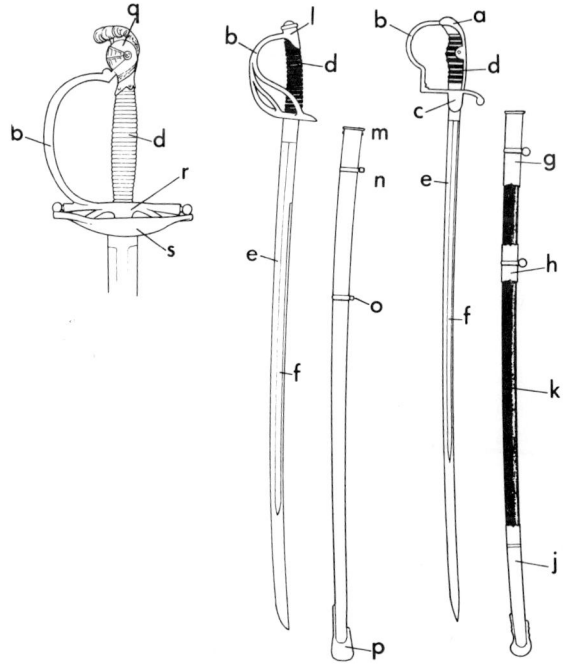

Fig. 1. Parts of a Sword. a) pommel and backpiece with ears. b) guard. c) langet. d) grip. e) cutting edge. f) fuller. g) top mount or locket. h) middle mount. j) chape. k) scabbard body. l) cap pommel. m) mouthpiece. n) top band. o) middle band. p) shoe. q) pommel. r) quillons with *pas d'âne* rings. s) Sheel guard.

The sword was probably the last edged weapon invented by man, except for the bayonet – an adaption of the knife or dagger which appeared in the middle of the seventeenth century. The reason for this lateness was that there was no suitable substance available from which to fashion a blade of reasonable proportions and strength. There had been attempts to produce a workable weapon from hard wood which was in appearance more like a club with a sharpened edge, or a club with pieces of horn or stone set and bound in.

The Stone Age produced the first really effective edged weapons used by man in the form of knives, both domestic and for hunting and fighting, hatchets, arrow heads and spear heads. The prevalent stone used was flint, although in areas devoid of deposits of this stone, basalt, obsidian, granite and other stones were used. Fine grained rock was the most suitable for working, as it tended to break when struck in a more or less dependable way.

The oldest known humanly made stone blades and points come from the Pleistocene period of geology which began nearly two million years ago and ended around 10,000 years ago. The implements were fashioned with stone strikers such as hard pebbles, and the finer work of flaking carried out with a wood or bone hammer.

The Neolithic or new Stone Age period saw many refinements in the flint blades, axe and arrow heads. They were now more skilfully worked and polished all over by hand work and in some cases decorated and bored with holes to receive the wood shaft. Figs 2, 3 and 4 show a number of flint weapons of this period.

Bones and antlers were also fashioned into primitive weapons, such as daggers and spearheads.

Bronze Age

It was not until the discovery of copper and altering it by its amalgamation with tin to form bronze that effective edged weapons were feasible. The discovery of metal, however, did not change weapons with any speed and flint weapons continued in use side by side with metal weapons during the Bronze Age The mining of copper was probably first carried out in Anatolia around 3700 BC and the Egyptians had copper mines about the same time. The knowledge and skill in working this metal slowly spread to Europe and probably reaching Britain in about 1900 BC.

Copper itself is a soft metal and when fashioned into a blade form would have to be frequently sharpened. Early copper bladed knives were cast in one piece and then hand finished and fitted with either a wood or bone grip riveted to the tang. In order to obtain a suitable cutting edge the cast blade was hammered with stones to thin the metal and then worked by hand with an abrasive material, probably sandstone. With improved casting methods that came with greater knowledge and experience of the metal, lighter blades were made but the need for strength meant that a central rib or bar had to be incorporated in the design. Copper swords were undoubtedly manufactured but the majority of weapons were knives of various types.

However, the use of copper was purely transitory and the discovery of smelting methods for various metals and their subsequent amalgamation produced harder and better substances more suited to a cutting edge. It was discovered that copper could be hardened by adding a small amount of another metal. In most parts this 'other metal' was tin, an easy substance to smelt but in parts of the world where this was not available, pure copper continued in use. Where neither was available it appears that zinc was added. While copper and tin produced a copper coloured metal called bronze the latter mixture produced a yellow mixture called brass.

The true Bronze Age, as opposed to the short period when copper prevailed saw swords of this amalgamation prevalent in the large armies of the Middle East where the great early civilisations existed. Arrow heads in many parts still continued to be made in stone, as being an expendable weapon the arrow did

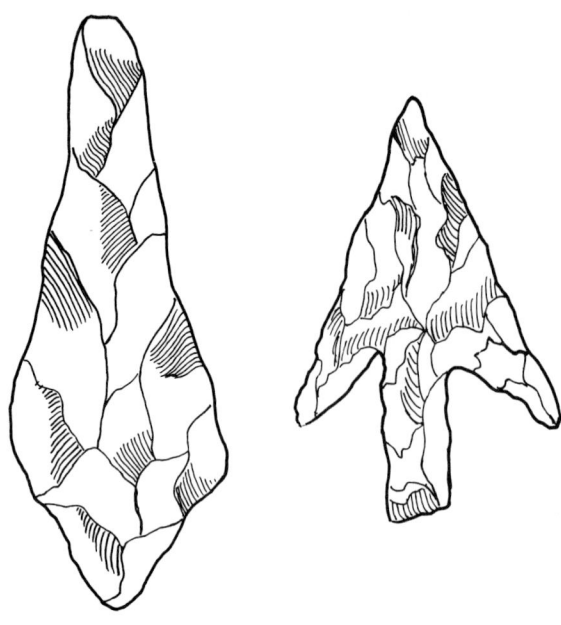

Fig. 2. Flint implements. Left to right; early stone dagger; barbed arrowhead.

not warrant the use of bronze heads. Bronze was however used for axe heads and for the heads of spears not intended to be thrown such as the thrusting spear carried by the hoplites.

Early Egyptian swords in bronze had a straight tapered blade and were meant solely for thrusting, and in appearance with their grips riveted to the tang looked like oversized daggers. Around 2500 BC the first cutting sword appeared with a sickle shaped blade. Known as the *khopesh,* it had the grip riveted to the broad tang and a formidable power because of the shape and the edge. The superiority of the Egyptian methods of casting gave the swordmaker an outlet for his artistic skills. A model of the intended weapon was made in beeswax and then covered with

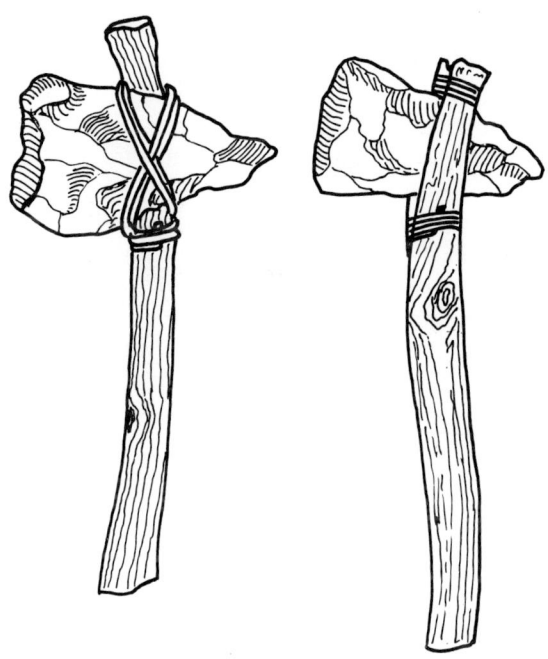

Fig. 3. Two axes showing different types of mounting.

clay, leaving a pouring hole at one end. The mould with model inside was then placed in the sun and the beeswax soon melted and ran out as the clay hardened leaving a mould ready to receive the molten metal. Once this had been poured and left to harden and cool, the clay was knocked off leaving the metal sword. Because of the brittleness that accrued in this method, the blade had to be annealed. Another method eliminating the brittleness but not allowing for decoration was to make the blade from a heated ingot. Scabbards were either made in wood covered in leather or in bronze or brass which by casting could be decorated in an appropriate manner. Axes and spear heads were also cast in bronze in moulds, leaving a hole in the former and a socket in the latter in which to fit the wooden shaft.

The Assyrian army were well supplied with swords and these were carried in a scabbard fitted to the belt so the weapon was worn horizontally. The blade was short measuring some 20 inches or so and was probably double edged with a thick diamond shaped cross section for strength. The grip was round resembling a modern file or screwdriver handle and ornately turned before being fitted to the tang. Assyrian swords were most decorative and usually incorporated some form of decorative cross piece below the grip with the same style being fitted as a chape or ferrule to the scabbard. In some of the more decorative weapons, gold was used for the decorative parts.

Fig. 4. Flint headed lance.

The early Greek sword had a straight blade some 36 inches in length and was made purely for thrusting. The blade, cross guard and tang were made in one piece with a thick central rib to give added strength. Later the sword became leaf shaped, a typical style associated with the Bronze age copied later in other parts of the world. The leaf shape gave the added strength and weight of metal required without resorting to a thick blade. Some of the later Greek swords used mainly by the hoplite were cruciform in shape with the blade broadening slightly at the tip. Others used the slightly inward curving blade reminiscent of the later Gurkha kukri called a *kopis*. This weapon had a single edged blade and the tang as an integral part of it. The *kopis* dated from about 700 BC while the cruciform sword first appeared about 1500 BC.

Iron Age

The discovery of iron and its infinite capabilities heralded the dawning of a new age in the history of man. Described by Pliny as the king of metals 'that breaketh in pieces and subduetn all things', ironworkings were first opened and the metal smelted in Asia Minor as early as 3000 BC. The Hittites were the first to make weapons of this metal in any quantity and the superiority of their swords must be judged by the vast conquests of territory they made but not until some 1500 years after the discovery of the metal.

Although iron had been known for many years before its use as a metal for blades, this gap was due to the lack of skill on the part of artisans who found it difficult to work with. In about 1400 BC it was discovered, probably by accident that if iron and carbon was heated together and then hammered into shape and quickly cooled in water, the subsequent blade produced was harder and more durable than bronze. This secret was, however, closely guarded by the Hittites and it was not until their empire was attacked and broken up that the 'secret' of wrought iron became widely known in the Middle East.

However, the armies of the Middle East appear to have relied mostly on the spear rather than the sword as their main weapon, the sword being the weapon used for close combat once the spears had been thrown at the enemy.

The Roman sword was like others, firstly leaf shaped but developed later into the *gladius,* a short double edged bladed sword which was carried by the famed legions. This style of sword appears to have been adopted in about 216 BC when the Romans invaded the Spanish Peninsula. In 192 BC they captured Toletum or as we know it Toledo, later famed for the quality of its sword blades. The legions were also armed with the *pilum,* a throwing spear with a soft iron head with a long socket fitted to a wooden shaft. Prior to the battle of Cannae (216 BC) a mixture of bronze and iron weapons were used, but after the battle, the iron sword prevailed.

Long after the blade was made of steel, the hilt of the *gladius* was still made in bronze with wood grips with metal rivets, probably in copper. The swords of high ranking officers, however, had bone and ivory grips, silver and gold hilts and scabbards decorated with raised patriotic scenes (plate 5 shows the sword and decorative scabbard).

The sword up until now had been a short bladed weapon intended only for close combat and it was not until the Romans faced the Gauls that they learned the full use of cavalry. The Gauls had mounted men with long double edged swords with simple wood or horn grips and it was only during the third century AD that they began to inflict defeats on the Romans and start the break up of their once vast empire. The barbarous hordes that descended on the Romans brought with them the style of the long sword soon to become universal.

The Saxons, Vikings and Normans

The Saxon sword was of simple design having a cross hilt, a straight grip and a round pommel. The grips were usually of wood or horn and slotted on to the tapering tang. The blade was double edged and used for both cutting and thrusting with a wide central fuller. The blades were manufactured with amazing metalworking skill, involving the complex method of twisting together strips of iron, heating and hammering and repeating the process until the blade had been forged. The hard cutting edges were hammer welded to the blade, and the complete blade polished. The twisting and hammering of the iron gave the blade a pattern on the surface of a series of lines running the length of the blade. Some blades were however made in a mould, hand finished, tempered and polished. The scabbards were usually in wood covered in leather with an iron chape and mouthpiece. On occasions, sheepskin with the wool innermost was used as a lining to the scabbard, the natural oils preventing rusting of the blade.

The Saxons also carried a smaller dagger like weapon named a *seax* or *scramasax* which had no fixed blade length. The single edged blade was often engraved. This was perhaps the last edged weapon of the knife or dagger style to be used offensively until the twelfth or thirteenth century when it was once again revived for the fighting man. In the inbetween years it was purely a personal, hunting or domestic implement.

The Viking's sword was similar to those of the Saxons, but they were heavier, and stronger than those of their opponents. The blade, manufactured by the method of twisting together strips of iron and hammering them under heat until the desired shape was attained, were double edged and tapered to a point, which made the blade less heavy at the point giving freer movement. The blades were fitted with bronze or iron crossguards which were either straight or downpointing towards the tip of the blade and distinctively 'Brazil' nut shaped or semi circular pommels. There were however many variations in pommel design. The Vikings like the Saxons still continued to be great users of the spear and the axe.

When the Normans under William invaded Britain in 1066 their sword differed little from those of the Vikings and the Anglo Saxons. It had a longish blade, double edged with a tapering point with wide central fuller to reduce weight but add strength, plain simple cross guard and largish pommel. The pommels were of varied designs but the 'Brazil' nut shape appears to have been a popular design. The scabbard was usually two pieces of wood, suitably hollowed out on the inside to conform to the shape of the blade and then covered in leather with the addition of a metal mouthpiece and chape, the former to cut down wear when drawing and returning the sword and the latter to protect the end of the scabbard where the point came.

Swords changed little in the twelfth and thirteenth centuries, still retaining the basic simple cross hilt features (plate 6), but there was a slow evolution in design, necessitated by the evolution in armour. Armour had evolved from the chain mail, *cuir boulli* (boiled leather), and leather jerkins with studs, rings and other metal protection sewn on to plate armour during the fourteenth century. While armour evolved to produce the absolute in protection against arrows and swords, the sword evolved to combat the new armour.

Sword Versus Armour

The swordsmiths devised various solutions to the problem. One answer was to produce the falchion, a wide bladed weapon with a short single edged blade widening at the point, while others produced longer thinner bladed swords with stiff unyielding blades used solely for thrusting at the armour in the hope of piercing the links or slipping between the lobster like joints of armour. During the fourteenth century, knights were often armed with two swords, one the broad bladed double edged cut and thrust weapon and the other the thinner bladed thrusting weapon. There is evidence to suggest that this sword was used like a lance with the pommel against the shoulder and the hand gripping the lower bar of the cross guard. To get a better grip, the top portion of the blade was left unsharpened and the hand looped over the cross guards. At this point it then became necessary to protect the fingers that were on the 'wrong' side of the crossguard and small iron rings were fitted to the crossguard.

The simple crossguard was now developing into more complex forms, with the addition of rings and extensions to the quillons. These joined beneath the crossguard forming a hand protection for the fingers which gripped the top of the blade. A natural development from this was to fit a further curved bar from the crossguard up to the pommel to protect the rest of the hand. *Landsknechts,* the German mercenaries recruited by Maximilian I of Austria wore a short double edged blade cutting sword with characteristic 'S' shaped cross guard and simple grip. Their main arm was the great two handed sword (plates 7 and 8) with an overall length of about 5 ft 6 in. The sword had a long double edged blade, often with a wavy edge (see jacket illustration) and with two hook projections at the top of the blade below the *ricasso* which more often than not was covered in leather acting as a grip for the second hand. The cross guards were usually of simple design with additional rings and drooped downwards. While the two handed sword was favoured by dismounted men, the hand-and-a-half sword, a smaller version

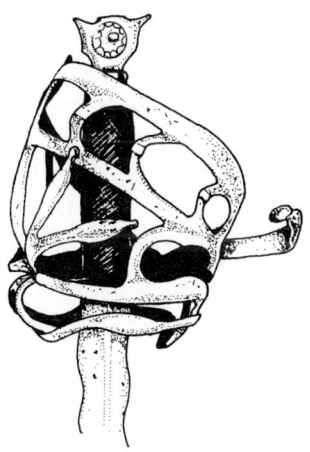

Fig. 5.
Hilt of the schiavona, the sword of the guards of the Doge of Venice. (See page 25.)

of the two handed was adopted by mounted soldiers. There were also long bladed executioners' swords, not to be confused with the two handed sword. The executioner's sword had a double edged blade with no taper and was either slightly rounded at the tip or cut off square. Another large two handed weapon was the Scottish claymore or *claidheamhmor* used during the sixteenth and early seventeenth centuries. The pommel and long straight quillons were usually ornamented with pierced quatrefoils.

The development of both sword and armour were seriously affected during the fourteenth century with the 'discovery' in Europe of gunpowder and the slow spread of firearms. It was soon not practical for the mounted man to have armour that protected him from the musket ball as this would entail a huge weight of iron and subsequent loss in mobility. Armour of course did not change overnight and it took until the beginning of the eighteenth century before it was entirely abandoned except for some mounted troops who retained the helmet and cuirass.

The sword, however, evolved owing to the adoption of new fighting techniques, and while previously there had been one style of sword for civilian and soldier alike, the formation of professional armies divided the evolution of the sword into two basic types. There remained the cut and thrust weapon for the military but there evolved for the civilian a more slender bladed weapon requiring a new art of fighting.

The Rapier

The *espada ropera* (the Spanish for a dress sword) or the *epée rapière* as described in a French document of 1474) was probably adopted in the late fifteenth century although its exact form is uncertain. By about 1530, however, the word had come to mean a light civilian sword designed for thrusting rather than cutting with a hand guard of rings and bars. In Italy, swordsmen concentrated on the use of the point and in the art of 'the fence' or what we today term as fencing and their slender double edged blades at times reached a length of nearly 5 feet. The spread of the Italian Renaissance through Europe naturally carried with it their art of 'the fence' and the rapier became universal. The weapons of the sixteenth and seventeenth centuries have a slender double edged blade primarily intended for the thrust but also capable of being used for cutting. Rapiers fitted with triangular blades or blades of square section were referred to as *tucks*.

The use of the rapier brought about a revival in the use of the dagger. The *main gauche,* the dagger carried in the left hand was used to parry the opponent's blade. The blade was double edged and strong enough to check the blows of the opponent's blade. To protect the hand, the quillons were curved away from the hand towards the point of the blade. Later examples had the additions of rings. Another variety prevalent in Spain had longer straighter quillons and the addition of a triangular shaped metal guard. Some examples had the addition of a shell on the guard conforming in design to the companion rapier. As the rapier itself declined so did the *main gauche,* going out of fashion in the 1660's but continuing in use in Spain until the early 1700's. Variations on the *main gauche* were numerous, the most favourable being the 'sword breaker'. This weapon had a thick blade notched at regular intervals to snag the opponent's blade and then to try and break it (plate 10h).

By the 1570's the earlier long blade of the rapier – some examples were as long as 5 feet – had been shortened to a more manageable length and the guard had become more ornate. The combination of bars for hand protection produced the style described as the swept hilt. This was the most popular of the styles. However, the designers and swordsmen continued to alter and improve the hilts, fitting in place of the lower rings, a single or double plate, pierced with decorative work. These plates, later grew in size to become shells and eventually a cup or bowl giving rise to the name of the cup hilt rapier. There was an infinite variety of designs in both the swept and cup hilt rapiers depending on the maker, wishes of the purchaser and his wealth and simple fashion. The effect of the Renaissance can clearly be seen in the decorative work and the inlays of gold or silver on the rapiers and their companion daggers (plate 10).

The Hunting Sword

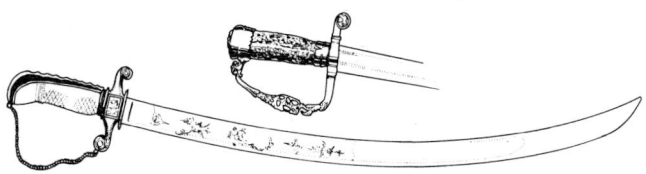

Fig. 6. Hunting swords.

Besides military and civilian swords there was the hunting sword, carried by those rich enough to be able to pursue the sport. The swords were short bladed either straight or slightly curved with a stag horn or other bone grip, knuckle bow with small shell guard and perhaps a decorative scene on the side shell guard. The weapons were used for self defence as well as killing wounded game and a number are to be found with a saw back to the blade. By 1750 or so the hunting sword had a plain round pommel, a horn or bone grip, the latter worked with spirals and often bound in the grooves with silver strips, a simple knuckle bow sometimes replaced by a loose chain handguard and a slightly curved single edged blade, sometimes to be found with a sawback. Some examples had the addition of a shell to the guard usually embossed with hunting scenes. Hunting swords continued to be carried during the nineteenth century especially in France and Germany, although they were to be seen in England. Hunting swords are still carried in certain parts of Germany and France today.

The Small Sword.

Although the rapier remained popular in Italy and Spain as late as the 1720s, its place had been taken as early as the 1660s in France and England by the small sword, 'Town' or 'Walking' sword. There was not an immediate change from one style to another, and the transitional weapon, often referred to as a *flamberge* had a long diamond or square sectioned blade, a simple hilt devoid of any knuckle bow and two short quillons above the shell guard if one was fitted.

From this *flamberge* evolved the true small sword which had a blade of some 32 in. with the basic hilt consisting of a shell guard with knuckle bow with a single quillon and two downward curving bars or rings which touched the shell guard, grip and pommel. The blade was usually triangular in section, tapering to an acute point and carried in a leather scabbard of the same cross section with top mount or mouthpiece, middle mount and bottom mount or chape.

The early small swords had a blade based on the rapier but it was not long before a blade form exclusive to the small sword evolved. This was the so called *colichemarde* blade form named after the inventor Count Von Königsmark a well known Swedish swordsman. The *forté* or the top portion of the blade was about 1¾ in. for a length of about 8 in. and then abruptly narrowed to a width of about ¾ in. This blade form was popular in the last quarter of the seventeenth century and the first 30 years or so of the following century appearing to fall into disuse in about the 1730s, although examples of this blade form, especially in France are known as late as 1780.

The most graceful part of the small sword was the hilt design, which incorporated the finest workmanship in the piercing, inlaying and chiselling. With the formation of standing armies, the possibility of a gentleman being called on to fight at short notice was slim indeed and if he was an officer in an army he would also possess a strong cut and thrust military style sword in addition to his small sword or swords. The small sword then became an indispensable part of the dress of the gentleman: the richer the man; the more elaborate his clothes; the more his sword. Hilts were made detachable so that they could be changed to suit the clothing or the occasion; Black hilts were used when in mourning with black scabbard while silver hilts, finely inlaid and chased metal hilts were used for other occasions.

By the early eighteenth century, silver hilts were popular, but towards the end of the century, cut steel hilts, highly polished were in 'vogue'. These hilts, still in use today were made from highly polished steel and inlaid with faceted studs, cut like a diamond. They were plainer than the earlier form of sword, but their highly polished faceted hilt devoid of the chasing and inlay of the earlier swords have a striking beauty in their simplicity.

By 1760, the two shells lost the dishing they had had and now appeared flat similar to a figure '8' while the down-drooping rings or bars decreased in size until they became purely decorative and of no practical use. By 1780, however, the small sword was fast becoming outdated and was abandoned. A small variation of the 'Town' or 'Walking' sword was a weapon without shell guard or knuckle bow. Legend has it that the sword was kept by the bed or under the pillow in case of intruders at night but there is absolutely no evidence to substantiate the claim. It was however, still used as a presentation weapon (plates 23, 24 and 25) many examples being made in gold, studded with precious stones and inlaid in enamels. The style of sword, was and is still used by diplomats and as a court sword and as the sword of civic dignitaries, while in military circles it was retained as a dress sword for formal social occasions.

2 *The Military Sword*

The military sword fell into two distinct categories, the swords of the man fighting on foot and the sword for the mounted man. The foot soldier who was armed with the pike and some with the fast emerging musket carried short swords or hangers as a last line of defence and the officers of infantry regiments, armed with the pike would have had a light strong bladed cut and thrust weapon with a hilt design with boat shells and knuckle guard evolved from the small sword. The cavalry, however, were armed with the sword as the main weapon and pistols and carbines as ancillary equipment. The weapons were heavy with a strong cut and thrust blade and a half or whole basket guard to give protection to the hand. The hilts were formed from an elaborate series of bars fitted to the pommel in as many as three places, emerging in as many as five or six places from the round plate guard at the base of the hilt. The heavy round pommel, the bars and the plate of the hilt were in iron, elaborately chiselled in many cases with foliage, soldiers and scenes. A well known pattern of this style of sword in England was dubbed the Mortuary sword because the basket hilt was decorated with the chiselled head of Charles I, but examples of this style were well known before 1649 (the date of the execution of the King), so the name was possibly not adopted until the nineteenth century.

Another distinctive style of basket hilted sword was *schiavona* carried by the Sciavoni, the guards of the Doge of Venice. This had an elaborate hilt composed of interlaced bars completely enveloping the hand and with a distinctive flat pommel in the form of a shield. More often than not this pommel was in brass. The blade was straight and double edged with a short fuller at the top in which the maker usually marked his name and mark.

As armies were formed on a permanent basis it became necessary for supplies of weapons to be made available to arm the men. It also became necessary to have every man armed with the same sword as his fellow soldiers. The usual practice at the time was that the colonel who was the proprietor of the regiment, ordered the clothing and weapons to his own design, which meant that 'regulation' weapons were purely, at this period, regulation for a particular regiment. A certain amount of uniformity did, however, prevail because the manufacturers from whom the swords were ordered tended for their own ease of working to have certain stock styles of swords from which the colonel could choose unless the commanding officer was himself an expert with specific ideas on what a sword should be and be able to do.

As with military uniforms, certain countries exercised an influence over others and countries with large and flourishing swordmaking industries such as Germany and France could influence the styles of countries such as England whose swordmaking industry was in a sorry state in the middle and late eighteenth century and who had to order from abroad. At this period and during the nineteenth century, Solingen was the largest supplier of edged weapons in the world.

The German influence on swords was also spread by craftsmen who left their homes to set up business in places such as England, Sweden, Russia and North America, taking with them their patterns, moulds and tools.

Britain

In Britain there was no standardization of swords for officers or men of cavalry and infantry until 1788. Prior to this date, regimental variations existed in abundance. In that year, however, the authorities decided on greater uniformity than that afforded at regimental level. All cavalry commanding officers were asked to send in a pattern of their sword. The Board of General Officers having duly deliberated, they decided that the heavy cavalry sword should be half basket, the same as in use in the 6th Regiment of Dragoons and that the light cavalry should have the sword in use with light dragoons which had a 36 in. curved wide single edged blade, a plain grip and a single stirrup hilt knuckle guard. Officers were ordered to have the same sword as the men. By 1796, however, it was found that the swords were too long in the blade, badly weighted and badly made, there being no system of proof at this period and although the swords were of a set pattern they were still obtained by regimental purchase. Because of the poor quality and bad design, a new pattern was authorized with plate handguard with pierced holes and a shorter blade. The ordnance also decided that swords would in future be purchased by them and issued against payment to the various regiments. It was not until 1844 that swords became free issue. The light cavalry sword came in for less criticism and was retained with minor modifications.

In 1821, a new pattern of heavy and light cavalry trooper's sword was adopted but manufacture was slow and neither patterns were in the hands of the troops in any quantity until the 1830s. The light cavalry sword had a curved single edged blade with a three bar guard, backpiece and leather covered wood grip. The heavy cavalry had a slightly curved blade, a similar grip and backpiece with an 'ear' each side through which a rivet passed through the grip, tang of the blade and the other side of the grip and a bowl guard. Both these swords continued in use until 1853 when they were superseded by a universal pattern for both heavy and light cavalry. The 1853 pattern sword employed the same three bar guard as the 1821 pattern of light cavalry sword, a curved single edged cut and thrust blade and a new patent grip designed by the swordmaker Charles Reeves. In his design, the tang instead of tapering from the shoulder to fit the hole in the centre of the grip, continued the same width, the grips of chequered leather in two parts being riveted to the tang (plate 63).

In 1864, as a result of complaints received, the sword was altered to a new pattern. The change in pattern, however, only involved the hilt. The three bar hilt was done away with and a sheet steel hilt with pierced out 'Maltese Cross' device was substituted. The hilt had no lapping on the guard which gave rise to complaints about damage to uniforms, but no action was taken because at this period cavalry were not actively engaged in the many small campaigns and wars. In 1882, however, a new pattern sword was issued with the same guard, but with lapped down edges, and the blades in two differing lengths. The patterns were known as the 1882 Long and 1882 Short, the former was issued to heavy cavalry and the latter to light cavalry. Severe criticism of the sword resulted in the formation of a committee to consider the question of cavalry swords. This committee of officers and representatives of the manufacturers reported in 1885 and produced the 1885 pattern sword in a single blade length. Except for differences in weights and slight modifications the 1885 sword was still basically the old 1864 and 1882 patterns. The new sword also came in for severe criticism as a result of the many breakages that occurred during the Sudan Campaign. Swords broke and bent in action as a result of poor tempering and inspection. A new experimental blade was fitted to the 1885 hilt in 1889 and formally adopted in 1890 becoming the Sword, Cavalry, Pattern 1890. The new sword was however heavier than the original pattern of 1864 which had started off the controversy about cavalry swords resulting in the various patterns and modifications described above.

However, the search continued for the perfect sword, and in 1899 a new pattern was introduced. It had virtually the same pattern handguard which soon proved too flimsy and a longer grip which was not liked by the users. After the Boer war, the experiments continued resulting in limited issues of an experimental sword in 1904 and 1906 until the Sword, Cavalry, Pattern 1908 was issued. What was considered by many as the most perfect sword ever designed was finally issued to the cavalry at a time when horsed cavalry was slowly losing its place on the battlefield. The sword had a limited use during the Great War but mechanization in the inter-war years which saw the removal of the horse also saw the withdrawal except for ceremonial occasions of the sword.

Cavalry officers were ordered a new sword in 1822 with a straight single edged blade with gilt hilt with knuckle bow and boat shell guard. In 1834 a new pattern with pierced bowl was ordered which in turn gave way in 1856 to a pattern of sword with scroll hilt. In 1822, all light cavalry officers had adopted a three bar hilt sword with slightly curved single edged blade. This they carried until 1896 when a universal sword was adopted for both heavy and light cavalry officers. This sword was an adaptation of the 1834 hilt and the 1856 blade. It survived only sixteen years when it was replaced by the 1912 pattern sword, similar to the troopers' pattern in size and shape except that the bowl guard was chased and the grip was wood covered in fishskin and bound with wire (plate 67).

Infantrymen who had been traditionally armed with a short brass hilted hanger discarded this in 1767 except for grenadiers who retained it a few years longer. The infantry officer had until 1786 carried a spontoon, a staff weapon similar to the partisan carried by the Yeoman of the Guard (plate 125). In 1786, however, officers were ordered to carry a straight bladed cut and thrust sword with a hilt in either steel, gilt or silver '. . . according to the colour of the buttons on the uniform.' Although there is no further evidence of the design of the sword, it is generally thought to be spadroon with a five bead guard. The grip was either in ivory or dark horn and often bisected with a metal band which matched the hilt with an oval bearing the title and number of the regiment or a crown over the royal cypher.

In 1796, a new pattern was ordered with a gilt hilt with pommel, knuckle bow and two shell guards. The grip was to be bound with silver wire and the sword carried in a gilt mounted black leather scabbard. This style of sword was widely copied throughout Europe and Russia but was probably first adopted by the Prussians in the 1750s. There were three basic styles, the

Prussian style, adopted by Britain and Denmark, the Russian style with distinctive flattened top piece to the ball pommel and the French style. All varied in some small way in the shape of pommel and shells.

In 1803 a curved bladed sword, similar in shape to that carried by the light cavalry was adopted for light and grenadier company officers. It had a lion head pommel to the backpiece, a knuckle bow with the crown above the royal cypher 'G.R.' with for grenadier company officers a stringed bugle horn. Regimental officers who carried this in place of the 1796 version had nothing above the crown and cypher. The grip was either wood covered in fishskin or wood covered in leather then bound with silver wire. General and staff officers carried this sword but with a carved ivory grip. There were also regimental differences incorporated in the hilt.

In 1822, a completely new design of sword was ordered for all infantry officers, foot guards and rifles. The sword had a gilt half basket hilt and in the oval cartouche the blade had a quill, pipe or ramrod back but in March of 1846 it was replaced by the 'Wilkinson' pattern without pipe back and a wide deep fuller. In 1827, the rifles obtained permission to have the hilt and scabbard fitting in steel and to replace the crown and royal cypher by a stringed bugle horn while in 1855, the foot guards were allowed a steel hilt with their regimental badges in the cartouche. In the army of the Honourable East India Company, the royal cypher was replaced by the Company's lion emblem which was used until control of the Indian Army came under the crown. When Victoria was created Empress of India in 1877, the cypher in the cartouche was altered to 'V.R.I.' interlaced and intertwined.

In 1892, an entirely new pattern was introduced (plate 65) with a sheet steel hand guard with the crown and royal or imperial cypher. The blade was a complete departure from any pattern used previously. It was a thrusting blade only having no cutting edge until the final few inches. The outside of the guard caused complaints about wear on the uniform and in 1895 the inside edge was turned under. The guards and rifles continued to carry their own pattern while the Royal Army Medical Corps, created in 1898, continued with the gilt 'Gothic' hilt sword until 1934.

Various corps also carried the infantry pattern sword and it is today worn by numerous Commonwealth countries who replace the royal cypher with their national emblem.

In the Royal Navy, officers had up until 1805 roughly followed the army officers in their choice of sword, the most popular being the bead hilted spadroon, or the slotted hilt with either engraved anchors on the pommel or inset into the knuckle guard. In 1805, however, the Admiralty ordered a standard pattern of sword to be worn by all naval officers. It had a single edged straight blade with a lion head pommel and backpiece with a stirrup hilt with a langet each side of the cross piece. On the langet the badge of a crown and foul anchor was engraved. Officers of flag rank had ivory grips to the swords, other officers having wood covered in sharkskin and bound with wire. Warrant officers had a similar sword but with a plain pommel and backpiece.

This pattern was carried until 1827 when it was replaced by a copy of the military 1822 pattern. In the naval version the parts between the bars were filled in solid and the cartouche bore the crown and anchor badge. The plainish military pommel was replaced by a lion head pommel and backpiece. This hilt with minor changes in style and of course crown remains in use today and was much copied by other navies of the world. In 1846, the pipe back blade was replaced by the Wilkinson pattern. In 1929, the slightly curved blade was ordered to be straight.

There was also a vogue in the 1870s for officers to fit a broader blade than laid down, the favourite being that used on the Scottish military broadsword or claymore. There were other notable variations in the design of naval swords, that of the Royal Naval Artillery Volunteers having a usual lion head pommel and backpiece in gilt brass, the grip covered in sharkskin but the guard being a steel guard of cutlass pattern.

In 1842, officers of flag rank were given permission to wear an ivory hilted scimitar similar to that adopted in 1831 by General Officers in the Army. The swords had the crown and anchor badge raised on the crossguard but were not popular and were finally abandoned in 1856. It is interesting to note, however, that at least one officer, Admiral of the Fleet Sir Henry Keppell who did not attain flag rank until the year after the sword was abolished continued to wear one as late as 1896.

Cutlasses supplied to ships had been crude affairs cheaply made but effective. The pattern in use at the beginning of the nineteenth century had a figure '8' guard consisting of two circles, a straight single edged blade and a cast iron grip grooved horizontally and vertically for better grip. In 1845, a new style with solid cast grip with horizontal grooving, a large bowl guard and straight blade was adopted. Another new model was adopted in 1889 with a similar guard except for the pierced out 'Maltese Cross' used on the cavalry sword of 1882. The last pattern of cutlass was issued in 1900, with the same guard but with leather grips riveted to the tang as was done with the 1853 and subsequent cavalry swords. The cutlass was finally withdrawn from ships in 1936.

However, because of cost etc., there was a considerable amount of conversion done to old cutlasses to up date them and even the cutting down of obsolete cavalry sword blades and rehilting them. In 1891 for example, tables of small arms in service record four patterns of cutlass, one with a 19 in. blade, one with a 27 in. blade which was slightly curved, one with a 25$^1/_2$ in. blade which was straight and the 1889 pattern with an 18 in. blade!

The most recent of swords in the British armed forces is that designed in 1920 for the new Royal Air Force by the Wilkinson Sword Company. The gilt guard was based on the infantry pattern sword – which was worn by the Royal Engineers who ran the early balloon establishments. A raised cartouche with the albatross in flight, the Royal Air Force badge, was fitted to the guard and the grip was white as used on the naval officer's sword. The pommel was an eagle's head with the feathers reaching down the backpiece (plate 69).

France, Belgium and Netherlands

The heavy cavalry sword used in France in the mid eighteenth century was similar in style to that used in other armies. It had a hilt consisting of a knuckle bow with auxiliary bars, a shell guard, wire bound grip and rounded pommel. The blade was straight and either single or double edged. An iron hilted sword with half basket guard was introduced in 1781 but replaced by a brass hilted version three years later. The hilts of these swords were made from sheet metal to form the bars fitted to a cast knuckle bow guard. The sword had a cap pommel with leather bound grip and the side bars or scrolls touched in two places on the knuckle guard and rejoined it as the base. Between knuckle guard and scroll was a brass *fleur de lys*. In the dragoon broadsword used from 1794 to 1815 and termed the Pattern of AnIV (Sept. 23, 1785–06) the hilt was in steel but of the same design but the cap pommel was slightly different and the *fleur de lys* was replaced by a *fasces*. In 1788 a further version of heavy cavalry sword was issued for officers. This had a flat cap pommel, and a stirrup hilt with five auxiliary bars which connected with a pierced shell on the left side. The grip was in wood covered in leather and bound in the grooves with wire. The blade was straight with a rounded point and carried in a leather scabbard with brass mounts. The same style of hilt but fitted with a curved blade was used by dragoon officers between 1806 and 1814.

The cuirassier's sword, a monster weapon with a heavy cast four bar guard was adopted in AnIX and takes its designation from that year (Sept. 1800–01). It had a cap pommel with the cast four bar guard fitted to it and a leather bound wood grip. The blade was straight and single edged with two fullers each side. As with French sword bayonets, the model date, place of manufacture and date of manufacture were engraved on the back of the blade. At this date a typical inscription might read 'M^{fture} Imp^{le} du Klingenthal Octobre 1813.

A further version was produced in AnXIII (Sept. 1804–05) which had a hatchet point to the blade with false edge, and was carried by dragoons up until 1815. A new pattern of the heavy cavalry sword was in the same style produced in 1816 with a straight single edged blade with two fullers and in 1822, heavy cavalry were issued with a curved bladed weapon. This sword had a brass hilt with four bars, but unlike its predecessors the bars where they joined the base of the guard did not have rounded ball finials, the whole hilt being cast in one in the flat and then curved up over a block. Another radical departure was the the grip tilted forward at the top as did the cap pommel. The blade was single edged and curved with a wide fuller. In 1854, however, a return was made to the straight single edged blade with two fullers of the 1816 pattern fitted to the 1822 hilt.

In 1882, when there was a general rationalisation of swords, a new version was introduced for heavy cavalry. This had a three bar guard with cap pommel and grip and a straight single edged blade with one fuller. It was carried in a steel scabbard with two bands and rings.

The light cavalry carried a number of styles of swords, hussars keeping to the pattern of the single stirrup hilt which was also adopted by lancers and light cavalry. In AnXIII (Sept. 1804–05) a new pattern of sword was adopted for light cavalry. This had a three bar brass hilt with cap pommel connected with a backpiece to the grip ferrule and a lozenge in the centre of the leather covered wood grip which secured through the tang. The blade was curved and single edged and the sword was carried in a steel scabbard with two rings. In 1816, however, a new pattern was introduced for light cavalry. This had a straight single edged blade and a three bar cast brass hilt with forward leaning grip and cap pommel. In 1822 a return was made to the curved single edged blade. Mounted artillery adopted a new pattern sword in 1829 having, during the Napoleonic wars, been equipped with the light cavalry sword. The new pattern had the standard cap pommel but a single cast knuckle bow and a curved single edged blade and a steel scabbard with two bands and rings.

There were other patterns of sword made for the Imperial Guard and the Royal Guards at various times, the Imperial Guard Dragoons having a sword with brass hilt of cap pommel knuckle bow with two auxiliary bars and between the top and middle bar an oval pierced out with a grenade badge. The *Mousquetaires de la Garde du Roi* of 1814–16 had a similar sword but in the oval, a cross topped by *fleur de lys* and surrounded by rays. The later *Cente-Garde* were armed with long sword bayonets based on the heavy cavalry sword (see page 106).

The light cavalry sword of 1822 survived and still is in use today by the *Garde Republicaine* in a steel scabbard with a single band and ring but officers were authorized a new pattern sword in 1923 with straight blade and pierced half basket guard, the bars of the basket being embossed with a leaf pattern.

The infantry in the 1790s were armed with a hanger with cast brass hilt with grip and knuckle guard in one. This weapon widely copied in Europe had a curved single edged blade and was usually carried in a leather scabbard with brass mounts. This pattern continued in use until 1833 when a new pattern was adopted. This sword had a straight double edged leaf shaped blade and a 'Roman' style hilt with rounded pommel and grip with the cross piece cast in one. With the universal issue of the sword bayonet, the side arm was made obsolete except for the Imperial Guard who retained it until 1870.

During the Revolution a great variety of sidearms were used with the basic three bar style of guard, pommel and backpiece and leather covered wood grip. In this pattern the pommel sometimes varied and was either the cap style in the shape of a helmet as in the case of the *Garde National Chasseur* hanger of 1792, or had superimposed on the bars of the guard a shield with a variety of badges or emblems on them. The foot artillery also wore a hanger with a double edged straight blade, the earlier pattern having a grip in the form of an eagle's head and neck while the 1833 pattern was similar to the infantry but had a scaled grip (similar to the American version) and a badge on the pommel.

At the beginning of the nineteenth century, infantry officers carried a straight bladed sword with elaborate cap pommel stirrup guard with large langets extending downwards and up the grip which was of ebony with cross hatching. More elaborate versions included extra embossing and engraving on the metal parts of the hilt. A new pattern was adopted in 1821 with a more orthodox cap pommel with leaf work in the portion that covered the top of the back of the grip, a single knuckle bow guard with an engraved band in the centre and a curved single edged blade. In 1845 another new pattern of similar style was adopted. This had a cap pommel but a single knuckle guard that swelled out at the base into a pierced shell. The blade was straighter than the last pattern and single edged. This was modified in 1855 and used until 1882 when a steel hilted sword was adopted. This weapon had an elaborate five bar guard, with an inner fall down, wood grip covered in leather and an embossed and chased pommel and backpiece. In place of the previous black leather scabbard with gilt mounts, an all steel scabbard with two bands and rings was adopted. In 1923, a new sword was adopted for all officers of the army. This had a gilt hilt with a single knuckle guard but a small bowl guard each side pierced with slots and embossed with leaf patterns. The pommel was the cap variety also with leaf decoration, but in the French army as in the German army, slight variations on regulation swords were allowed, the most popular having a lion head pommel and backpiece and a slightly more ornamented guard. The blade was single edged and slightly curved.

In the Navy, as in the Royal Navy, the choice of style of sword during the eighteenth century was an individual matter and there was no fixed pattern until 1800. Officers had previously had their own designs but their main choice lay in copying the infantry pattern. The new sword had a simplified version of the light cavalry hilt with single knuckle guard and curved blade with langets bearing the foul anchor, ebony grip and cap pommel. In

1805 a new pattern was authorized without grip langets but with a block bearing the anchor superimposed on crossed flags. In 1837 a new design was authorized with a half basket guard with pierced out designs which incorporated the anchor and crown. Minor changes occurred in 1848 when the crown was removed and in 1852 when a slightly different crown was included when the Second Empire was established. In 1870 a new pattern was authorized which did not include the crown. All these patterns had black leather scabbards with the top mount bearing a foul anchor. Once again there were more elaborate versions with more embossing and engraving available for those who wished to spend their money.

Ratings in the Navy were armed with the cutlass introduced in 1771, having a brass pommel and backpiece with prominent tang button and a single knuckle guard with the addition of two extra bars joining the guard and the shell at the base into which the guard had widened. A new version was adopted in AnXI which had a sheet iron covered grip with an oval iron shell to form the knuckle bow and a sheet iron half basket guard fitted to it. After 1816, no more cutlasses were made until 1833 when a variation was produced with thicker blade. In 1872 another pattern was issued. This had a pommel and backpiece with ears riveted through the leather covered grip with a guard with 'ears' each side and a wide knuckle plate engraved with criss cross lines and pierced in the centre of each lozenge so formed with a hole. The top of the pommel was fitted with a lug holding a loose ring.

Besides the swords described, the French were great users of dress swords. These took the form of a small sword having a pommel, grip, knuckle guard and downpointing shell guards.

Belgium who did not gain independence until 1831 after that date copied the French styles of sword usually adopting new weapons a few years after they became regulation in France. Cavalry were armed with various French patterns of sword, heavy cavalry adopting the sword of AnIX (page 33) and later the curved bladed 1822 pattern and light cavalry, the pattern 1822. Some regiments were for a short period armed with the three bar hilted *'Sabre Montmorency'* of 1802 imported from Germany. This weapon had a curved single edged blade with pommel and backpiece with ears and a leather covered grip. In 1852 the Belgian *Gendarmerie* adopted the old French heavy cavalry sword AnXIII and used it up until 1873 when they reverted to the regulation heavy cavalry sword of 1822.

The infantry soldier was armed with the hanger of French design but termed of Dutch pattern possibly because they were supplied from Holland. This had the hilt with knuckle guard cast in one and a curved single edged blade. Officers carried the French infantry officer's pattern of 1821, designated the pattern of 1833, then adopted the 1845 pattern which they designated in 1850, the year of adoption, and then in 1889 made a radical departure from the current French pattern by adopting a sword with a French cavalry style guard of four embossed bars and cap pommel with straight single edged blade. Officers, as in the French army also had their small sword style dress swords.

Regiments of *Chasseurs,* however, had a different pattern more befitting their dashing status. This had a lion head pommel and backpiece with stirrup guard and langets pointing down bearing the bugle horn badge. The blade was slightly curved and carried in a gilt mounted leather scabbard.

In the Navy, the French pattern of 1837 was adopted in the same year to replace a model adopted in 1832. The original pattern was similar to the *Chasseurs'* sword but with an anchor on the langets. However, by the last quarter of the nineteenth century the British pattern had been adopted with the Belgian crown over the anchor in the cartouche and with pipe backed blade.

During the last part of the nineteenth century, Holland had restricted the number of patterns of swords. While they followed the French in the style of trooper's sword, the infantry officer's sword was typically German. It had a lion head pommel and backpiece with stirrup guard with langets and a curved single edged blade. In the Navy, the sword had a lion head pommel and backpiece with the crown over the anchor. The blade was slightly curved and pipe backed. Ratings in the Navy carried a cutlass which was of French pattern until the end of the nineteenth century when a new style was adopted. This had a curved falchion shaped blade with a sheet metal guard pierced out to give the impression of knuckle guard and bars and a pommel and backpiece. It was carried also by colonial troops and pioneers in the Army.

The Dutch Marines, however, adopted a sword on the French infantry style which they still wear.

Prussia, Germany and Austria

The sword carried by Prussian cuirassiers in 1732 was a broadsword adopted in that year. The blade was straight and double edged and the hilt a basket design incorporating bars and scrolls and a side panel with the crown eagle with the initials FR on the breast. The pommel was round with a prominent tang button. Similar pattern swords were carried by the Baden Dragoons, their weapon having a lion head pommel and incorporated into the brass guard was the arms of Baden, while the sword used by the Saxon cuirassiers had a lion head pommel, straight knuckle guard with three bars coming from it to a side panel decorated with the crown over the initials FA. Prussian dragoons carried a sword similar to that adopted in Russia, with an eagle head pommel and guard of intersecting brass bars.

In 1819, a Russian pattern of sword was carried by cuirassiers. It had a brass cap pommel, straight grip and a brass three bar guard. The blade was straight and double edged with two deep fullers extending from the shoulder to almost the point. It was carried in a steel scabbard, with two bands and rings. The officer's version was similar in design but had a four bar gilt hilt, a slightly shaped grip and forward leaning cap pommel. A leather finger strap was fitted to the ferrule of the grip. By 1854, the cuirassier's sword now had a straight single edged blade with one fuller each side and a four bar hilt, shaped grip and forward leaning cap pommel. The issue of this sword was extended in

1876 to cover all German cuirassiers.

In 1889, a universal cavalry sword was adopted. This had a steel cap pommel with composition grips screwed to the tang and a half open basket guard with in the cartouche the arms of the state to which the regiment belonged. Cuirassiers and lancer officers, however, retained their own distinctive patterns. There had been a previous universal pattern sword which had been issued to Prussian cavalry in 1852 but was extended to cover a number of other regiments of the states that made up the German Empire in 1871. This sword, issued to troopers had a rounded pommel and backpiece with 'ears', shaped wood grip covered in leather and a steel half open basket guard composed of the knuckle guard and three additional bars on the outer side and one on the inner side. There was a leather finger strap fitted to the ferrule. The blade was single edged and curved and the sword carried in a steel scabbard.

Officers of Uhlan or lancer regiments carried a sword with gilt lion head pommel and backpiece with stirrup hilt and langets each side over the blade which was slightly curved and single edged. Other ranks carried the typical light cavalry style of sword widely adopted in other countries. This had a rounded pommel and backpiece with 'ears', stirrup hilt and curved single edged blade. There were various patterns, that of 1811 having a heavier hilt and wider thicker blade while the pattern of 1873 was lighter with a thinner blade.

The infantry, like other nations had armed the private soldier with a sidearm as well as a musket and bayonet. There is very little to distinguish the eighteenth century patterns from those used by the British, except for the markings on blade and hilt. The hilt consisted of a cast brass grip and pommel and a small double shell guard. The blade was short, curved and single edged. By 1818, a pattern almost exactly the same as the French hanger had been adopted. Although these were manufactured during the 1820s, the first supplies were weapons captured from the French after Waterloo.

The infantry officer carried a sword that was similar to the 1796 sword of the British infantry, although the Prussian weapon seems to have served as the model, being adopted in the 1750s. Although this type was used during the nineteenth century as a dress sword, it was discarded during the last quarter except for a few regiments, mainly Guard regiments, who retained it. In 1889, a new pattern of sword was adopted for the Prussian infantry officer, which was also used by infantry officers of Württemberg, and Mecklenberg. The sword had a straight single edged blade with a gilt brass guard consisting of three narrowly spaced bars on which was fitted the badge of the state. The grip was bound in black fish skin and topped with a French style cap pommel. The Prussian version had the crown and cypher of the Emperor fitted to the middle of the grip. Jaeger and Fusilier officers had adopted a sword with a single stirrup hilt with a backpiece that incorporated a lion or eagle as a pommel depending on the state.

The cavalry and artillery had also adopted a sword with a single stirrup hilt with a lion head pommel and backpiece. On each side of the lower part of the guard there was a langet on which was placed a motif to show the arm of the service; crossed swords for cavalry and crossed cannon barrels for artillery.

On the formation of the *Deutsche Marine* in 1848, a sword was adopted for officers that was based on the British pattern of 1827. The German sword had in the cartouche a foul anchor and a bone grip in place of the fish skin on the British sword. The blade was slightly curved, single edged and pipe backed. In 1871, with the proclamation of the German Empire, the Imperial crown was placed in the cartouche above the foul anchor. There was a great variety of German naval swords from rather plain versions to highly elaborate swords which in some cases incorporated coloured stones in the eyes of the lion head pommel, green for starboard and red for port.

To show the extent of the variations that might be encountered, the Carl Eickhorn catalogue, *Musterbuch der Waffenfabrik* of 1908 illustrates ten different styles of sword and seven different versions of the scabbard. In 1919, the Imperial crown was removed from the cartouche which now only contained the foul anchor. This style remained in use throughout the Nazi regime without change.

There was a wide variety of sword used by the Austrian army, the cuirassier's sword of 1769 had a rounded pommel and backpiece – nco's had a lion head pommel – with single knuckle strap reinforced at the base with a flat pierced disc with two langets extending over the shoulder of the blade. The blade was straight with a rounded 'hatchet' point and single edged. In 1775, a modified version was issued which had 'ears' to the backpiece and langets extending both sides of the guard, and yet a further version was issued in 1798 to nco's which had the knuckle guard and disc in one with two slots behind the grip for the sword knot and a plain pommel. In 1824, this pattern slightly modified in the shape of the pommel and backpiece was issued to all other ranks. In 1845, however, the distinctions between the various branches of the cavalry in relation to swords was abolished and a universal pattern issued for officers and another pattern for the men.

Before this, hussars, light dragoons etc. had their own patterns. The light dragoon sword of 1798 had a straight single edged blade with spear point, a straight grip with pommel and backpiece and a knuckle guard widening into a shell pierced with slots. Hussars and lancers in 1808 were ordered a typically curved bladed sword with stirrup hilt and pommel and backpiece with shaped grip. A further pattern was issued in 1825 and in 1830 officers adopted a very curved bladed weapon with exaggerated stirrup hilt. In 1837, this model was modified by the inclusion of larger langets to the guard and the knuckle bow which was narrower at the base and widened towards the pommel.

The universal pattern issued to cavalry in 1845 had a slightly curved blade with half bowl guard, backpiece and rounded pommel. The guard was pierced out at the base with round holes. The officer's version was similar but slightly smaller. A further pattern was issued to both officers and men in 1861 and another version in 1869. This was similar in design but had the sides of the guards curved upwards to form more of a bowl and had the edge beaded to stop chaffing the uniform. In 1904 the sword was modified by having a slightly smaller guard and a nearly straight wide single edged blade.

Light cavalry and artillery received a new sword in 1877 which had a rounded knuckle bow, pommel and backpiece with ears and an almost straight single edged blade. This replaced a very curved bladed sword with stirrup hilt with folding extra guard introduced in 1861. The double guard could be opened when needed and then shut back when worn.

The infantry officer's sword of 1811 was of the small sword type with round pommel, wire bound grip and knuckle guard with double boat shells. The blade was straight and double edged. In 1837 the pattern was altered slightly by widening the knuckle bow into a strap but in 1850 a Germanic sword with single stirrup hilt was introduced. In 1862, a half pierced basket hilt was authorized with slightly curved single edged blade. The basket was pierced out with circles and slots.

In the Navy, the sword introduced in 1827 had a cap pommel with stirrup hilt with a rounded lozenge shaped langet which displayed the anchor badge. The grip was in two halves in cross hatched bone and fitted to the wide tang. In 1837, a new sword was authorized which had a brass knuckle bow with straight quillons and double oval shells for the guard. The grip was bound in wire and the pommel was ovoid with a prominent top nut or tang button. The blade was straight and single edged.

In 1846, a further pattern was introduced which was similar to the British pattern of 1827 except that the half basket guard was pierced with designs of foliage, sea monsters and scallops and the pommel and backpiece decorated with embossing. The blade was slightly curved and pipe backed. However, this was a short lived sword being replaced in 1850 with a newer version. The pierced half basket guard now incorporated the double headed Austrian eagle with the foul anchor supported by two mermaids. The grip was covered in fish skin and bound in the grooves with gilt wire. Once again the pommel and backpiece were heavily ornamented with embossing and chiselled work. The top locket of the black leather scabbard was adorned with a foul anchor badge. Besides this, officers were also ordered a dress sword which took its style from the small sword. It had a lion head pommel, knuckle bow in the form of a cable with oak leaves on the upper portion and mother of pearl grips. The upturned shell guard bore the cypher FJI (Franz Joseph I).

Other ranks were armed with the cutlass, that of 1862 having a pipe back blade, a sheet steel guard pierced with two slots and a grip covered in fish skin and bound with copper wire. In 1891, a version was issued for warrant officers with a more elaborate hilt design to replace the officer's sword which they had adopted in 1873.

Russia and Asia

Until the liberation of the serfs by Alexander II in 1863, all weapons whether for officer or soldier were made in government factories, except for those swords obtained from abroad by officers. After this date swordsmiths set up their own private manufacturies to cater for the demand by officers of decorative and elaborate swords.

During the eighteenth century, the principal centre of weapon production in Russia was at Tula where the individual armourers were required to fulfil a certain quota per year before being allowed to accept any private work. Failure to reach the set quota was punishable and slackness in passing bad work by appointed inspectors was a flogging offence.

Other arms centres were situated at Sestroretsk, Olonets, Ijevsk and Zlatoust, the last factory specializing in sword, bayonet and sidearms manufacture. The encouragement given to German craftsmen to emigrate from Solingen together with equipment and machinery of the latest design made the weapons produced at Zlatoust mechanically and uniformally of the highest quality.

The Russian swords in use in about 1800 are typical of the

styles to be found in many armies. There were nine basic patterns for various arms of the service, the Guard Cuirassier having a straight double edge bladed sword with an elaborate guard of a knuckle bow and bars with incorporated into the side design, the Imperial Russian crown over the double headed eagle. In some styles, the pommel was in the shape of an eagle's head but in others an oval plain pommel was used. The scabbard was in undyed natural leather with two large brass mounts. The top mount or locket had a single loose ring for suspension and was pierced with a long slit and three holes while the chape which reached to within 4 inches of the locket had a ring for suspensison and two long slits and five holes. The line cuirassiers had a brass half basket hilted sword with double edged blade with eagle head pommel. The half basket had a single knuckle bow and intersecting bars, and where they cross the metal was formed into a circle, being plain for troopers but with a circle bearing the double headed eagle for officers who also had a plain oval pommel. The dragoon sword was the same as that of the cuirassiers except that it had a lion head pommel and the scabbard had a simple mouthpiece oversewn in the leather body and a small chape. There was also only a hook for suspension in a frog. After 1816, the leather body of the scabbards were blackened.

The light cavalry had a stirrup hilted curved bladed sabre with single edge, so common in many armies at this time. The scabbard was similar in design to that of the Guard Cuirassiers except that it was curved.

Cavalry officers also carried a small sword or dress sword which had a shell guard, knuckle bow and oval pommel surmounted by a prominent tang button. This type of sword (plates 84 and 86) were common in many armies with officers.

In 1806, however, the French influence was starting to be felt and the dragoons adopted a new sword. This had a brass-gilt for officers – three bar guard and shell and round wood grip covered in leather and bound with twisted wire and a French style cap pommel (plate 84). The straight blade was single edged with two fullers reaching from the shoulder of the blade to the spear point. The scabbard was in brown leather with three mounts.

For the cavalry, except cuirassiers, a new sword was introduced in 1809. This had a three bar hilt in brass with a brass pommel and backpiece, the pommel having a distinctive forward leaning shape. The blade was curved and single edged and carried in a steel scabbard. The cuirassiers of the guard and line received a new sword the same year, which was exactly the same as the dragoon sword of 1806 except that it was carried in a steel scabbard. Dragoons also adopted the new 1809 cavalry sword.

It was not until 1826 that new patterns were issued for the cavalry. The heavy cavalry sword was based on the 1809 pattern but had a four bar hilt similar to that of the French heavy cavalry sword *'System AnXI'*. The light cavalry sword with three bar hilt was the same as the French light cavalry sword *'System AnXI'* and in fact many of the swords issued were captured French swords repaired in Russian factories, the rest being Russian made copies. The distinctive feature of the sword was the large oval brass button in the centre of the grip which in fact held the grip firmly to the tang of the blade.

The change from the French style to the Russian style occurred in the 1830s after intensive fighting in the Caucasus where the Russians found that the swords used by the local population were superior to their own. Officers of the Caucasian Cossack units armed themselves with captured or locally purchased weapons. In 1834 the first issue of the 'Asiatic' pattern sabre was made. The sword had a curved single edged blade and the hilt was shaped the same as the grip. The scabbard was wood covered in leather with mouthpiece, two bands and a chape. The distinctive feature was that the rings were on the outer side of the curve and not on the inner curve as was the usual practice. This placed the grip in a more convenient place for drawing.

In 1838 a new pattern was issued with the same blade but with a hilt of the same shape as the 'Asiatic' pattern but covered in leather and with a brass backpiece and ferrule. The rings on the scabbard were on the usual inner curved side. This was issued to all Cossack regiments.

The influence of this pattern was soon seen in swords for the rest of the cavalry. In 1841, dragoons were ordered a sword with curved blade, tilted forward grip with brass cap and single knuckle bow. The rings on the leather covered wood scabbard were on the outer side of the curve. Troopers carried a similar pattern but with a fixed bar on the top band and a loose ring on the bottom band.

There were no changes in the design of swords until 1881, when like other countries a commission was set up to enquire and report into the suitability of existing weapons and to provide suggestions and designs for new improved patterns. The commission produced a single sword for all cavalry, artillery, and infantry corps, the only variation being the continuation of the Cossack style of hilt for those regiments. The sword 'System of 1881' had a curved single edged blade and a black wood grip with brass cap pommel and single knuckle bow. The quillon of the knuckle bow was pierced to carry the sword knot. The scabbard was wood covered in leather with mouthpiece and top band together, the band having a 'D' on the inside face, a middle band with loose ring on the outer curve and a chape. Soldiers carried the same weapon but with the addition of two extra bands to the scabbard. These bands with the middle band were fitted with brass fitments to take a socket bayonet. This weapon was issued to all cavalry of the line who at this time were converted into dragoons. The old pattern swords were kept by the Imperial Guard for full dress ceremonial wear.

The Cossack version was identical but had a black wood grip with beak shaped brass cap, bored to take the sword knot and a brass ferrule. There was no provision on the scabbard for a bayonet.

In 1904, a new improved version of the 'Asiatic' pattern *shashka* for the Caucasian Cossacks was approved. This was virtually the same style of weapon but with horn grips with a wedge shaped split at the top of the grip. The officer's sword was improved in 1909 by the substitution of a composition grip and with decoration to the knuckle bow and cap pommel. The Imperial cypher was also included engraved on the back of the cap pommel. This cypher which also appeared on the reverse side of the blade was that of the Czar in whose reign the officer had first been commissioned.

In the same year, an order allowed officers of the line artillery and cavalry to wear the old 1826 pattern light cavalry sabre when not on duty, dragoon officers of former cuirassier regiments however being allowed the old heavy cavalry sabre. New versions of these swords were introduced in 1909 for those officers who wished to take advantage of the order. They differed slightly from the original by having the Imperial cypher on the rear of the cap pommel.

The Cossacks also were ordered that they might carry swords used by their ancestors if they were still in good repair and serviceable. For those not possessing 'heirlooms' a new pattern was introduced in 1909 similar to the 1881 pattern but with composition grip, and Imperial cypher on the back of the peak pommel.

At the beginning of the 1800s the infantry officer had been armed with a version of the small sword which prevailed in the infantry of other armies including Britain, France, Denmark, Prussia and others. This weapon had a single edged blade and a hilt in gilt brass consisting of urn pommel, knuckle bow and shell guard. The grip was bound in silver wire. The scabbard was in leather with a locket and chape, the former having a hook for frog suspension. The other ranks carried a hanger with single edged curved short blade and cast brass ball pommel, grip, knuckle bow and shell guard. The scabbard was in leather with a brass locket with hook for frog and brass chape. The hanger was carried in an enlarged frog fitted to the cross belt which also housed the bayonet. In 1817 an improved version was issued which in appearance differed very little from the sidearms of numerous countries, France, Denmark, Prussia and others. The grip, backpiece and knuckle bow were cast in a single piece and hammered on to the tang, the tang extending through the top being hammered over for a firmer fit. This pattern continued in use until after the Crimean war when it was made obsolete.

The next change for officers occurred in 1826 when a distinctively French style was introduced. This had the cap pommel with a single knuckle bow broadening into a shell guard at the bottom. The blade was curved and single edged with a deep fuller from the shoulder until about 8 inches from the point. The scabbard was in black leather with top mount with frog stud and chape with button end. This was carried until the universal pattern of 1881 (described page 47) was ordered for all. In 1909 they adopted a new pattern but in 1913 wore it in an all steel scabbard fitted with rings on the inner curve in the usual way.

In 1916, an order allowed war department unit officers when not on mounted duty to wear a *kortik* or dirk in place of the sword. This had a decorative ball pommel, black composite grip and cross piece with one quillon upturned and the other facing down. The blade was diamond sectioned and carried in a black leather scabbard with three gilt mounts, there being a ring on the mouthpiece and middle mount.

In the Russian Navy there was no set pattern of sword until the 1820s when finally one of set pattern was approved. This had a straight blade with a three bar hilt, brass backpiece with flat top and a pronounced top nut. This was worn until after the Crimean war when in the 1860s a new pattern was introduced. The main difference was that the blade was changed from straight to curved. This pattern was worn for many years and still appeared to have been in use as late as 1958.

Siam, China and Japan

All these countries had armed forces, mostly armed and formed in a feudal manner. It was not until the nineteenth century that they organised their armies and navies on European lines and adopted European uniforms and weapons. The style of dress, equipment and weapons depended largely upon whose 'sphere of influence' the country came under or which by treaty or trade

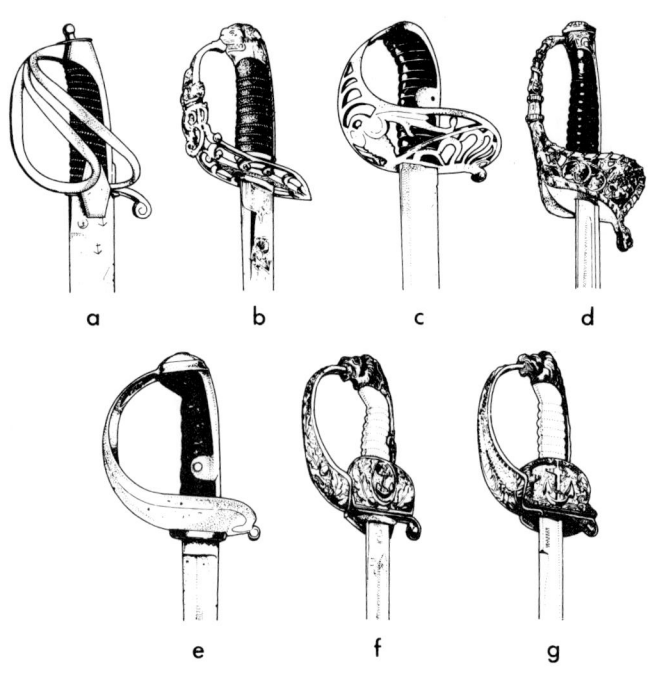

Fig. 7. Military and Naval swords. a) Russia, Navy officer 1861. b) British. 1803 Infantry officer. c) British, 1834 Heavy Cavalry officer. d) French, Navy officer 1870. e) British, 1821 Heavy Cavalry trooper. f, g) German, Navy officer 1889.

was the most favoured by the ruler.

In Siam, the influence was British and both military and naval forces copied the British style of weapon. The infantry sword was based on the 1822 British pattern but in place of the moulded backpiece it had one with an elephant head pommel with the trunk following the strap of the guard. In place of the royal cypher, the Siamese pattern incorporated the arms of Siam. The hilt instead of being gilt was silver plate and the blackened fish skin covered grip was bound with silver wire. The cavalry officers utilized the British 1856 pattern with the Siamese coat of arms incorporated in the guard (plate 98). The navy adopted the British pattern of sword but with only the anchor in the cartouche and in place of the lion head, an elephant's head.

In the cavalry other ranks were armed with the British 1864 pattern until after 1900. These weapons were sold to them by Wilkinsons having been refurbished and reproofed. They were carried in wood scabbards covered in brown leather with an internal mouthpiece and chape. The rings for suspension were also fitted internally and were fixed.

In the Navy, obsolete cutlasses, refurbished and with new scabbards were sold to the Siamese.

One feature about Siamese swords was that the hilt proportions were slightly smaller than the European, to suit the smaller hand.

In China, westernization came late, and it was not until a few years before the end of the nineteenth century that there were troops dressed and equipped in the western manner. They fought against Japan in the Sino-Japanese conflict of 1894–5 but had not acquired the skill or training of a western styled army to prevent the Japanese from overwhelming them. The Chinese copied the style of the United States (see page 68) while their navy adopted the British style of sword. This had an anchor in the cartouche which was surrounded with a corn wreath and foul anchor. The pommel and backpiece differed from the British pattern having a *li-ting*, an ancient Chinese symbol looking like a cauldron with three hands and lid on a tripod in place of the lion head. Warrant officers had the same sword but with a black grip in place of the white grip of the officer's sword and a plain rounded pommel and backpiece.

One force which was uniformally armed at an early period was the Chinese Maritime Customs. This force formed in 1868 by the instigation of Sir Robert Hart lasted until the opening years of the Second World War. The uniform and weapons of this force were British, their job being to 'keep up communications with the lighthouses, for the protection of the revenue and to assist in the suppression of piracy.'

Officers carried a British pattern naval officer's sword with dragon head pommel (plate 99) and plain anchor in the cartouche. In 1872, a new pattern of sword was introduced with, in the cartouche, the anchor with dragon superimposed. This badge was also adopted for belt plates, cap badges etc. The other ranks carried the naval cutlass pattern 1845 and were also armed with the boarding pike. This weapon continued to be carried on board Royal Naval vessels until 1926 when they were withdrawn but were still in use with the Hong Kong Police as late as 1950.

In Japan, the ancient feudal systems were reorganised on European lines in the 1860s with the abolition of the ancient Samurai. Although influenced by European fashions in uniforms and weapons, the Japanese clung to their traditional blade shape which they combined with a western style hilt. The French and American influence can be seen in the hilts of the swords of the late nineteenth century but with the coming of German military advisors, the style soon changed to the hilts that Solingen was turning out for the export market. These hilts, faithful to those carried by the soldiers in Germany, South America and other countries were mated to ancient blades or had modern 'ancient' blades fitted to them.

In the Navy, the British style was adopted and the pattern altered by putting in the cartouche an anchor with cherry blossom device (plate 105). Flag rank officers had the cartouche surrounded with an edge of rope joining the top of the anchor. The fouling of the anchor differed from the British pattern as it entwined the top bar of the anchor and not the shaft.

The latter influence on the sword design came from the United States, although their swords were mainly of the French design. The Japanese swords on the whole seem strange in appearance, having the western style of hilt with elongated knuckle bow and grip to suit the traditional Japanese blade.

In the diplomatic services of these countries the small sword, as in others, was the regulation wear. While basically they conformed to the small sword style, they incorporated various national symbols or emblems. The Chinese Ambassador in the 1870s had a small sword with bi-convex blade and gilt hilt with decorated round pommel, knuckle bow with down drooping quillons and a simple downpointing shell guard with beaded edge. The grip was in ivory and engraved with an oval design depicting a fir tree. The Siamese Ambassador in the same era had a sword with pommel of three elephants facing outwards, a simple knuckle bow, two outward pointing quillons and a downpointing shell guard with on it in relief, an elephant flanked by flags. Japanese Ambassadors also followed suit, their sword being similar to the Chinese pattern, but incorporating the cherry blossom device as decoration on pommel, shell guard and knuckle bow. Scabbard mounts of the sword were also decorated in like style as the hilt.

India

The army of the Honourable East India Company followed the design of swords used by the British army except that for certain native cavalry troops, the tulwar was used rather than the regulation British pattern of swords. The native Indian swords were renowned for their sharpness and as Captain L. E. Nolan, more famed for his part in carrying the order for the charge of the Light Brigade at Balaclava than for his far sighted criticism of British cavalry and their weapons, recorded in his book *Cavalry; its History and Tactics:*

> 'At Rumnugger . . . the troopers of the light cavalry had no confidence in their swords.
> . . . a regulation sword in his hand which must always be blunted by the steel scabbard in which it is encased.
> The native's sword-blades were chiefly old dragon blades cast from our service . . . they all had an edge like a razor from heel to point, were worn in wooden scabbards . . . are never drawn except in action.'

The native cavalry of the new Indian Army formed after the Indian Mutiny of 1857–8 were armed for the most part with obsolete British cavalry swords, until the Government of India, after advice from the Army, procured blades and swords of a special pattern for the cavalry. These weapons were always carried in a wood scabbard covered with leather as Nolan had recorded and were made with special small hilts and grips for the Indian hand.

In the 1860s a sword with a curved blade was adopted for all Indian cavalry, Madras and Bombay having a 31½ in. blade while Bengal had a 33 in. blade. Although of differing lengths, the blades were termed as of the 'Paget Pattern' No. 6480 India Stores Sealed pattern. The swords usually had a three bar hilt with back piece and leather covered wood grip, although certain regiments who were allowed the native 'Tulwar' style hilt had the blades hilted in India, the rest with the three bar hilt having them made in Britain by Mole or Wilkinson.

Officers carried the British officer's pattern with the Imperial cypher rather than the Royal cypher and the regimental emblem etched on the blade. In 1918, all the variations of sword in the Indian cavalry ceased with the issue of the India Pattern 1908 Mark I, the Indian version of the British 1908 trooper's sword. The Indian version differed in the hilt having a wood grip and a small bowl guard with no reinforcing piece. The officers of the Indian cavalry also adopted this pattern but with engraved guard incorporating the Royal cypher and wood grip covered in fish skin.

In the infantry, the Indian army followed the British army by using the 1822 pattern with Imperial cypher in the cartouche, then the 1892 pattern with Imperial cypher on the guard.

Denmark, Sweden and Norway

In Denmark, weapons had been regulated by the early years of the eighteenth century. Like other armies, the heavy cavalry carried a broadsword, which was similar in style to the pattern used in Russia. The blade of the 1774 pattern was straight and single edged with a brass basket hilt with double oval shells and a round pommel, filled with lead for weight to which the basket guard was screwed. The scabbard was in leather with a top mount with two rings and a long bottom mount or chape, reaching more than half way up the scabbard with a further ring. Officers carried a more elaborate version, the pattern of 1780, again with a straight single edged blade, engraved and gilded at the top part, with a basket hilt with, to the left side a large oval bearing the arms of Slesvig for the Slesvig Cavalry Regiment, others having differing arms. The pommel was in the form of a helmet and the whole sword was carried in a brown leather scabbard with three gilt mounts.

Dragoons carried the double edged bladed broadsword approved in 1785. This had a brass basket hilt, the outer side incorporating the Danish coat of arms, the whole joining a round brass pommel. The grip was wood covered in leather and bound with brass wire in the grooves. The scabbard was in brown leather with internal mounts.

In 1808, the dragoons received a new pattern sword. This was a single edged bladed weapon with brass French style three bar hilt with langets, plain flat pommel and backpiece. It was from this pattern that the later 1818 light cavalry sabre was evolved.

In 1789, heavy cavalry troopers received an issue of swords. The weapons were, however, not new but a conversion of the 1774 pattern. The blade had been shortened and some of the bars removed from the hilt. The lead had also been removed from the pommel in an effort to produce a lighter more manageable sword. A new scabbard of the Dragoon pattern with internal mounts was issued with the sword. For officers a new sword was approved in 1798, but again this was only another modification this time of the 1780 pattern. The conversion or modification (for some officers had new swords made) consisted of removing the large shield bearing the arms on the left of the guard, removing the existing bars and adding one curled bar each side from the shell guard to just beneath the helmet pommel. The scabbard in leather had three large mounts with extra gilt reinforcing strips down each edge of the scabbard.

The next new pattern of heavy cavalry sword was issued in 1831. This was a straight single edged bladed weapon with a gilt brass hilt in the French and Prussian style. The hilt consisted of a knuckle bow forming a shell guard where hilt joined blade with additional bars fitted each side, three on the outer side and a single one on the inner side. The scabbard was steel with two rings for suspension. This was carried until a new universal pattern cavalry sword was approved in 1843. An improved pattern with slightly differing arrangement of the bars of the hilt was approved in 1838.

Officers in the Guards adopted an ornamental broadsword in 1772. This weapon had a straight blade, single edged, and was engraved at the top with arms and trophies and gilded. The hilt, in silver or white metal had a single knuckle bow forming a shell guard with bars both sides, the outermost portion having a large shield with the Danish coat of arms. The sword was carried in a leather scabbard with three large silver mounts, the long chape having a slot in the centre. This sword continued in use, mainly for ceremonial, until the regiment was disbanded in 1866. For every day wear, a steel three bar hilted sword with straight blade was introduced in 1828. This had a plain round pommel and chequered backpiece with hatched ebony grip.

Hussars in the Danish army carried the typical curved bladed hussar style sword with simple single knuckle bow, back piece and pommel (the latter sometimes ornamented) and curved leather scabbard with three mounts. The pattern in use about 1790 had a single knuckle bow with backpiece and pommel, the latter having in relief a lion's head mask, and a single knuckle bow with an extra side bar on the outer side. The blade, engraved at the top was single edged but double edged at the point. The scabbard was in leather with three ornamental gilt mounts. Some other examples had a lion head and mane pommel and backpiece and a double langet each side of the guard engraved with trophies of arms etc.

In 1818, a light cavalry sabre was introduced in a distinctive French style. The blade was curved and single edged and the hilt in brass (gilt for officers) had a single knuckle bow with two outer bars joining and forming a ring over the langets. The pommel and backpiece in brass were plain, the former with flat top and top nut to the tang. The grip was in wood covered in leather and bound in the grooves with brass twisted wire. This sword was carried by all regiments of light cavalry until the universal pattern of 1843 was introduced. In 1836, it was adopted by the artillery.

Some regiments of dragoons, however, received a new issue of swords in 1829. The new or improved pattern had a single edged blade but the three bar hilt with rounded pommel and chequered backpiece was in iron. This sword was made obsolete by the issue of the new pattern in 1843.

Lancers had their own particular style of sword approved in 1816. This had a single edged curved blade carried in a steel scabbard and a steel hilt with single knuckle bow and flat topped pommel and backpiece. The sword was used by the lancers until they were abolished in 1842 when the sword was relegated to the reserve artillery.

The universal cavalry sabre introduced in 1843 was intended for both officers and men. The blade was single edged with a deep fuller starting at the shoulder and terminating some eight inches from the point where the blade becomes double edged. The hilt was in sheet iron in the form of a flat knuckle bow widening at the outer side. This outer side was pierced with a short slot giving the appearance of a flat bar to the knuckle bow. The pommel was flat and the backpiece was faceted each side. Where the leather bound wood grip joined the guard there was an iron ferrule with a loop to take the short leather strap through which the forefinger was placed. The scabbard was in iron with two bands and rings for suspension and a steel shoe. The version carried by officers was slightly smaller in dimensions than that issued to nco's and troopers. Officers had themselves been ordered a new sword in 1837 with a curved single edged blade with a steel hilt with six bars. This short lived pattern was superseded by the 1843 sword.

In 1899, an improved sword known as the pattern 1843–99 was issued. This was similar in appearance to the old model with the same guard but with plain rounded backpiece and top nut surmounting the flat pommel. The loop on the ferrule was also removed as was the leather strap for the forefinger. The sword was carried in a new pattern scabbard approved the year before which had only a single top hand and ring for suspension.

The sword for Guards officers approved in 1852 was based on the universal cavalry sabre and differed in having silver or German silver fittings and being carried in a leather scabbard with metal mounts.

In the infantry, other ranks had carried a hanger in addition to musket and bayonet. These were withdrawn in the mid eighteenth century for all except grenadiers. The 1753 grenadier pattern hanger had a short curved single edged blade with a cast brass knuckle bow and double shell guard in one and cast round pommel and grip with spiral grooving. The blade was ornamented with royal cypher and date of manufacture. The scabbard originally of brown leather and later black had an internal mouthpiece and chape and hook for frog suspension. This pattern was later issued to all infantry and some were still in use during the 1845–50 war.

In 1788, a different pattern was approved for light infantry. It was single edged and straight bladed with a lion head pommel and backpiece and simple squared knuckle bow. Some of these swords were still in use in the 1880s with artillery and engineer units.

In 1793, more hangers were ordered for light infantry. They were provided by the simple expedient of converting the cavalry broadsword of 1750. The blade was shortened and ground down leaving part of the original engraving on the central rib and the original guard with side plate bearing the royal cypher was unscrewed from the pommel and cut from the single knuckle guard leaving the lion head pommel and backpiece and single knuckle guard as the hilt.

In 1834 a new pattern of hanger was produced for the infantry.

It had the same hilt as the grenadier pattern of 1753 but with an improved blade. Four years later a new version with the grip cast in two parts was approved. They continued in use well after 1854. The light infantry received a new sidearm in 1847. It had a straight single edged blade with a brass grip and pommel in one piece with a stirrup hilt fitted to it. Abandoned by light infantry in 1854, it was used by artillery until finally withdrawn in 1923.

In 1854 a new pattern version of the sidearm was issued. The first pattern had a hilt and knuckle bow cast in one piece. It was a copy of the French style of sidearm adopted by many other countries. It was in use with the infantry until 1869 when it was relegated to the Life Guards. Another sidearm issued the same year had a 'Roman' hilt, again popular in many armies. This too had a long life being withdrawn in the 1860s and relegated to non-combatants and finally made obsolete in 1924.

The sword adopted by infantry officers in 1766 was based on the small sword and was of the style popular with infantry officers in many armies including France, Prussia, Russia and Britain. The blade was single edged and straight and engraved from the shoulder for about 8 inches with the Danish coat of arms, foliage and trophies. The hilt was in gilt brass with double shell guard with curved single knuckle bow fitting into an urn shaped pommel. The grip was bound with twisted brass wire with ferrules top and bottom and the sword was carried in a brown leather scabbard with brass top mount with single ring and brass chape. This continued to be carried until 1789 when a hussar styled sabre was approved for officers of the army except for the King's Guard and the Military Academy. The sword had a single stirrup hilt with a side bar, plain pommel and backpiece and curved single edged blade carried in a black leather scabbard with three mounts. Officers of the King's Guard and the Military Academy adopted the same style but in silver rather than gilt brass.

In 1831, an unusual style of sword was adopted for infantry nco's. This had a straight single edged blade with a brass grip and knuckle bow with the addition on the left side of two extra bars forming a scroll. The scabbard was in black leather with brass mounts but had an extra channel into which a long bayonet was fitted.

In 1836, officers adopted a new sabre with single knuckle bow, rounded pommel and backpiece and langet with shell pattern each side of the shoulder. However, this pattern was short lived and a return was made the following year to the small sword style. The 1837 pattern had a straight single edged blade with shell guard, single knuckle bow and rounded grooved pommel. This was superseded in 1858 by a simple sword with slightly curved blade and a hilt with plain rounded pommel and backpiece and guard with two bars. Officers whose regiments had white metal buttons and silver lace had white metal fitments while others had brass or gilt brass. This was carried in a steel scabbard with two bands and rings and pronounced shoe. The shoe was removed from the scabbard in 1904, the same year a new pattern sword was introduced. This was a smaller sword in length and hilt size and had a single knuckle bow with a langet and rounded plain pommel with back piece with an ear each side. The blade was a return to older styles being slightly curved with a pipe back. The blade was nickle plated. The scabbard was in brown leather with metal mouthpiece with a 'D' for suspension and chape with button end.

In the Navy, there was no regulation pattern until 1849 when a gilt hilted sword was approved for all officers. Prior to this a variety of styles were popular especially the curved bladed 'fighting swords' with stirrup hilts and lion head pommel and backpiece. Another popular weapon was the straight bladed sword with 'five ball' hilt. Variations of the 'five ball' hilt with curved blades were also popular. The main difference between the British 'five ball' hilted sword and the Danish was that the latter tended to have a squared pommel and a smooth ivory grip, but both had the side ring with foul anchor which often leads to confusion when identifying these swords.

The 1849 sword had a solid gilt brass half basket hilt with raised bars and a foul anchor badge in the cartouche similar to the

Royal Naval sword. The grip was in gilt brass with side pieces in mother-of-pearl fitted each side. The pommel in gilt brass was composed of acanthus leaves and swept forward in the French style, the guard fitting into the foremost part which was split resembling the beak of a bird. There was a great variation in blade design some being flat and single edged while others such as the one illustrated on plate 87 has a piped back blade. All the blades, however, were slightly curved and were carried in a black leather scabbard with three gilt brass mounts. The locket or mouthpiece with its suspension ring bore the design of a dolphin superimposed on a trophy of arms, the middle mount had a military trophy of arms and the chape a foliage design. The only officers not to wear this pattern were those of the Engineering Branch whose warrant engineer officers (*Overmaskinmestre*) carried an adaptation of the small sword. This weapon had a knuckle bow with a dolphin at the halfway point terminating in a quillon over an upturned trefoil shaped shell guard, with the badge of crown and foul anchor in the centre and a wreath of oak and laurels around the edge of the shell. The pommel was almost hemispherical with the flat side joining the black fish skin covered grip.

The cutlasses issued to the Danish Navy were numerous in design, partly because of shortages of weapons when conversions and cutdown swords were pressed into service and partly because of new designs. At the beginning of the nineteenth century, the cutlass had a curved blade and a hilt composed of an upturned shell on the outerside with a knuckle bow finishing halfway up the grip and a down pointing quillon on the other side. The grip was bound in wire and topped with an onion shaped iron pommel.

After the British raid on Copenhagen and the subsequent loss in weapons, 'new' patterns were hastily converted for service. One such weapon had the blade taken from the dragoon sword of 1775, shortened and fitted with the basket hilt of the cavalry broadsword of 1789. Another weapon introduced at the same time was the 'Holstein' pattern cutlass which was in fact only the

1767 pattern French grenadier hanger with its hilt with knuckle guard cast in one and curved blade which was single edged. Yet another weapon was the so-called 'Stralsund' sword, said to have been obtained as part of the plunder at Stralsund. This weapon, originating from Prussia, had a brass stirrup hilt and backpiece and pommel and a leather bound grip. The blade was curved.

Around 1825, a new pattern was introduced to replace the variety of cutlasses then in use, although the so called 'Stralsund' pattern having been relegated to naval buglers continued until 1875. In the artillery it was issued in 1824 and withdrawn in 1854 but was supplied to the artillery school in 1832, suffered minor conversions in 1849 and 1856, and was finally withdrawn in 1912. The new pattern cutlass had a straight single edged blade with a round iron guard and knuckle bow reaching to a round pommel. The grip was tubular and also in iron. The whole hilt was painted black. Another cutlass was introduced in 1836 with an iron bowl guard pommel and tubular grip and a straight single edged blade. In about 1840 yet another new pattern was introduced with an iron bowl guard and backpiece but with a leather covered grooved wood grip. The blade was straight and carried in a leather scabbard with internal locket and chape. This pattern continued in use until 1875, although some ships retained them until after 1900.

There were also a variety of swords issued for nco's in the navy, the pattern of 1817 having a brass stirrup hilt with lion head pommel and backpiece. The blade was single edged and straight. In 1856 this was replaced with a new pattern having a solid brass half basket guard with a slit at the front similar to the universal pattern cavalry sword, the lower part of the basket being embossed with the crown and foul anchor. The backpiece and pommel were plain and the grip covered in black leather and bound with brass wire at intervals.

In 1882, this weapon was replaced by a shorter bladed sword with half basket guard in brass without the cut out slit and with the crown and foul anchor in a raised cartouche. The backpiece and pommel were of the same design but the grip was covered in fish skin. The scabbard was in black leather with two mounts in brass.

In Sweden, the heavy cavalry carried a broadsword introduced in 1777. This had a straight double edged blade with a basket style gilt composed of flat bars joining the single knuckle bow at the front and forming an oval (plate 86). The light cavalry carried the typical hussar style sabre with stirrup hilt being adopted in 1759. In the early nineteenth century the cavalry were armed with brass hilted French style swords with three bar guard, French pattern cap pommel and slightly curved blade, hussars retaining the sword with stirrup hilt and mounted squadrons having a steel disc hilted sword similar to the British pattern of 1796.

In 1854, a universal pattern sabre was introduced very similar in style to that adopted in Denmark but with a slightly fuller guard and wider slit in it. This continued in service until 1867 when a new pattern was introduced with narrower guard with beaded edge and a design of pierced out holes. The forefinger loop of the previous pattern was still retained, but the ferrule had the addition of two langets which passed through slots in the guard.

The artillery had adopted a stirrup hilted sword in 1831 with a simple rounded pommel and backpiece with ears and langets to the guard. The blade was single edged and curved. Officers in the artillery adopted a decorative dress sword in 1889 with typical French cap pommel, exaggerated stirrup hilt with langets and a straight double edged blade with two narrow fullers.

In the infantry, privates carried the brass hilted hanger similar to that adopted in Denmark, continuing to wear it well into the 1830s while officers as would be expected wore an adaptation of the small sword so beloved of infantry officers at this period. The sword had a straight double edged blade with central fuller and was decorated with blue and gilding at the top (plate 86). The hilt was gilt brass with round grooved pommel, knuckle guard and groove shell guard. In 1859, however, a new style of sword was introduced with pierced and decorated cast gilt brass guard, plain rounded pommel and backpiece and leather grip bound in the grooves with wire. The blade was slightly curved and pipe backed and decorated with scrolls, and emblems which were blue and gilt.

In the navy, the British 1805 style of sword was adopted in 1824, but with the pommel in the form of a dolphin's head rather than a lion's head. The blade was straight with a single edge and decorated at the top with engraved designs and blue and gilt. This pattern survived until 1860 when a new pattern again modelled on the Royal Navy sword was adopted. This had a solid half basket guard with raised ribs with an anchor in the cartouche. The pommel and backpiece were in the form of a lion's head and mane and the blade was slightly curved and pipe backed. In 1878, the pipe back blade was replaced by a flat curved single edged blade.

Cutlasses in the Swedish navy also followed the British pattern of the early 1800s with a figure '8' guard, cast ribbed grip and straight blade. In 1846 the cutlass issued had a simple knuckle bow hilt and a falchion blade.

Norway having no fully independent existence until 1905 being at various times united with Denmark and Sweden, used the swords of those countries. The Norwegian navy, however, even after the union with Sweden in 1814 still continued as a separate force. The swords carried by officers from about 1860 were of a distinctly French pattern as many Norwegians served with the French during the Napoleonic wars and the French influence was strongly felt. The sword very similar to the French naval sword of 1837 had a pierced half basket guard in gilt brass with the crown above the foul anchor pierced out on the left side of the guard where it swelled out and upwards. The pommel and backpiece were very decorative being worked with floral designs which stretched a little way down the backpiece. The blade was slightly curved with a single cutting edge and wide fuller. The scabbard was in black leather with three mounts, the top mount with the crown over foul anchor and the chape was plain with large rounded shoe.

United States and South America

During the American War of Independence, the swords used were basically of British pattern as well as those captured from the mercenary troops employed in the service of Britain. For the infantry soldiers, the most common weapons were the British pattern hangers with their brass hilts and short curved blades as well as a number of French weapons of this type. American made hangers also appeared but in small quantities. These had a barrel shaped grip in wood covered in leather with a foreign made blade – French or German – and a flat shell guard with knuckle strap. The knuckle strap was secured to the cap pommel by hammering over.

Officers carried a great variety of swords usually of civilian pattern. The basic small sword in silver or brass was a popular weapon with its slender blade and hilt with knuckle guard, shell and rings as was the civilian hunting sword with its straight or slightly curved blade, simple hilt of stone, bone or ivory bound with silver strip and usually having a flat pommel and chain guard. As it had a short blade it was usually carried by high ranking officers who were not expected to indulge in close quarter fighting with the 'red-coats'.

Other styles of swords had a similar blade to the hunting sword but a hilt with knuckle guard and additional bars, while some officers equipped themselves with a cavalry type of sword. The most common style of this sword had a lion head pommel in brass, wood grip covered in leather but sometimes in ivory or bone and spirally grooved with a single knuckle bow developed into an additional bar each side where it formed the junction with the blade. The blades were usually single edged, slightly curved and of the light cavalry weight. The fittings were usually in brass but depending on the wealth of the buyer, silver was sometimes used. Brass was popular because it was easy to cast and work and therefore many more swords could be made when they were wanted with the minimum of equipment.

The cavalry who used the sword perhaps more than anyone

else had two basic types of sword, the curved sabre and the broadsword or basket hilted sword. Some of the swords were of home manufacture but others were usually captured weapons. When sufficient quantities of any one pattern were captured they were issued out to one particular regiment. In 1778, General George Washington ordered that the swords of the Brunswick Dragoons captured at the Battle of Bennington should be issued to Colonel Sheldon's Second Continental Dragoons.

The curved bladed weapons carried usually had a simple stirrup guard, plain back piece and pommel and wood grip covered in leather and bound in the grooves with wire. Some patterns had rounded pommels and slotted guard, that is the knuckle bow widened out where the grip joined the blade into a shell and was cut out with slots. The guards themselves were either of the stirrup pattern or rounded and the pommels sometimes round or shaped like the Adam style urn used on many infantry pattern small swords. Some patterns went to the trouble of incorporating lion head pommels and in this case as in the cases mentioned there was no backpiece but the pommel alone. Captured weapons included British swords, Brunswick swords and French weapons which were left from the French presence in America or specially purchased in France.

Local made weapons include a credible copy of the British light cavalry sword and it is known that 1,000 of this pattern were made at Rappahannock Forge in 1781 by James Hunter. This had a curved single edged blade without fullers – although swords with imported blades did have fullers – a simple stirrup guard, plain backpiece with tang button and curved quillon. The grip was almost round covered in leather and wired in the grooves. Although varying in detail, most of these sabres were of simple design with a very basic type of guard, although models are known with two and three bar guards.

After independence, and with the establishment of a standing army, equipping and clothing in a uniform style became of paramount importance. The cavalry sword pattern 1789 had a simple stirrup guard, plain flat topped pommel and backpiece, wood grip covered in leather and a curved single edged blade. Two thousand of these were made under contract in 1789 by Nathan Starr, perhaps more well known for his firearms and undoubtedly other makers supplied this style of sword. A more suitable method of supply was assured when the Virginia Manufactory or State Armoury was established in 1789.

In 1803, the manufactory produced a new pattern of cavalry sword. This had a steel hilt composed of a flat top pommel and backpiece, a knuckle guard widening at the base with cut out slots. The grip was in wood covered in leather and bound in the grooves with wire. The blade was single edged and slightly curved with a fuller each side measuring just over 40 in. and carried in a steel scabbard with two bands and rings. This pattern was used until 1820. In 1812, however, another type of sword was produced under contract and 10,000 were supplied by Nathan Starr. This was very similar to the British light cavalry sword of 1796 with steel stirrup guard, rounded pommel and backpiece and single edged curved blade. Another version, also produced by Starr in 1812 had a single edged curved blade with a fuller each side, and a hilt with round knuckle guard and a rounded forward leaning pommel and backpiece.

By 1833, however, a standard pattern of cavalry sword replaced the various odd patterns in service. This weapon had a three bar steel hilt, rounded pommel and plain backpiece and a slightly curved single edged blade. These swords were supplied under contract by N. P. Ames of Springfield. This weapon had a short life and was replaced in 1840 by a French style of sword. The heavy cavalry pattern of 1840 had a three bar brass guard, and French style cap pommel with wood grip covered in leather and bound in the grooves with brass twisted wire. The blade was single edged and curved and the sword was carried in a steel scabbard with two bands and rings.

In the same year, the Light Artillery adopted another French pattern of sword. This was modelled on the French horse artillery sabre and had a curved single edged blade and a single brass knuckle bow, cap pommel and leather covered grip bound in wire. The Foot Artillery were armed with a French style short sword with 'Roman' style hilt with the eagle engraved on the pommel, scaled grip and crosspiece with rounded finials. The blade was leaf shaped and double edged.

Officers carried the same pattern swords as the men in the cavalry and light artillery but often had extra decorative designs incorporated in the hilt and on the blade.

The infantry officer after the War of Independence carried a spadroon without beaded guard and this sword was also adopted by nco's. In 1821 a new sword was adopted which had a beaded guard. This had an eagle head pommel, silver plated brass grip and knuckle guard with 'five balls' and a side guard with a further 'five balls'. The weapon had a straight single edged blade and was introduced in the uniform regulations of 1821. A further style of weapon was also available to officers and this was a small sword with an Indian head pommel, ribbed grip and ornate knuckle guard and downpointing shell guard. The blade was single edged and straight. Nco's adopted a pattern of their own in 1840 with cast brass hilt of knuckle guard, shells, round pommel and grip, this pattern without shells being adopted by musicians in the same year.

By the time of the American Civil war, swords had been regulated to a small number of styles. General officers carried a small sword with gilt hilt of knuckle bow and shell guard with an embossed eagle with a silver wire grip, straight blade and a brass or steel scabbard while officers of the cavalry carried the three bar hilted sword previously described and artillery, infantry and foot riflemen had a sword on the French infantry pattern. This had a knuckle bow broadening out into a pierced half basket guard with forward leaning French cap pommel and leather bound grip with wire in the grooves. Field officers, however, and the officers of supporting troops, Adjutant General's office, Quartermasters etc., wore a differing pattern. Medical cadets were ordered the same pattern as worn by nco's.

In 1902, a new pattern was ordered for all officers. This had a nickle plated four bar hilt, black shaped moulded grip and slightly curved single edged blade. In 1913, cavalry troopers were issued with a new pattern of sword whose design was greatly influenced by the British pattern of 1908. This had a straight double edged blade and bowl guard with grip and backpiece cast in one piece. Like the British pattern, the backpiece had a thumbhole on the back, but it was never as efficient as the British grip.

In the Navy, the first pattern of regulation sword was adopted in 1813 but the description was so vague as to allow plenty of latitude in design. In 1827, however, a sword based on the British infantry officer's pattern of 1822 was adopted with an eagle with outspread wings in the cartouche and an eagle head pommel and backpiece. In 1841, a further sword was introduced with an eagle head pommel and backpiece, a decorative knuckle bow and a small downpointing shell embossed with oak leaves and acorns. However, in 1852, as with the army, the French influence came to bear and a sword based on the French naval pattern was introduced. This incorporated in the design of the half basket guard the letters USN. Officers of the Revenue Service had the letters USRM. The Revenue Service was amalgamated with the Coast Guard in 1915 and all officers carried the naval sword with the letters USCG in the guard. During the War of Independence, cutlasses used were of the British style but with a turned wood grip. In 1808 a new pattern was adopted with slightly concave guard tapering from pommel to the shell guard and eight years later a variation was issued with shorter blade. In 1841 a pattern not dissimilar to the 1833 artillery short sword was adopted but it had a brass knuckle guard, slim at the pommel but widening at the base. In 1861, a French style cutlass was adopted. This had a cap pommel, knuckle bow with riveted to the outer side of the bow a solid half basket guard. The grip was wood covered in leather and bound with wire and the blade was single edged and slightly curved. Cutlasses were abolished in 1949.

Officers of the United States Marine Corps were ordered swords in 1804 which were referred to as 'yellow mounted sabres' but in 1825 a new pattern was authorized. This had a mameluke style hilt with ivory scales held to the tang with gilt stars. The blade was single edged and slightly curved. In 1850, the sword was withdrawn in favour of the infantry pattern sword but in 1875 officers managed to get permission to revert to the mameluke hilted sword. Enlisted men of the Corps carried the same pattern sword as infantry officers (plate 96).

The swords of South American countries were usually modelled on swords of some European country, Germany being a strong influence and also the main source of supply. In Argentine the cavalry sword had a half basket hilt with black plastic grips and rounded pommel and backpiece. In the cartouche of the guard – very similar to the British 1822 – were the arms of the country. The naval sword had a lion head pommel and backpiece with a black moulded grip and a stirrup knuckle guard which was highly decorated with oak leaves and acorns.

In Brazil, the basic military sword had a half bowl guard with a turndown on the inside edge with a plain ridged pommel and backpiece. The arms of Brazil were stamped on the outer side of the bowl guard. Troopers carried the three bar brass hilted sword of the French style. The Brazilian Navy adopted a sword along the lines of the French and American patterns with the anchor in the pierced work of the guard. Warrant officers however, had a sword with a three bar hilt with a cartouche between the top and middle bar, a cap pommel and single edged blade.

In Chile, the police carried a very German style sword, in fact a copy of the cavalry sword of 1889 but with the arms of Chile in the cartouche. Small brass hilted French style hangers were worn by other ranks. In Cuba, the Navy had a sword based on the British pattern with lion head pommel and the backpiece, a solid half basket guard with the star over the anchor in the cartouche. The cavalry had a French style sword with four bar hilt, cap pommel and curved single edged blade. The infantry wore a plain stirrup hilted sword with langets to the guard, rounded pommel and backpiece and straight blade. Peru also adopted the cavalry styled sword of Cuba as did Costa Rica, while Equador adopted the British 1822 pattern infantry sword and the 1829 Royal Naval sword replacing the British badges in the cartouche with their own national ones, the Navy having in addition the anchor.

In Guatemala a sword similar to the sword adopted in 1902 by all offices in the United States army was carried but with a cartouche fitted to the bars of the guard bearing the national emblem, while in Venezuela, the naval sword was of a unique design (plate 87). The infantry sword, however, was a direct copy of the British 1822 pattern but the cavalry sword was the same as the Prussian officer's sword of 1889.

In Mexico, the navy adopted a sword similar in design to the British pattern but without the lion head pommel which was replaced with a condor's head and this bird with anchor appeared in the cartouche. The cavalry however, carried the same three bar brass hilted 'French' design sword as the US cavalry and the infantry wore a German style sword with single simple knuckle guard.

3   *Scottish Weapons*

The large double handed claymore or *claidheamhmor* had by the early seventeenth century acquired a large solid shell guard upturned towards the pommel to protect the user's hand but because of the advances made in firearms and the demise in the use of armour was soon abandoned in favour of the broadsword, which since the eighteenth century has erroneously been called a claymore.

The Scottish broadsword was developed from the broadsword in use on the continent, especially in Germany but how the influence came to Scotland during the early seventeenth century is difficult to ascertain. There were various styles of broadsword but all employed a double edged blade, wide at the shoulder and tapering towards the point. There were usually a single or number of fullers in the blade. Scottish broadswords tended to have a smaller basket guard and grip than the broadswords in use in various parts of Europe as a cavalry sword. They tended also to have a distinctive pommel shape in the form of a flat topped cone, which usually had the tang riveted over it. Various types of broadsword are shown in plates 28 and 29.

At the beginning of the eighteenth century, the broadsword was carried as an integral part of Highland dress, worn by clan members, in the style of European gentlemen of the same period who carried the 'Town' or small sword. With the broadsword, was worn the dirk (see pages 74 to 76) and the 'targe' or shield, and side pistol(s). Ten years following the 1715 rebellion, the Disarming Act was passed making it a penal offence to have, use

or wear, 'Broadsword or targe, poignard, whinger or dirk...'
To induce the natives to hand in their weapons, the government empowered generals to offer a cash payment for each prohibited weapon. Later, however, in view of the 'rubbish' that was handed in, cash payments were suspended. In the same year, however, a number of independent companies were formed from those clans favourable to the House of Hanover to act as police. These men were armed with muskets, broadswords and dirks and it was only in these companies that Scots could bear arms. The independent companies were, in 1743, formed into a line regiment, the 43rd (re-numbered 42nd in 1749) – the Black Watch.

In 1746, following the '45 rebellion, a further act was passed for the 'Abolition and Proscription of the Highland Dress', which was brutally enforced, those wearing highland dress or carrying any highland weapon being shot on sight by the military.

The sword and dirk were now solely the weapon of the Scottish regiments, except for those chiefs who supported the Hanoverian Government, but in about 1757, the enforcement of the Act was relaxed. In 1782, the Act was repealed due to the pressure of the Highland Society of London and highland dress and weapons were once again worn by civilians.

After the repeal of the act, the sword was not generally adopted by civilians and remained basically a military weapon, although used by pipers, drummers and for the sword dance. The dirk, however, was generally used with civilian highland dress.

The Scottish dirk had evolved from the fourteenth century 'Ballock' knife (see page 17) but by the early 1500s had already taken on a special form in Scotland. In the Scottish version, the two side balls on the grip became larger and the pommel flattened. Up until the early eighteenth century, the grip had been plain but afterwards started to have Celtic interlacing carved into it and decorated with small nail heads between the strap work. The side balls now became flat at the front and back. The blades had been in the past made from old broken sword blades, having a number of decorative notches along the back of the blade and this gave the style for later 'made' blades. As early as 1512 a contemporary account records that highlanders were noted for their 'large daggers sharpened on one side only, but very sharp'. In the early forms of dirk, the scabbard was not made to incorporate a companion knife and fork which later became a feature of this weapon, although some examples are known. Another feature of the dirk following the revival of interest in Highland dress after 1782 was the setting in on top of the grip in place of a flat metal pommel, of a cairngorm stone in a metal setting. This later also became a feature of military dirks, although those carried by pipers except where purchased by the officers of a regiment, had and still have a metal top with embossed crown.

Highland regiments raised for military service were supplied with long arms but 'dirks, highland pistols and targes' were either supplied by the colonel against payment from the men or by the men themselves. The dirk carried by the soldiers appears to have had a carved 'bog wood' grip with interlacing, a flat pommel with a small top nut, carried in a black leather scabbard with brass top and bottom mounts. The flat pommel possibly bore a regimental number or the crown. In 1776, the dirk and broadsword seemed to have been abandoned by privates being only carried by officers and sergeants. In an inspection return of the 42nd for May 1775, it appears that the grenadiers' swords – enough for all the grenadier company – were wanting. It was, however, explained that the highlanders 'declined using broadswords in America, that they all prefer bayonets, and that swords for the battalion men, though part of their dress and establishment, are an incumberence.'

Sergeants, pipers and drummers continued to wear the broadsword and dirk: the pattern of dirk carried by sergeants and drummers was probably with a carved grip surmounted by a flat brass pommel engraved with the crown; while the dirk carried by pipers, who were not officially sanctioned or carried 'on the strength' was of varying patterns as they were equipped and paid for by the officers.

Officers carried the traditional broadsword from the beginnings of the Scottish regiments and it was only in 1798 that any regulation referring to swords was passed. The sword ordered was a basket hilted weapon with a double edged blade and a gilt metal basket hilt. The basket hilt was often engraved or pierced according to regimental or individual preference and lined on the inside with a crimson cloth covering lining edged with a fringe. Plate 49 shows the gilt hilted broadsword of the 93rd about 1820. In 1822 with the first issue of Dress Regulations, the 'Gothic' hilted infantry sword was ordered for *all* but this was on oversight and the Highland regiments continued to wear the gilt hilted sword until 1828 when a new pattern with a steel hilt was ordered. The gilt hilted sword continued in use with some officers as the authorities allowed old patterns to be used 'until worn out.' The new pattern continued and continues to be worn by officers of Highland regiments, although from the late nineteenth century, the hilt was nickle plated and not of polished steel.

The original scabbard was in black leather with metal mounts but in 1868, all steel scabbards were ordered. With the wearing of the 'Sam Browne' belt for active service at the end of the nineteenth century, a wood scabbard covered with brown leather with a metal chape was ordered. One distinctive feature of the scabbard of officers' swords was that the chape of the leather scabbard and the metal scabbard had a ball finial.

In the 1870s, the cross hilt was introduced to replace the cumbersome basket hilt on active service. This took various forms for the individual regiments. The basket hilt was removed by placing a key in the hole in the tang button and unscrewing; the basket hilt with its crimson lining edged in blue silk was removed as was the crimson silk fringe leaving only the grip to be re-used. The cross hilt was slotted on to the shoulder of the blade, the grip replaced and the tang button put on and tightened.

When officers wore the cross hilt, field officers adopted a different hilt or at least in one case a different sword. There were two basic designs of hilt, one being a pierced shallow bowl guard engraved with thistles with the regimental badge in the centre and the other being a steel version of the scroll hilted sword carried by Royal Engineer officers from 1856 until 1892. This was also the same as the heavy cavalry officer's sword ordered in the same year. The thistle design was adopted by The Royal Scots, Royal Scots Fusiliers, King's Own Scottish Borderers and the Gordon Highlanders while the scroll hilt was used by The Black Watch, Highland Light Infantry and the Argyll and Sutherland Highlanders. In the Queen's Own Cameron Highlanders, field officers adopted the 1822 light cavalry officer's sword.

Sergeants continued to carry the brass hilted broadsword until 1828 when the iron hilted one was issued in place of any swords that had worn out. In 1852 swords were withdrawn except for staff sergeants who received a new pattern in 1857. This sword with minor alterations in weight and design continued in use for Highland and after 1881 Lowland Regiments (except for the Scottish Rifles) until 1929 when all the variety of swords were made obsolete and a new pattern introduced, the No 1 Mk III, which was similar to the pattern in use with officers. The basket hilt was removable and could be fitted with a cross hilt. The scabbards were the No 1 Mk II in black leather with nickel plated locket and chape with ball finial or for service dress wear the No 1 Mk III in wood covered with brown leather with the same chape.

Pipers and drummers of Highland regiments were equipped with the broadsword, firstly the brass hilted version and then an iron hilted pattern. The brass hilted broadsword appears to have been carried until 1857 when a shorter version of the staff sergeant's sword pattern 1857 was issued. The scabbard in black leather had only locket and chape for frog suspension as opposed to the three mounts on the staff sergeant's pattern. The sword was withdrawn in 1871 and the dirk issued in its place. Bandsmen carried the broadsword until 1872 when it too was replaced by the dirk.

The Ordnance issue dirk, designated the Dirk, Piper, Band and Drummers Highland Regiments Mk I was introduced in 1872. It was in the traditional form, with a carved wood grip with interlacing and German silver nails at various points where the strapping crossed. It had a round flat pommel with a raised crown on the top and a German silver ferrule. The blade was the same as used on dirks supplied to officers being single edged with a thick back with decorative scallops. The scabbard was in 'best mahogany' covered in black leather with four mounts in iron. Each of the mounts was decorated with an embossed design of thistles and leaves. There was no companion knife and fork fitted. The scabbard Mk I and II had iron mounts while the Mk III had nickle plated mounts. The difference between the marks of dirks was as follows. Mk I: Name of the regiment and or number etched on the blade. Mk II: No name or number but general design incorporating thistles and foliage. Mk III: Blade had no scallop edge to back and was plain. Sometime in the 1920s, the carved ebony grip was abandoned in favour of a moulded grip.

Officers had carried dirks since the formation of highland regiments but no weapon was regulated, but it is certain that by the beginning of the nineteenth century regimental patterns had been adopted 'by custom'. *Dress Regulations* of 1822 stated that the dirks should have 'Plain gilt mountings; black ebony grip, plain steel blade, scabbard fitted with knife and fork. Scabbard in black leather worn on right side'. Further editions of *Dress Regulations* throw no more light on the designs simply stating 'Of established Regimental pattern'. These patterns can be identified from surviving examples and from drawings in manufacturers pattern books. The following is taken from detailed drawings in the Pattern Book of Henry Wilkinson (later The Wilkinson Sword Company). The descriptions date from about circa 1850 and 1881 following the regimental amalgamations brought about by the Cardwell reforms.

42nd: Black carved grip with interlacing and studs, forward leaning pommel with cairngorm stone, thistle pattern ferrule. Blade etched with St Andrew and cross over 42. Later examples include battle honours. Reverse of blade crown and VR. Blades decorated with thistles and foliage. Scabbard black leather with four mounts. Top mount St Andrew and cross with thistles, other three mounts thistles only. Chape with ball finial. All metal fittings gilt. No alteration in pattern after 1881, officers of old 42nd and 73rd adopted this pattern.

71st: Black carved grip with interlacing in centre portion, lower portion had carved highland bonnet with crossed claymores behind. Forward leaning pommel with cairngorm and thistle pattern ferrule. Blade etched with regimental badge and crown and VR on reverse side with thistles and foliage decoration. Scabbard black leather with four mounts. Top mount French bugle horn with crown above and '71' in centre, border with thistles. Other three mounts thistle embossing with border. Flat bottom to chape. All metal fittings gilt. 1881, on formation of the Highland Light Infantry this pattern was adopted with the new badge in place of the bugle horn on the top mount.

72nd: Black carved grip with interlacing and studs, plain flat pommel with cairngorm stone, grip carved with leaves just beneath pommel. Thistle pattern ferrule. Blade with regimental number with crown above and on reverse crown with VR beneath. Both sides decorated with thistles and foliage. Scabbard black leather with four mounts. Top mount embossed thistles with number '72' in centre. Other three mounts thistle embossed with flat bottom to chape. Companion knife and fork with carved wood grips tapering from shoulder to flat pommel with cairngorm stone. 1881, amalgamated with 78th to form the Seaforth Highlanders (see below). All metal fittings gilt.

74th: Black carved grip with interlacing in centre and top portion, lower portion with wide band in gilt brass with thistles and regimental device. Flat pommel with cairngorm. Blade with regimental badge, and crown and VR on reverse side with thistles and regimental battle honours. Scabbard black leather with four mounts. Top mount with St Andrew and Cross on star edged with thistles. Next mount edged with thistles with the elephant and scroll above 'ASSAYE'. Lower mount edged with thistles with regimental number '74'. Chape with thistles, flat bottom. Companion knife and fork with flat pommel embossed with thistles and with cairngorm. All metal fittings gilt.

78th: Black carved grip with interlacing and studs in centre portion, lower portion had carved highland bonnet with crossed claymores behind. Gilt metal thistle pattern strips each side of lower part. Thistle pattern ferrule. Forward leaning pommel with cairngorm stone. Blade etched with regimental number and the elephant with 'ASSAYE' beneath. Reverse side crown with VR beneath. Both sides decorated with thistles and foliage. Scabbard black leather with four mounts. Top mount with St Andrew and cross flanked by thistles. Other mounts with thistle embossing. Chape of special pattern terminating in a trefoil. On amalgamation of 72nd and 78th, this pattern was adopted. All metal fittings gilt.

79th: Black carved grip with interlacing and studs in centre portion. Slightly leaning forward pommel with long portion with thistle embossing with cairngorm stone. Lower portion of grip covered at front with gilt panel with embossed thistles. Blade with regimental number with crown above and on reverse crown with VR. Scabbard black leather with four mounts, top mount embossed with thistles with '79' in centre. Other mounts embossed with thistles. Special pattern chape with long decorative portion reaching up and nearly touching the third mount. Knife and fork had grips tapering from narrow at the shoulder to large gilt pommels with cairngorm stones. 1881, top mount of scabbard altered to have crown above thistle in place of '79'. All metal fittings gilt.

91st: (Only restored Highland dress in 1864. Description of dirk drawing proposed by Wilkinsons and accepted 1864.) Black carved grip with interlacing and studs. Flat pommel with cairngorm stone, thistle pattern ferrule. Blade with number and thistle and foliage design. Scabbard black leather with four mounts. Top mount with thistle and ribbon interlacing with '91' in centre. Second mount with same interlacing with Star of Order of Thistle in centre. Other two mounts with thistle and ribbon interlacing. Chape with rounded bottom. All metal fittings gilt. New pattern probably adopted in 1866. Black carved pommel with interlacing and studs. Round 'door knob' type pommel with flat top with cairngorm stone. Ferrule with raised words 'ARGYLLSHIRE' above 'HIGHLANDERS'. Blade with thistle etching and number 91st in panel. Scabbard with three mounts. Top mount with St Andrews cross with at the top of it the crown, between the two left arms the letter 'V' and between the two right, the letter 'R'. Below a thistle with leaves. Middle mount with letters 'XCI' with thistle and leaves beneath accommodating both knife and fork with grips similar to the dirk. Chape had thistles and leaves. (See Argyll and Sutherland Highlanders.) In 1881, amalgamated with 93rd to form Argyll and Sutherland Highlanders.

92nd: Black carved grip with interlacing and studs. Flat open work pommel with cairngorm stone, thistle pattern ferrule. Blade with regimental number and crown above and crown and 'VR' on reverse. Scabbard black leather with four mounts. Top mount with sphinx on tablet inscribed 'EGYPT' over '92'. Second mount with single thistle, third mount with double intertwined thistles, chape with three thistles and rounded bottom. Knife and fork with barrel shaped grips and smaller versions of dirk pommel. All metal fittings silver.

Argyll and Sutherland Highlanders:
Black carved grip with special interlacing and studs. Forward leaning pommel with leaf carving to top portion of grip and cairngorms stone. Special pattern ferrule with stopped engraving. Blade with regimental badge, number and battle honours, reverse side with crown and 'VR'. Scabbard with four mounts, top mount with the double cypher of H.R.H. the Princess Louise with coronet above, the whole surrounded with interlacing. The second mount with boar's head and scroll beneath with *Ne Obliviscaris* all surrounded by interlacing. Third mount with cat above scroll with *Sans Peur* surrounded by interlacing. Chape with flat bottom and interlacing and sea monsters which also appear on the mounts for knife and fork. Knife and fork grip of special carved pattern with forward leaning pommels with cairngorm stones. All metal fittings in silver. The title Princess Louise's was given to the 91st Argyllshire Highlanders in 1870, and this pattern was probably adopted shortly after (see 91st).

Officers and pipers also wore another knife, a short bladed weapon carried in the right stocking. This Highland weapon dates from the revival of Highland dress in the eighteenth century. It was called a skean dhu which is Gaelic for black knife. The version carried by pipers had a scaled down version of the dirk blade with a flat carved grip with nickel plated flat pommel and ferrule. The scabbard had locket and chape. Officer's skean dhu's had a carved grip with studs and a pommel with a cairngorm. The grip was without badge in the Seaforth Highlanders but the other regiments had the following badges. The Black Watch had on the grip St Andrew and his cross, a differing version being worn by the Gordon Highlanders while the Highland Light Infantry had their badge in the centre of the grip and the Cameron Highlanders had above the ferrule the Sphinx on a tablet inscribed 'EGYPT'. The scabbards had plain mounts.

4
Staff Weapons and Lances

Bill

This was one of the most common of staff weapons used by many countries to arm the foot soldier. It was in continuous use from the middle of the thirteenth century until the seventeenth century. The head of the weapon was in iron and was long with a single cutting edge which divided at the top into a forward curving 'bill' and a spike. In the centre of the back was a further short spike. The head was fitted to the shaft by a short socket and two langets through which rivets passed.

Gisarme

The gisarme was in use in England and on the continent from the twelfth century until the mid 1400s. The curved half moon shaped blade with cutting edge on the outer curve was fitted to the staff by a single socket. The top curve of the blade extended beyond the shaft while the lower curve fitted into it.

Glaive

The glaive was much used in France and Germany and had a single edged blade with a double edge on part of the back. It was made with a thick neck and shoulder with langets to secure it to the shaft. Some examples have hooks, extra blades and spurs on the blunt top edge.

Halbard

The halbard came in varying styles but the most distinctive feature was an axe type blade with a spike above it on the other side of the shaft. It was similar to the poleaxe except that the blade continued in the form of a double edged spike. First used in Switzerland in the thirteenth century, this weapon continued in use in some armies until the nineteenth century as a parade weapon for officers and nco's. The shape of the axe type cutting blade varied some examples having an inward curving edge while others had a backward facing top blade. The heads can often be found with pierced work and also engraving. During the early years of the sixteenth century the blades tended to have the edge drawn out to a point, while later in the century the blade with inward curving cutting edge already mentioned, and long spear pointed extension became popular. During the eighteenth century the halbard used by British infantry sergeants had a slightly convex blade with two hooks and a backward leaning top blade. The extension had a round base and a wide double sided blade. All of these weapons were fitted to wooden shafts by langets and rivets and later screws.

Lance

From earliest times, the term lance meant a spear but by the end of the sixteenth century was used exclusively for the staff weapon carried by horsemen. The heavier longer lance was carried by the heavy cavalry and the lighter somewhat shorter *demi-lance* by the not so heavily armoured cavalry. Jousting lances were in the beginning exactly the same as fighting lances but with a rebated head and a small hand shield or vamplate. From the end of the fifteenth century when jousting was more of a sport, lances were made hollow for lightness and so that they would break on impact hopefully not injuring the vanquished too much.

The demi-lance came into prominent use during the late

fifteenth and early sixteenth centuries but were themselves replaced by horsemen armed with pistols and swords only because of the changing tactics of warfare brought about by the discovery of gunpowder, handguns and artillery, and its widespread use.

It was only during the Napoleonic wars that the weapon was revived in the French service, adopted in 1816 by Britain and later by other countries and continued in use until mechanization finally ousted the horse. In France the lance had a long wooden shaft with iron head with triangular sectioned hollow ground blade secured to the shaft by two wide langets. Beneath this were three 'D's for securing the pennon. The shoe was pointed similar to a shell head and fitted to the shaft by langets and rivets. This pattern with only slight modifications in shortening the length of the ash pole continued in service for many years.

In Britain, the lance was adopted in 1816, the first pattern being some 16 ft long! This had been taken from the length of the French *Gendarmerie* lance which was two foot longer! After some deliberation it was decided that a 9 ft lance was more manageable and this was accordingly adopted. This remained the standard length until the demise of this weapon. In Britain, ash was used for the shaft from 1816. This wood was impregnated with linseed oil and tar as a preservative. At first the original pennon was red with the union flag in the corner but this was abandoned in favour of the red over white swallow tailed pennon.

The 1846 pattern lance had an ash shaft and a spear head attached to it with langets some 30 inches long and rivets. A sling was tied to the shaft at a convenient height for the user to slide his arm through when carrying or using it on horseback. The shoe was a plain rounded iron tip with langets held by rivets. In 1860 a further pattern similar to the last was ordered but with differing shoe which now had a swell in it to sit firmly in the 'bucket' carried on the stirrup irons and had keyed slots in the langets to take the pennon. In 1868 a new pattern was ordered with a male bamboo pole (female bamboo is unsuitable as it is partially hollow), being a triangular sectioned hollow ground spear head with long socket and the same pattern shoes as previously used minus the langets. The head and shoe were held to the pole by glue. This pattern also had a protector in addition to the sling, and the pennon was tied on with rawhide thongs. The protector was situated 2 ft from the tip of the shoe and stretched for 18 inches. It was made in brown leather and was securely sewn to the pole or shaft. This served to protect the wood from rubbing and damage. In 1885, the bamboo pole was again replaced by ash and the lance designated the pattern 1885 and at the same time the protector was removed. However, by 1890, a return had been made to the 1868 pattern with protector, which was discontinued except for ceremonial use in 1903. It was revived shortly afterwards in 1909 and used during the Great War and finally abolished in 1927. Not to be confused with the lance is the Naval boarding pike. This had the head of the 1846 pattern lance with shorter langets and no shoe to the pole. They were still in service in 1899 and not withdrawn until 1926.

The lances of various other countries followed this style of having an ash shaft – Britain adopted bamboo in 1868 because of its association with India – and varying types of heads and butts, but the German Uhlans were equipped prior to the Great War with lances with metal shafts or poles usually in two pieces which were then fitted together.

Linstock

The linstock was not truly a weapon but a shaft with decorative head. The spear head was flanked each side with a branch, sometimes decorated with serpents' heads into which was clamped the slow burning match for the gunners. The linstock was thrust into the ground by the guns and kept burning in action serving as a ready source of fire for the gunners' slow matches which were used to ignite the vents of the pieces.

Lochaber Axe

This was a Scottish weapon with an almost semi-circular blade; the cutting edging on to the rounded part with two sockets to hold it to the shaft. Attached to the flat back of the head was a hook useful for disengaging defences etc. This weapon was carried during the eighteenth century by the Edinburgh Town Guard.

Partisan

The partisan was introduced in the middle of the fourteenth century and became popular because of its blade shape which was easy to handle and inflicted fatal wounds. The original blade of the weapon was long and triangular in shape but later this shape evolved into a more tapering blade with the shoulders hooking up. Eventually when this became a popular parade arm, a number of hooks were incorporated at the shoulder and the blades highly decorated. Plate 125 shows a partisan of the Queen's Bodyguard of the Yeomen of the Guard with the blade decorated with blue and gilt, the royal cypher and coat of arms. With any change in monarch, this decoration is altered to incorporate the new coat of arms and cypher.

Pike

The pike was the weapon of the infantry until the widespread use of the firearm. Usually ranging from 16 to 22 ft long, it had a simple leaf shaped head. Tactics of pikemen involved forming a shield to repel cavalry behind which the musketeers could retreat. With the introduction of the bayonet and the widespread use of muskets on the fields of battle, it became obsolete. During the Second World War it was revived during the emergency of 1940 for issue to the LDV and later Home Guard. This weapon ironically consisted of a length of gas piping with a bayonet – the weapon that had played its part in ousting the pike – welded to the end.

Poleaxe

The poleaxe was a long shafted axe used by men fighting on foot. The long shaft gave more reach than the conventional axe. The head had an axe blade one side and usually a short blade or hammer the other, the shaft being surmounted by a spike or another double edged blade.

Ranseur

This weapon had a long triangular blade with central ridge, and two shorter blades radiating from the base to form a three pronged head which was fitted to the shaft. It was in use in France, Germany and Italy from the latter part of the fifteenth until the early seventeenth century.

Spontoon

The spontoon from the French *espontoon* was a short form of spear or pike. It had a broad spear shaped head with rounded shoulders and a cross piece similar to a civilian hunting spear or two small lugs. It was used in the British Army during the eighteenth and nineteenth centurues, the first order being in 1743 ordering all foot guards officers to carry them. In 1769, an order stated that commanding officers were 'to take post with their espontoons' when leading their regiments. In 1786 they were abolished for officers which left only sergeants carrying them which they had done since the 1750s when it replaced the halbard. It continued in use by sergeants until abolished in 1830, sergeants of artillery however, retaining them until 1845. The military spontoon had a spear shaped head, cross piece and socket to fit the shaft. Usually they were made in three pieces and screwed together.

5 Dirks, Knives and Daggers

Except for the Highland and Scottish dirks described in Chapter 3, the main wearers of dirks were the Navy.

Britain

The naval dirk itself only originated towards the end of the eighteenth century, although daggers, short swords, hangers and the like had been carried for many years by naval officers. Although certain uniform types of dirk had been worn from the late eighteenth century, no regulation pattern was authorized until 1856. The two basic designs of dirk carried during the Napoleonic wars were the straight bladed dirk and the curved bladed dirk. The straight bladed dirk usually had a double edged blade of diamond section with a simple cross piece, sometimes slightly decorated, a turned round ivory grip tapering from pommel to shoulder and a simple cap pommel. A large number of this type however have no pommel at all, the grip being glued to the tang. The blades were invariably decorated with engraving and blue and gilt work and were carried in leather scabbard with two or three gilt mounts. Some dirks of this type were carried in an all metal scabbard, usually gilded with engraving and the maker's name engraved by the mouthpiece.

During the 1780s, a straight bladed dirk with a single edge and central fuller to the blade seems to have been adopted by some. The guard was similar to the 'five Ball' guard adopted for the sword, except that no knuckle bow was fitted.

The curved bladed dirk had a single edged blade with the usual blue and gilt work and a carved ivory grip with rounded pommel and back piece – later a lion head was incorporated into the design as a pommel – and an 'S' shaped crossguard which sometimes had an upturned side guard incorporating the foul anchor. Many of this style of dirk had a chain knuckle guard, that is a gilt chain connecting the upturned quillon of the crossguard with a loop on the pommel. The scabbards were either in leather with gilt mounts or all gilt metal. The dirk on plate 126b has an engraved scabbard incorporating a sailing ship, a figure and eagle amidst foliage work.

The dirk was worn at the beginning of the nineteenth century by midshipmen, volunteers and masters' assistants, but in 1825 dirks were forbidden and swords substituted. However, two years later volunteers were allowed to resume the wearing of dirks and the style worn seems to have been the curved variety with plain or lion head pommel and back piece, carved ivory or ebony grip and simple 'S' cross piece with or without a chain guard.

In 1856, a regulation dirk was ordered for midshipmen, naval cadets and masters' assistants. It had a straight blade about $13\frac{1}{2}$ in. long with a single cutting edge, a simple 'S' shaped cross guard, the ends of the quillons terminating in acorns and a wood grip bound with white fish skin and bound in the grooves with twisted gilt wire. The pommel was in the form of a lion's head with the mane forming the back piece. The scabbard was in black leather with locket and chape, the former having a stud for frog suspension. At a later date, two rings were fitted each side of the locket for sling suspension.

In 1879 a new pattern was introduced with a $17\frac{3}{4}$ in. straight single edged blade, the 'S' shaped cross guard of the previous pattern but with a medallion each side with oak leaf surround with crown above bearing the foul anchor and the same lion head pommel and back piece. The lion head, however, had a ring in its mouth to take the dirk knot, a diminutive version of the sword knot.

France, Belgium and Netherlands

In the French navy, dirks were never authorized for any officers but officers wore them unofficially. As there was no set pattern, there was a great variety of design.

The Belgian Navy, formed in 1831 did not adopt a pattern of dirk until 1893. This pattern closely resembling the British pattern of 1856 was not exclusively for the Navy and was carried by the Army. It had a straight single edged blade with a false edge at the point and a straight cross piece with acorn type finials. The pommel and backpiece were in the form of a lion's head and mane with a ring in the mouth for the knot. The grip was black and bound in the grooves with gilt wire. The scabbard was in black leather with chape and locket, the latter with two rings, one each side for suspension. In 1893, the blade shape was altered by the inclusion of a wide fuller.

In the Dutch Navy, dirks had been worn during the eighteenth century but were not mentioned until the dress regulation of 1808 which allowed the dirk for undress wear. Even then, the style was left to the individual, the regulations stating that the blade could be straight or curved but that the mounts were to be brass and the grip in white bone. This pattern was worn by all officers. Midshipmen however were ordered a dirk in 1806 and again there was the same latitude that was later accorded to the officers. The curved version soon lost popularity and the straight bladed weapon continued during the nineteenth century. The established style had a long straight blade of diamond section, a turned bone grip with two groups of bands, a horizontal disc pommel with hollow conical tip and tang button and a cross piece with square shaped quillons with acorn finials protruding from a block on which an anchor was placed. The scabbards were in brass with two bands and rings for suspension with an engraved anchor between the bands.

This style continued to be carried until the twentieth century but there were alterations in dimensions in the 1870s when the blades became longer and at the turn of the century when blades were nickel plated. In 1888 a white metal version was authorized for supply branch midshipmen.

Prussia, Germany and Austria

The dirk adopted in 1849 by the *Deutsche Marine,* set up under the control of Prussia (which in 1871 became the *Kaiserliche Marine,* the German Imperial Navy) had a straight double edged blade, a turned ivory grip with spiral grooving, a cross piece with button finials to the quillons and a tablet in the centre on which appeared a foul anchor placed diagonally and a round pommel engraved with leaf pattern. The scabbard was in gilt brass with two bands and rings for suspension. The scabbard was engraved from top to bottom with foliage and 'ermine spots'.

Dirks were worn by all officers, rank being denoted by the sword knot or the absence of it but in the 1860s the dirk was withdrawn for officers and in 1872 from midshipmen and cadets who were ordered a brass hilted side arm.

This weapon had a cast brass grip incorporating the backpiece with two rounded quillons, with between them, the Imperial crown. Beneath the grip there was a small downpointing shell with the foul anchor. The blade was straight and single edged. Presentation versions exist with the Imperial crown as a tang button and engraved backpiece to the grip. When the dirk was re-introduced for midshipmen in 1890, the side arms continued to be worn by engineering cadets until 1918.

The 1890 dirk was almost the same as the 1849 pattern but in place of the global pommel engraved with leaves, a pommel in the form of the Imperial crown was substituted. In 1901 officers were again ordered the dirk. The variations encountered in the scabbard of dirks had very little to do with rank and were dictated solely by cost. In a German swordmaker's catalogue of 1908, *Musterbuch der Waffenfabrik,* eighteen different styles of Naval dirk scabbard are shown.

In 1919, the provisional Navy ordered a new pattern of dirk. This was the same as the Imperial dirk but with a blackened or black grip and the global pommel in place of the crown. The scabbard was also painted black and the lower band and ring removed. Following complaints about the dirk and the chipping of the paint, the old style scabbard was restored in 1921 and the white grip in 1929.

In the Austrian navy, the first regulation dirk appeared in 1827. It had a straight slim blade of flattened oval section with a deep, narrow fuller each side. The grip was square sectioned and made from ivory with cross hatching on it fitted to a simple cross piece and a 'pillow' pommel as found on British 'five Ball' hilted swords. The scabbard was in black leather with three mounts, the upper two fitted with rings for suspension.

This pattern lasted until 1854 when a dirk with a straight blade of diamond section, a fluted ivory grip, an 'S' shaped cross piece and an Imperial crown pommel was introduced. The scabbard was in gilt brass with two bands and rings and engraved with foliage designs. In 1873 dirks were abolished for officers.

In 1907 a new dirk appeared for cadets of the Naval Academy. The dirk was similar to the 1854 pattern but had a blunted blade and point nearly rectangular in section and engraved with trophies and the foul anchor with Imperial crown above. The scabbard was in black leather with locket and chape, the former engraved with a foul anchor and with two rings, one each side for suspension.

Russia and Asia

Dirks had been introduced in Russia as early as 1769 when they were ordered for petty officers but midshipmen did not receive theirs until 1803. In 1828, the dirk was withdrawn for all except officers of flag rank and in 1855 a dirk was again introduced for all officers.

The 1855 pattern had a straight blade with ivory grip and simple cross piece and squared cap pommel. The dirk was carried in a leather scabbard with three plain gilt mounts. This pattern lasted up until 1917. In 1921, the same dirk minus any traces of

Imperial cyphers that were sometimes included on blade and pommel, was introduced for the Red Fleet but abolished in 1926.

In Turkey, a dirk modelled on the British pattern of 1879 was introduced. It had the same straight single edged blade, grip pommel and backpiece but in place of the crown and foul anchor on the medallion fitted to the cross piece it had the cyher of Abdul Hamid II. It was carried in a leather scabbard with two mounts, the locket having two rings for suspension. In 1890, however, this pattern was abandoned in favour of a German style when Turkey looked to Germany for assistance with the Navy and Army. The dirk had an 'S' cross piece and in place of the Imperial crown pommel, a turban pommel.

In Siam, a dirk based on the British pattern of 1879 was also adopted but with in place of the lion head pommel and backpiece, an elephant head pommel and plain backpiece and a plain foul anchor in the medallion. The embossing on the blade included the arms of Siam. Both China and Japan also adopted the British style of dirk, the former with an anchor within a wreath of corn in the medallion and a dragon head pommel and backpiece and the latter with a cherry blossom device (plate 105) in the medallion. However, this pattern did not last and a dirk based on the traditional Japanese dagger was introduced in 1883. This had a wood grip covered in white fish skin with wire binding in the spiral grooves, a cap pommel, a slightly 'S' shaped cross piece and a single edged blade. The scabbard was in black leather with a locket and chape, the locket with two rings, one each side for suspension. The locket and chape were decorated with engraved cherry blossoms.

Denmark, Sweden and Norway

As in other navies, the dirk was worn long before it was officially recognised and in Denmark this was not until 1822. Prior to this various types had been carried, many resembling British dirks of the same period. The curved bladed dirk was particularly popular in Denmark and one theory is that the British copied this style and even used Danish dirks captured at Copenhagen in 1807, but there is no evidence to support this. The 1822 dirk probably had a straight double edged blade with a turned ivory grip and a simple cross piece. In 1842 the wearing of dirks was extended to Army officers and it was ordered to be the same as that used in the Navy. After a few years, however, the Army started to adopt a black horn grip to their dirk.

By the 1860s a uniform style of dirk had been adopted. It had a turned ivory or bone grip (modern versions have plastic) with hemispherical ivory pommel in place of the previous gilt one and three distinctive annulets. The cross piece was straight with ball finials and the blade of oval section at the shoulder and then double edged. The locket with its ring bore the arms of Denmark, the middle mount with ring and foul anchor and the chape was decorated with foliage. An all gilt metal scabbard was adopted at a later date bearing the same decoration on it as on the mounts of the leather scabbard. (It is interesting to note that the dirk used in the Greek navy is exactly the same as the Danish pattern except that the scabbard bears the Greek arms in place of the Danish arms.)

In Sweden the dirk in use in about 1800 had a straight double edged blade with an ivory turned grip, simple gilt cross piece and an octagonal pommel. This was carried in a gilt mounted leather scabbard but after the 1820s all gilt metal scabbards came into use.

United States and South America

At the beginning of the nineteenth century, a variety of dirks were in existence and worn by officers in place of swords when required. There was no established pattern, but examples have the eagle head pommel or other distinctive features applicable to the United States. The dirk was never authorized for wear in the United States Navy.

In South America, various influences of France, Spain, Britain and Germany in naval affairs dictated the designs of dirks carried. In Colombia, the 1879 pattern dirk was introduced, the only difference being that the Colombian arms was substituted wherever the crown appeared on blade or medallion. In Mexico, the dirk for the navy and army was based on the British pattern of 1879. In the naval version, the medallion bore a condor with outspread wings holding a snake surmounting two crossed foul anchors. In the army version, the medallion bore the condor with wings outstretched with 'REPUBLICA MEXICANA' above and 'COLEGIA MILITA' beneath (Military College). On both patterns the lion head pommel and backpiece were replaced by a Condor head pommel with feathers stretching a little way down the backpiece.

In Paraguay, a dirk was used with lion head pommel with mane forming a short backpiece in the style of a French cap pommel, a cross guard with circular block with the arms of the Republic and a diamond section blade all carried in a hammered German style all metal scabbard. This dirk was issued to cadets at the Defence College who intended to serve on inland water craft.

Bowie Knife

Perhaps the most famous of all the hunting types of knife was the Bowie knife, named after the designer Colonel James Bowie. The knife had a large wide blade, with clipped back which was sharpened and had a simple cross piece and wood or horn pieces riveted to the thick tang. However, after 1830, the year that William Stenton of the firm of George Wolstenholme and Sons of Sheffield arrived in America with his sample bag of blades, most 'Bowie' type knives had Sheffield made blades or were entirely made in Sheffield. There is a great variety of this style of knife, in differing sizes and with different grips and scabbard. The blade decoration also differed greatly from patriotic scenes and legends, to eagles and portraits of the famous, President Zachary Taylor, 'Old Zac', hero of the Mexican war, being a favourite subject. Scabbards were in leather with locket and chape and usually had on them in gold embossing the name of the firm or in some cases 'IXL' ('I EXCEL') the famous trademark. Some scabbards can be found with such legends as

CALIFORNIA TOOTHPICK.

The grips vary enormously from wood, horn, bone, ivory and silver reminiscent of cutlery handles of the period. Some had plain cross pieces, others elaborate ones and decorative pommels.

The Bowie knife survived and was popular up until the 1850s but after the Civil War it was once more relegated to the role of a hunting knife. While Wolstenholme followed by other Sheffield knife makers had a large and lucrative market during the period 1830–1880, the years that followed saw the market for Sheffield made knives decline rapidly with the introduction of heavy import tariffs and fierce competition from the cheaper knives produced in Solingen. Another significant factor was the competition from American knife manufacturers and Wolstenholme's representative in America wrote to him stating that 'The Americans make a knife which is apparently good enough for the average American.'

Others in the cutlery trade tried to cash in on the 'IXL' mark: firms such as Frederick Warn concocted 'B4 ANY' (Before ANY); while others dreamed up even more contrived trade marks.

Other companies produced numerous styles of hunting knives, Solingen being a large exporter of this style of weapon. In Britain, Wilkinsons produced various types of knives for the military man and the sportsman – amongst them the famous 'Shakespeare Knife' designed by Colonel Shakespeare of the Indian Army. This had a double edged blade of round cross section with a simple chequered grip which was waisted with no cross guard. The scabbard also in wood covered in leather which was chequered had a stud for the frog and a spring clip to keep the knife in the scabbard. This knife was produced in various sizes as was the Wilkinson 'RBD' knife, a popular knife amongst sportsmen.

Commando and Fighting Knives

Commando or fighting knives were born during the First World War when trench raiding parties at night called for a knife. At first nothing was available except for the commercially made hunting knives and ground down bayonets of obsolete patterns which were pressed into service. A number of nineteenth century British bayonets were utilized for this purpose. In Germany a variety of knives were specially manufactured. They had a simple Bowie style blade, small cross piece and wood grips usually with the diagonal grooving found on the grips of German bayonets. In Britain there was little official movement to produce a special knife but the Colonel of one of the volunteer battalions of the Welch Regiment had made at his expense a fighting sword. This weapon had a leaf shaped blade with central rib reminiscent of early Bronze age and Iron age swords, a swivel cross piece that lay flat when worn but formed a circular guard when held and a simple bound grip.

In America, a combined 'knuckle duster' and knife was produced in 1917. The early model had a wood grip, knuckle guard with spikes and blade but in 1918 a knife with solid brass hilt incorporating four rings as 'knuckle dusters' was produced.

During the Second World War a knife was designed for the Commandos formed in 1940 by Captain Fairburn, Captain Sykes and J. Wilkinson-Latham (the author's grandfather) of the Wilkinson Sword Company. From the various discussions was born the 'FS' Fighting Knife which had a tapering double edged diamond section blade, a small cross piece and a turned brass grip with chequering. The knife, never intended to be thrown was so balanced that it sat in the hand. Later versions had slightly differing styles of grips and blade and the name 'FS' was dropped in favour of the name Commando knife. All the metal parts were blacked and the knife was carried in a leather scabbard with metal chape. The scabbard had on each side two small tabs which could be used to sew the scabbard to the trouser leg to prevent it banging up and down.

6 Bayonets

The bayonet did not make its appearance until the seventeenth century when firearms were in widespread use in the armies of Europe. While the musketeer had a short sword or hanger for personal defence, he was still vulnerable to cavalry during the long re-loading exercise and any attack by cavalry could not be fought off with the hanger. The musketeer needed a weapon with the reach of a pike to be able to withstand a cavalry attack for, if cut off from the pikeman, there was no protective cover for the musketeer. The musketeers were grouped with pikemen so that the re-loading could be done behind the protective hedge of 16 ft pikes, but musketeers on their own were most vulnerable.

How a knife or dagger came to be used as a bayonet is impossible to discover. Many theories have in the past been put forward of how either a dagger or broken arrow – the old French word for arrow was *bayon* – were thrust into the barrel of the musket as a means of defence or that the word bayonet derived from the town of Bayonne famous for its knife and cutlery trade but there is no conclusive evidence for any of the claims and theories put forward. It is possible that the bayonet had a chance birth, possibly in a tight spot during a battle when a musketeer either hard pressed or out of ammunition strove to make a pike from his useless weapon by either thrusting his dagger into the muzzle or tying it on. He may have used instead of his dagger, a broken lance head or arrow, hence the name bayonet from the French for arrow.

In early drill manuals the bayonet is referred to as a dagger (*An*

Abridgement of the English Military Discipline 1686) even though in other official papers it was already known as a bayonet or *bayonette*. The French appear to have been the first nation to use the bayonet according to the *Mémoires de Jacques de Chastenet, Chevalier Seigneur de Puysegur* who recorded that in 1647 his men were armed with 'bayonettes' with blades and handles 12 in. long. In 1660, Louis XIV issued a proclamation forbidding the use of the bayonet stating that 'The frequency of accidents which happen almost daily by the use of bayonets and knives in the form of daggers which are placed in the muzzle of sporting guns or which are carried in the pocket . . .'.

The bayonet probably did not come into use in the English army before 1662 when captured French bayonets were issued to the Tangier Regiment. An order in the Public Record Office of the 14 March 1662 states that 'The French pikes and short swords or bayonettes that lately were received from Dunkirk be surveyed and an account presented to this office of their defect to the end a contract be made for their speedy repair.' Three days later the bayonets were issued out to Joseph Awdeley, Samuel Law and Robert Steadman the contractors responsible for the refurbishing. In 1672 when twelve troops of Dragoons were raised they were ordered muskets and '. . . also to have and to carry one bayonet or great knife'. In 1680, in *'English Military Discipline'* the author Robert Hartford states that some musketeers were issued with bayonets in that year. By the reign of James II (1685–1688) most musketeers and dragoons seemed to have been armed with the plug bayonet.

The plug bayonet, because it plugged into the muzzle of the musket, had a double edged blade of flattened oval section, a cross piece usually with decorative finials and often a small shell guard facing down towards the tip or the blade. The grip was either of turned wood with a metal cap or of ivory (for civilian weapons and sporting guns), and studded with silver wire inlay. Many of the bayonets had engraved blades with such legends as 'GOD SAVE KING JAMES II 1686' while others of the military variety were stamped with the crown and rose mark. The scabbards were usually in wood covered in leather with locket and chape but military weapons probably had a simple leather scabbard. There are blade variations, some being curved and single edged and others having waved edges. Short trowel like blades are also known as are longer blades with a shell guard similar to that in use on hangers.

Because of the disadvantages of the plug bayonet some other methods were sought for attachment. The plug bayonet could become stuck in the muzzle or worse could be broken off rendering the musketeer defenceless. Also it was impossible to fire a musket with the bayonet fitted. In Sweden, this problem was solved as early as 1685 by having two rings fitted to the barrel to take the hilt of the plug bayonet rather than place it in the barrel itself.

Other countries later fitted two rings to the handle of the plug bayonet so that they could be slipped over the barrel. By replacing the two rings with a metal tube or socket and dispensing with the grip, the socket bayonet came into existence. Who invented it or precisely when is unknown, there being a number of claimants for the honour.

There were various types of early socket bayonets with various ideas incorporated to hold them firmly on the non-standard size of barrels. The most common method was the split socket, that is the socket or tube which could be opened or closed over the barrel as required. In other countries such as Sweden, the socket was held firmly to the barrel by having a 'wing nut' in the socket which was tightened down on to the barrel. However, early in the eighteenth century locking rings were used in some countries which closed over the slot holding the bayonet to the lug or sight of the barrel.

Britain

In Britain there were a variety of bayonets in use as the following shows. Lord Mark Kerr wrote to the Board of Ordnance requesting a supply of bayonets for his regiment but received the following reply. '. . . all regiments raised since the disuse of pikes have provided Bayonets as they do swords and belts as their Charge . . . Few of the officers agree to the sort of Bayonet fit to be used or in the manner of fitting them to the Musquets as may appear by the various sorts that are of them in ye Army.'

By 1720, however, the socket bayonets of standard pattern were in use with muskets whose barrels had acquired a degree of uniformity. In 1722, the Board of Ordnance obliged colonels of regiments to have any new arms '. . . made according to the said pattern and proved and viewed by the Proper Officers of the Ordnance.'

The uniform bayonet had a 17 in. blade of triangular section, hollow ground on two faces with the socket held by a crooked neck. The socket was fitted with a zig-zag slot which fitted over the foresight block. By 1760, the socket had a reinforced collar fitted to it. The bayonet was carried in a triangular section black leather scabbard with brass chape and locket with frog stud for suspension. This basic pattern remained in use for over 100 years with the rank and file of the British Army until the advent of improvements in locking devices and springs introduced by George Lovell. Smaller versions of the triangular section blade socket bayonet were produced for sergeants and cadets. A further version was produced especially for the Irish Constabulary in 1840 with a spring clip in the top of the blade to hold the bayonet in the scabbard. In 1858, another version was produced with a socket with locking ring on the principle adopted in 1853 for the Enfield rifle.

In 1839, a socket bayonet with a thick collar was produced which engaged on a small spring fitted to the nose cap of the stock. In 1842, the collar was made with a small 'ear' to engage a leaf spring also fitted to the nose cap. Various other locking devices were fitted to volunteer bayonets and bayonets intended for the muskets supplied by the East India Company. The so called 'East India Company' spring had a retaining spring, was screwed to the socket and extended over the slot gripping the lug. The New Land Pattern muskets were introduced in 1802;

springs were issued with them. The new musket was a restricted issue, the bulk of the army being armed with the India pattern muskets brought from the East India Company and manufactured for the Government thereafter because they were easier to produce. The New Land pattern bayonet had a shorter lead spring which was behind rather than over the barrel lug, thus stopping the bayonet working forwards along the slot.

Sword bayonets were used by many of the volunteers but were not introduced into the army until the Baker Rifle was introduced for the Rifle Corps in 1800. This bayonet had a brass stirrup hilt, a cast brass grip with spring for retention and a straight single edged blade. In 1801, the knuckle bow was made curved. As a result of complaints received in 1815, the rifles were converted to take a socket bayonet with locking ring but by 1823 a return was made to the full stocked rifle with a 'sword' bayonet although the new pattern was in fact a knife bayonet. It had a brass grip with spring, a cross piece and a short triangular sectioned blade. There were also numerous variations used by volunteer units.

In 1836, when the Brunswick rifle was issued in place of the Baker, a brass hilted bayonet was also adopted but without guard. The blade was leaf shaped in the 'Roman' style. Various other bayonets in this style were also produced for the Brunswick rifle, as also for the constabulary, carbines and volunteers.

In 1853, when the British Army adopted the Enfield rifle, a socket bayonet with triangular section blade hollow ground on all three faces with locking ring was issued. This pattern remained in use until 1876 when a longer blade version was issued for the Martini-Henry rifle. Sword bayonets were also manufactured for the Enfield, Snider-Enfield and Martini-Henry rifle but these were issued to others other than the infantry except sergeants who used the 1856 pattern with 'yatagan' blade. This bayonet was also used on the artillery carbine and by rifle regiments while the engineers had their own pattern of brass hilted bayonet for the Lancaster carbine. The Royal Navy blended the cutlass with the bayonet to produce a monster weapon the cutlass bayonet. Later the artillery adopted a saw backed bayonet with long blade and knuckle guard while a special pattern invented by Lord Elcho with leaf shaped blade with saw back was produced in 1871 and saw service with officers in the Ashanti war. It was later revived in 1895 but for a short period only.

This great variation in bayonets for various weapons and various arms of the service could not continue and in 1886 a new sword bayonet was authorized to replace all other variations. This issue and its subsequent alterations in May 1887, June 1888 and July 1888 was soon abandoned with the approval in 1888 for the Lee Metford magazine rifle with short double edged blade, stepped cross guard and Rigby patent pommel. However, the socket bayonet still survived for in 1895 a long bladed weapon was produced for the Martini-Enfield rifle.

With the adoption of the 1888 pattern, variations still continued and individuality was continued by a variety of scabbards produced for land and sea service, there being seven different patterns. In 1903, with the adoption of the SMLE (Short Magazine Lee Enfield) another pattern of bayonet was produced after some trial patterns. It utilized the same blade as the pattern 1888, the same grips but a beaked shaped pommel. Here, too, individuality was retained in the variety of scabbard there being over nine differing patterns and conversions. After a series of trials, a new pattern bayonet was produced in 1907 with beak shaped pommel, shaped grips, cross guard with curved 'fighting' quillon to catch the opponent's blade and a single edged 17 in. blade. This pattern was retained in use until well into the Second World War before the 'spike' bayonet – a socket bayonet with spike blade – was produced. In 1916, the hooked quillon was cut off. This is perhaps the most common of British bayonet, many millions being made during both world wars (Wilkinson alone produced over 2,000,000 during 1914–18 and 250,000 during 1935–45).

France, Belgium and Netherlands

The French had standardized their socket bayonet for the infantry musket in 1717 but this like the bayonets of some other countries had a plain socket with slot and triangular section blade. The pattern 1746 which superseded it differed little in outward appearance except that the slot was not reversed 'L' shape as in the 1717 pattern but spiralled from the side before straightening. In 1763, however, the locking ring was adopted on the new bayonet. This had a shorter socket and a small straight slot with the locking ring at the top end of the socket. Once the bayonet had been passed over the barrel, the locking ring was rotated to block the slot. It is interesting to note that from the introduction of the musket pattern 1763, the bayonet locked on to a lug beneath the barrel rather than on to the block which acted as a sight as in other countries. The sight for French muskets was incorporated in the top band.

In 1774, another pattern of bayonet was introduced without locking ring but with two slots in the socket. The arrangement featured a straight slot with half way down and joining the main slot on the left side an 'L' shaped slot. The bayonet was fitted to the barrel in the normal way, but a spring on the underside of the barrel engaged the slot to retain it in position. It appears to have had a short and limited life and in 1777 a bayonet with locking ring was once again introduced. This pattern with minor variations stayed in service until the 1860s. The socket had a 'zig-zag' slot with reinforced ferrule to the socket with a raised portion over the slot opening. The locking ring was positioned in the centre of the socket so that when rotated, it closed firmly behind the bayonet lug. The bayonet underwent various changes in blade length and in other minor alterations as recorded in AnIX (Sept. 1800–1801. Republican Calendar), 1822 and 1847. In 1866 a version with a quadrangular section blade was introduced for *Gendarmerie*. In 1838 a special version of the socket bayonet was issued for the 1837 carbine and the 1838 Rampart gun. This had the usual socket with locking ring and a wide single edged blade. When not fitted to the barrel, a hollow brass handle with tools inside was provided which locked into the socket to form a 'sword'.

In 1840, however, a sword bayonet was introduced for carbines. This pattern which was destined to be copied by numerous other countries had a brass grip incorporating a leaf spring and slot for fixing, a shallow 'S' shaped brass cross guard with hole to fit over the barrel and a single edged blade of 'yatagan' shape (plate 132 for blade shape). In 1842 an improved version was issued with a steel cross guard and a longer blade. The scabbard was made of steel with a 'D' at the top to take the frog strap. In 1859, the bayonet was improved further by using an internal coil spring rather than the leaf shape, but a return was made to the leaf spring when the not dissimilar Chassepot bayonet was introduced in 1866.

This bayonet had a similar brass grip with horizontal lines, a leaf spring and a straight cross guard with hooked quillon for bayonet fighting. This bayonet continued in service until 1874 when the Gras rifle and bayonet was introduced. The Chassepot bayonet of 1866 was copied by numerous countries and during the Franco-Prussian war of 1870-71 many captured bayonets were issued to Prussian troops.

A special and unique type of bayonet was introduced by Napoleon III in 1854. This was of sword length and designed to fit the carbine issued to the *Cente-Garde.* The first pattern had a cap pommel with locking device, grips fitted to the tang not dissimilar to the style used on the heavy cavalry sword and a cross piece with slots to take the barrel of the carbine. The Imperial Guard was also issued together with a similar type of sword with a three bar hilt and different shaped pommel which had a raised portion to take the slot and locking device. There were also various other types of sword bayonets which were experimental or had a limited issue such as the Favre bayonet of 1866, the Manceaux bayonet of 1858, the 1861 bayonet for the double barrelled naval fusil and the special bayonet for the cadets at the School of Vincennes.

The Gras bayonet had a straight tapering 'T' sectioned blade with flat back, a cross guard with hole for the barrel and hooked quillon, shaped wood grips and a brass pommel. This bayonet was in service until 1886 when the Gras rifle was replaced by the Lebel. A bayonet similar to the Gras 1874 pattern was that designed to fit the Kropatscek rifle adopted by the French navy. This bayonet differs in having a straight rather than stepped back to the grip which was also slightly wider, and the blade was marked with the manufacturer Steyr on the blade and has an anchor on the cross guard.

Up until 1886, all French sword bayonets were marked on the back of the blade with place of manufacture, date of manufacture and Model (Pattern) date which simplifies identification. In 1886, however, this dating was abandoned with the introduction of the Lebel bayonet with its long thin cruciform section blade as there was nowhere this data could be engraved. The Lebel bayonet firstly had a white metal grip but later patterns have them in brass or steel. The bayonet locked on to the rifle by slotting the grip into a recess and putting the cross guard over the barrel where it was locked in place by a catch activated by a round knurled button situated just behind the cross guard. In 1893, the catch was modified by altering the shape and in 1916 in common with Britain, the hooked quillon was removed, and from then on the bayonet manufactured without it. A variation of the bayonet is that issued to the *Gendarmerie* in 1890; although similar in outward appearance it had a unique milled slot in the grip and an internal spring activated by a button at the top of the grip. In 1935, the bayonets were ordered to be shortened and the following year the MAS rifle with 'ramrod' bayonet was introduced.

There were other bayonets issued with Mannlicher Berthier rifles and carbines which had straight double edged blades, hooked quillon to the cross guard, shaped grips and squat pommel. The grips were either in composition or wood. The French also used the Remington bayonet (plate 142) supplied with Remington rifles by the U.S.A. during the Great War.

Belgium did not become an independent country until 1831. Because of the vast output of the Belgian Arms industry it is often difficult to know which bayonets were meant for the home market and which were purely export designs. Because of the vast export of Belgian arms, there were also many experimental bayonets developed. Up until 1868, the Belgian army were armed with a socket bayonet with locking rings on the French style but in that year, the Tersen rifle was adopted with the 'yatagan' bladed brass hilted bayonet similar to the Chassepot of 1866. The main difference between Belgian and French weapons was that on the former the leaf spring was held by a screw not a rivet and that brass mounted leather scabbards were used in place of all steel ones. A wide bladed version with saw backed blade was issued to Engineers in 1868 but a slimmer version with narrow straight blade was adopted in 1888.

In 1924, the same pattern of bayonet was used with the new rifle, the only difference between the two being the diameter of the muzzle ring, that of 1916 being slightly larger.

The Netherlands, like other countries, equipped their armies with socket bayonets at an early date, and as late as 1871 when the Beaumont rifle was introduced supplied it with a socket bayonet and a sword bayonet, the former for general issue and the latter for the Navy and Marines. The socket bayonet had a cruciform sectioned blade without shoulder which bends to form the elbow, being fitted to the socket on its right side. The socket was, as expected, equipped with locking ring. The sword bayonet resembled the French Chassepot and can be distinguished by their rather long leaf locking spring.

In 1888, the Beaumont rifle was converted to the Italian Vitali repeating system and in addition to the previously described bayonets a new pattern of socket bayonet was introduced. This had a cruciform section blade but the locking ring on the socket had two screws.

In 1895, with the adoption of the Mannlicher rifle, new bayonets were issued, folding socket bayonets being designed for the police and a sword bayonet intended for the Navy, Marines and the Army. The bayonet had a single edged tapering blade of 'T' section, becoming double edged near the point, a cross guard with muzzle ring and curved piling quillon, wood grips and an inverted pommel not unlike that of the British pattern 1888 bayonet. The version issued for cavalry and horse artillery had the same hilt but a short double edged blade. All bayonets have the grips secured by rivets, but after 1900 an increasing number were secured by screws to enable removal for cleaning. Bayonets produced after the Great War do not have the stacking hook as it was found superfluous and a hindrance.

In 1940, the Dutch purchased large numbers of the American Johnson self-loading rifle with its unique all metal bayonet. This bayonet, forged in one piece had a short tapering spike blade, with cross piece with muzzle ring and a machined metal 'hilt' to fit on to the rifle.

Prussia, Germany and Austria

Prior to the unification of Germany in 1871 with Prussia as the dominant power, there was a Confederation of states which dated from 1816. For this reason a single style of bayonet was carried by a number of the member states of the Confederation, but with slight variety in the bayonets issued to special troops such as pioneers and those worn when walking out which are termed as dress bayonets.

The early pattern of socket bayonet used by the Prussians was very similar in style to those used by many other armies at the period and it was not until the end of the eighteenth century that a distinctive pattern was adopted. The bayonet used with the model 1805 musket had a plain socket without any collar and a long triangular section blade, although a shorter bladed bayonet with the distinctive 'Kyhls' locking spring had been adopted in the 1790s. This spring which was mounted on the socket had two ears that were lifted which allowed the stud under the barrel to engage the slot in the socket. Once in position the spring was lowered which blocked the slot and kept the bayonet firmly in place. This spring was used for many years by the Prussians and features on a number of various patterns of socket bayonet. It was also copied by Denmark on their 1794 pattern and used until about 1848 when a locking ring was adopted.

The Prussians, however, were not great users of socket bayonets, preferring instead the sword bayonet. On the Jaeger rifle from which the British Baker rifle was copied, a large all brass hilted sword bayonet or Hirschfanger was carried. The hilt, which except for the knuckle bow, was cast in one piece had an oval section grip which broadened out towards the top. The knuckle bow, which was an inverted stirrup guard had a small down pointing shell guard on which is usually found engraved numbers and letters referring to the regiment to whom it was issued. A variety of hilt designs were used with this style of bayonet but nearly all have the slot for the bayonet bar in a separate 'box' brazed to the grip. Along the top edge of this 'box' is a steel spring with a catch which locked the bayonet in position on the bar on the barrel.

When Prussia introduced its revolutionary 'needle gun' or Von Dreyse pattern as it is termed, a socket bayonet was approved for the rank and file. This model had a 19 in. blade and as is expected employed the Kyhls locking spring fitted to the socket. In 1849 a brass hilted bayonet with a steel cross guard was adopted for Fusilier regiments and it was from this style of bayonet, with a falchion pattern blade that the better known model of 1871 was copied for use on the Mauser rifle of 1871. In 1865 another sword bayonet was introduced which although in appearance is styled similarly to the pattern of 1860 had a steel pommel and cross guard and chequered leather grips like many other types of sword bayonets of the period.

In 1871, when Prussia adopted the Mauser magazine breech loading rifle a brass hilted bayonet was used with it. The grip had an engraved panel in which was fitted the leaf spring and the panel engraved with lines at about 40 degrees. The scabbard which took the falchion shaped blade was in black leather with brass mounts. A variety of this pattern of bayonet exists, some with saw backed blades being pioneer weapons while others with slim blades which are engraved being dress models which in some cases have no fitment for the rifle and the leaf spring engraved in the grip. The pattern for Jaeger regiments had a chequered leather grip, while the standard infantry pattern had a slim blade with a central fuller and that of nco's having in addition a saw back. The cross guard of this pattern has a distinctive 'S' shape. There were also slight differences in blade shape and design between the various German States. In 1884, a short knife bayonet with a 10 in. blade was adopted. This bayonet was an all steel construction with wood grips. The first pattern can be distinguished by the shaping to the top of the grips and tang and the pronounced beak on the pommel. In 1888 a Commission for the trials of Small Arms recommended various improvements to the pattern 1871 rifle which changed its designation to Infantry Rifle Model 1871–84. In 1888 a new pattern rifle was adopted which took the 1871–84 bayonet, and also the brass hilted 1871 bayonet. In 1898, the famous Gewehr 1898 rifle was adopted and with it a new pattern of bayonet. A number of the 1884 bayonets were adapted for use on the new rifle and were designated 1884–98. One variety was a conversion of the old knife bayonet having the muzzle ring removed while the newly manufactured model had no muzzle ring, an oil drain slot above the cross guard and no beak to the pommel. The later model had a flat back to the grips and tang and with a shaped pommel, and a steel plate along the back of the hilt to protect the grips from muzzle blast.

With the new rifle, a variety of bayonets were used, the number and pattern increasing during the First World War to the staggering total of over forty variations and patterns. The original bayonets issued with the rifle were of three varieties, that with the long falchion shaped blade of 20¾ in., that with the so called 'Butcher' blade which swelled at the point of 14 in., with a pioneer variation with saw backed blade, and that with a short 10 in. blade. The hilt had the shaped pommel used on the

1884-98 bayonet and with a single sided cross guard and no muzzle ring. On the first two varieties mentioned the grips were lined but on the third they were plain. These three patterns formed the basis for the many variations found except for the all steel *Ersatz* or emergency models and the converted captured and obsolete bayonets. The book, *GEW 98* published in 1921 by Bannerman & Sons illustrates thirty-one bayonet variations for the Gew 98 rifle, and there are undoubtedly many more. The *ersatz* bayonets were of all metal construction and while having usually a good quality blade, the rest of the bayonet was poorly made and finished. The earlier versions had well machined metal hilts, but later models relied on pressed tin grips and open muzzle rings which could be made to fit the barrel of the rifle. The Germans also pressed into service a large quantity of captured rifles and bayonets and often adapted their own bayonets to fit captured rifles. It must be remembered that the crudeness of construction of some of these is not surprising as any small concern with the slightest knowledge of metal work was pressed to make them and railway repair yards also produced them.

There was also a great variety of German dress bayonets. These weapons, often elaborately chiselled and engraved were brought privately and used in undress or walking out dress. Plate 138 to plate 140 show a variety of German bayonets.

In Austria, the army was, at the beginning of the nineteenth century, armed with a socket bayonet without locking ring or spring but with a cruciform section blade and it was only in 1854 that on the flat bladed bayonet for the Lorenz rifle, a locking ring was incorporated. The slot for fixing on to the barrel on the Lorenz bayonet was helical which had been adopted some years previously for the standard infantry musket. The Lorenz carbine, however, utilized a sword bayonet. A flat bladed bayonet of similar construction but with a straight slot had been used on the 1849 Augustin rifle replacing an earlier version without locking nut.

Because of their swift defeat at the hands of the Prussians

armed with the Dreyse breech loading rifle in 1866, the Austrians started trials to find a new rifle to replace the Lorenz. In 1867, the Werndl rifle was adopted, and with it a sword bayonet for general issue, the socket bayonet being abandoned. The first pattern bayonet had a 'yatagan' type single edged blade, cross piece with muzzle ring with unusual rounded finial and a short hooked quillon on the opposite side. The grips were similar to the British sword bayonet of the period and were made from leather sewn together and chequered. These were held to the tang with three rivets, one above the other two, and a screw which held the leaf spring activated by a push button on the steel beak shaped pommel. In 1870 a new version of the bayonet was issued and the original model designated *'schwere gattung'*, or heavy pattern. The new version had the same outward appearance but had an adjusting screw on the muzzle ring for better fit to the barrel in place of the ring and finial. Three years later, a new rifle prompted the issue of a new bayonet. The hilt remained the same, except for the leaf spring which was replaced by a coil spring in the pommel beneath the press stud and the blade was shortened by some four inches and had only a gentle sweep to the inner cutting edge as opposed to the distinctive 'yatagan' shape. A version was issued for nco's which had a loop screwed to the pommel from which to hang a knot. Many of the original bayonets and the 1870 pattern were shortened at this time to conform to the new pattern. A socket bayonet was issued with the carbine version of the rifle. In 1881, probably following complaints about the swelling of the leather grips when wet, wood grips were used on the bayonet. In some of the conversions that took place there were variations in the number and positions of the rivets, some having two, some three and some even four.

In 1886, the Austrian authorities adopted the Mannlicher rifle with a short bladed knife bayonet. This had a short single edged blade with fuller, a one sided cross piece with adjustable muzzle ring, wood grips held by rivets and steel pommel with coil spring and press stud. In 1888, the rifle was reduced in calibre and a new bayonet issued. Identical with the pattern 1886 it can only be identified by having a smaller diameter muzzle ring. A version of these bayonets was issued for the nco having the distinctive swivel fitted to the pommel from which hung the knot. These bayonets usually had the addition of a hooked piling quillon to the cross guard. In 1895, another Mannlicher rifle was adopted with a new pattern of bayonet. This bayonet while looking quite conventional was unusual in that the cutting edge of the blade faced the muzzle ring rather than away from it. The cross piece, held by two predominant rivets in the centre had only a muzzle ring on one side below wood grips held by rivets and a beak style pommel with internal coil spring and press stud. Special troops armed with short rifles were issued with a bayonet which incorporated a sight on top of the muzzle ring. Once again the nco had his own version with swivel on the pommel and hooked piling quillon.

During the Great War, Austria suffered from the same supply problem as Germany and produced various *ersatz* bayonets. These were crudely made and usually consisted only of a blade with a tang on to which was fitted muzzle ring and locking device.

Russia and Asia

Russian troops were armed from the beginning of the nineteenth century with socket bayonets and by 1845 these were fitted with locking rings on the French principle. For the rifles, however, a rifle was issued in 1843 and this weapon made in Belgium was a version of the Brunswick rifle adopted six years previously. Besides the maker's name the Russian bayonet with its brass hilt, cross guard and leaf shaped blade can be distinguished from the British version by its large size press stud. The scabbard was unusual in that it had in the leather body a compartment for the ramrod.

The deplorable state of Russian muskets and bayonets during the Crimean war decided the authorities to consolidate the various patterns in use and to issue a new percussion weapon.

This was the pattern 1856 rifle which was over a period issued to the entire army. The bayonet was of the socket variety with a locking ring to the socket to close behind the sight when fitted. In 1866, the Russians converted these rifles to breech loading using the Krnka system with no alteration to the bayonet.

In 1868, however, the Russians purchased from the USA large quantities of the Berdan Rifle, a breech loading weapon with hinged block. The socket bayonet had a long triangular section blade with flat 'screwdriver' type point, short socket and locking ring. The idea of the point was that it could be used as a stripping tool if required. In 1870, an improved rifle the Berdan II was issued and with it a new bayonet with cruciform section blade, with 'screwdriver' tip, socket with arched collar to allow the sight to pass through and locking ring.

In 1891, the Russian army adopted the breechloading magazine Mosin-Nagent rifle with a socket bayonet. This weapon had a cruciform section blade, again with 'screwdriver' point with no arched collar to the socket but just a milled out slot and a locking ring working on a collar. There were no scabbards provided – although dragoons had a special fitment to the sword scabbard for holding them – as they were meant to be permanently fixed to the rifle. Any bayonets of this type found with scabbards are either Finnish or captured weapons utilized by the Germans. In 1930, the bayonet was improved by getting rid of the locking ring and putting in a spring loaded device to hold it to the barrel.

With the shortage and great loss of arms during the Great War, the Russians purchased the Mosin-Nagent from America and France and also imported a large number of Winchester pattern 1895 rifles with sword bayonets. These have a single edged blade with fuller, a single sided cross piece with muzzle ring, wood grips held by two rivets and a beak style pommel with coiled spring and release stud.

In China, the army was only formed on modern lines towards the end of the nineteenth century and was armed with imported Mauser rifles pattern 1871 and bayonets to fit them. The Chinese manufactured their own version of the German 1888 rifle terming it the Hanyang 88 and also the bayonet. Bayonets continued to be imported from Germany and conformed to the German pattern in current production at that time. As there was no home bayonet industry, or if there was it was not capable of the output, bayonets were imported at first from Germany but after the Great War, the Chinese turned to Belgium for their supply. From Belgium came a large assortment of odd bayonets. Using German *ersatz* hilts – as they fitted the rifles – various obsolete blades from socket bayonets were welded to them and cross pieces with muzzle rings were fitted. During the Second World War, British and American arms and bayonets were supplied but in 1949 with the take over by the Communists, Russia became the source of supply.

Siam, very much dependent on outside influence in the formation of her army and navy turned to Britain for the supply of arms. Many thousands of Snider-Enfield rifles and sword and socket bayonets were supplied and later Martini-Henry versions of them. In between the two World Wars, quantities of reconditioned British 1907 bayonets were supplied through commercial channels. These can be recognised by either the grinding off or the obliterating of British markings and the stamping of the arms of Siam. The Wilkinson Sword Company supplied many thousands of these reconditioned bayonets as well as a quantity of pattern 1903s. In the Wilkinson versions, the old markings have been ground off and their name etched on in the same way as on a sword blade. A large quantity of 1907 blades with simple cross guards and turned wood grips as side arms were also supplied to Siam and these again have their name etched on the blade.

In Japan, they adopted in 1880 a rifle designed by Major Murata Tsuneyoshi with a sword bayonet. This had a straight single edged blade with cross piece with muzzle hole and hooked quillon. The grips were in chequered leather and the beak pommel incorporated a stud pressing on a leaf spring to lock the bayonet in place. In 1885, a version with shorter blade and wood grips held with two screws; the top one also holding the leaf spring was issued and later in 1889 the bayonet was issued with a coil spring in the pommel in place of the leaf spring, and a slightly shorter blade.

In 1897, a new rifle designed by Colonel Arisaka was introduced. The original bayonet, not unlike the British pattern 1907 in appearance had single edged blade, cross guard with extended muzzle ring and curved quillon. The grips were in wood and fitted to the tang by two rivets and the pommel had an internal coil spring and press stud. During the Second World War, when there was no time for extra finishing, bayonets were produced with square pommels, straight unshaped grips and unfullered blades. Very late crude weapons had wood scabbards and a tang extension with hole rather than a pommel, so that the bayonet could be tied to the rifle.

The Japanese also utilized captured British and Dutch bayonets, sometimes cannibalizing them to use the blades for their own designs. In other cases 1907 bayonets were manaufactured in Japan to fit captured stocks of SMLE's. These can be recognised, apart from the markings by having the grips angled at the top to fit the angled pommel.

From the time that the Indian Army came under the Crown they were armed with British pattern bayonets and rifles, although the issue of new weapons always was some years behind. However, during the Second World War, quantities of short bayonets were manufactured in India for the SMLE rifle. These can be found in about four variations. The original pattern had the same hilt as the pattern 1907 but displayed a short single edged unfullered blade; the second was the same but with a false edge to the blade while the other two patterns had squared pommels and unshaped and straight grips, which as in Japan was to facilitate production by firms not used to the tight specifications and tolerances expected, and single edged blades with or without false edge.

Denmark, Sweden and Norway

Up until 1814, the countries of Norway and Denmark were united and they had the same pattern of bayonet in the army. These were the standard socket bayonet as used in other countries but in 1794, socket bayonets were fitted with the unique Khyl locking spring. This was a leaf shaped spring screwed to the socket and extending over the slot. The portion of the spring over the slot had a cutout to take the lug on the barrel and two 'ears'. The bayonet fixed by simply slotting it on and was removed by gripping the 'ears' between thumb and forefinger and lifting to free the lug and allow the socket to be slid off.

For use on various patterns of rifles, a sword bayonet was adopted. These were made by converting hangers and cavalry swords and have a cumbersome and heavy look about them. The 1801 pattern had a crude lion head pommel and backpiece with knuckle guard and a wire bound wood grip. A round bar with spring was welded on to the quillon of the guard and the weapon was fitted to the rifle by pushing this into a tube on the side of the barrel.

In 1831, nco's were supplied with an unusual combination of weapons. A sword with complicated guard of bars was supplied in a scabbard with compartment for a socket bayonet. The bayonet had a triangular section blade with elbow but no socket. In its place was a rectangular projection which fitted into a bar on the barrel. In some cases the retaining spring was in the bar on the barrel and in other cases rivetted to the projection on the bayonet.

In 1848, the Slesvig-Holstein rebellion broke out and the rebels were supported by Prussia and consequently supplied with Prussian arms of various sorts. Various patterns of bayonets found their way to Denmark including socket bayonets, Prussian *Hirschfanger* sword bayonets pattern 1810 and Prussian made bayonets with the Khyl locking spring.

After the end of the war, the various captured weapons were

issued to the Danish forces, the *Hirschfanger* going to the navy and the socket bayonets to the army where they survived until the 1860s.

In 1867, Denmark Sweden and Norway adopted the Remington rifle. The Danish bayonet had a 'yatagan' blade with cross guard with muzzle ring with a small lug above it and a curved quillon with ball finial. The grips were in chequered leather held to the tang with five rivets and the screw holding the leaf spring. The pommel was beak shaped and held the locking catch and push stud. The bayonet was carried in a leather scabbard with two mounts, the locket having a 'D' for the frog strap and the chape a ball finial. A later version of this bayonet had an internal coil spring in the pommel.

In 1889, the Krag Jørgensen rifle was adopted and with it a most unusual knife bayonet. This had the blade, tang and pommel forged in a single piece. The blade was single edged with a fuller each side and had a shoulder and no cross piece. The grips were in chequered leather and fitted to the tang with two rivets. After 1893, wood grips were fitted to these bayonets. The back of the tang was slotted and the pommel fitted with an unusual protruding release catch. The bayonet was carried in a leather scabbard with two mounts, the chape with ball finial and the locket with bar for the frog strap and a spring catch to retain the bayonet in the scabbard.

In 1915, a longer bayonet was issued with the shortened Krag rifle. The blade, cross piece, tang and pommel were again forged in one piece. The blade was 18 in. long of 'T' section single edged and tapering to a point. The back of the tang was slotted and held the muzzle ring stepped back from the shoulder of the blade and the spring release stud. The grips were in wood and held to the tang by two rivets. These bayonets are shown in plate 144.

In Sweden, the socket bayonet was adopted in 1696. This weapon had a flat double edged blade and a short socket with on the blade side a wing nut which was tightened to hold the bayonet firmly on the barrel. In 1699, with the issue of a new musket an improved bayonet was issued. Of similar construction, the socket had an extension piece into which the wing nut was placed. In 1701 a further version of this style of bayonet was issued with an even smaller socket and with the wing nut in the socket as in the 1696 pattern. A profusion of bayonets were issued during the eighteenth century with the same style of locking system and varying lengths of blade and a sword bayonet for the 1761 light infantry rifle while having a wide doubled edged blade, tubular grip and knuckle guard employed the wing nut system. In 1811, the first socket bayonet with locking ring was issued. This pattern was replaced in 1815 with another similar bayonet with shorter blade. Further socket bayonets were issued in 1840, 1851 and 1864. These were more modern patterns having a shorter elbow from blade to socket and the locking rings in various positions on the socket. In 1867 when the Remington rifle was adopted a socket bayonet was issued with it. This had a cruciform sectioned blade, short elbow and a zig-zag slot with locking ring. A sword bayonet was also issued with the rifle. This had a single edged 'yatagan' style blade, cross piece with muzzle ring and chequered leather grips with beak shaped pommel with leaf spring and push stud. This bayonet was similar in appearance to the many bayonets adopted by various countries at this time.

In 1889, when the calibre of the Remington was reduced a further issue of socket bayonet was made. This unusual bayonet had the cruciform blade of its predecessor and a short socket but without locking ring. Retention on the barrel was by means of a coil spring and stud situated in the socket.

In 1896, when the Mauser rifle was adopted a knife bayonet was issued with it. This had a single edged blade with cross piece with muzzle hole, a tubular metal grip with turning for better grip and the unique protruding locking catch in the pommel. This can be seen in plate 144. In 1914, when the Mauser carbines were adapted to take a bayonet, a new design was introduced. This bayonet shown in plate 144 had a double edged blade, cross piece with muzzle ring, wood grips to the tang and an inverted pommel with groove and locking catch. A version with longer blade was issued to the navy.

Although Norway was united with Denmark until 1815 and with Sweden until 1905, they tended to retain their own pattern of weapons. As with other countries the favourite and cheapest bayonet with which to arm the infantry was the socket bayonet and like Denmark, use was made of hangers as sword bayonets by the addition of a bar and spring.

In 1851, a bayonet with unique features was issued with the newly converted to percussion 1821 rifle. This bayonet had a single edged 'yatagan' blade with small cross piece and a tang with a wood grip on one side only. The other side showed the exposed tang with two slots. When the 1821 rifle was converted the tube on the side of the barrel to take the converted hanger bayonet was removed and replaced with two catches which engaged the slots in the exposed tang.

In 1859, a 'Yatagan' bladed bayonet of similar style to countless others adopted by many countries at this time was issued. It had a beak pommel with hole for sword knot and unlike many others, wood grips. This bayonet with differing sized muzzle rings was issued with the 1859 rifle, the 1860 rifle, the Remington in 1867 and the Krag Peterson in 1876. A special version with shortened blade, with saw back and with the beak of the pommel removed was issued to engineers.

In 1884, when the Jarmann rifle was issued a new bayonet was designed. This had a cruciform sectioned blade, a straight cross piece with muzzle ring with cut out collar, metal backstrap with slot and locking stud with coiled spring and metal pommel. The grips were wood and held with two rivets. A bayonet with short double edged blade but with the same hilt was issued to the Navy. In 1894, when the Krag Jørgensen rifle was adopted a bayonet not unlike the 1889 Danish bayonet was issued. The basic difference was that the Norwegian bayonet had a single grip screw and the protruding locking catch was replaced by a pivot and stud next to the shoulder of the blade. On pressing the stud the pivot worked against a cooled spring to raise the locked lug and when released the locking lug dripped back in place in the slot at the proper place. This system was later adopted on United States bayonets for the M1 Garand rifle. In 1912, a longer bladed version was issued for the Krag carbine and another version with different fullers in the blade was issued in 1914. During the Second World War a great number of these were shortened.

United States and South America

It was not until the late 1970s that the United States adopted a musket designed and manufactured by the US Armouries at Springfield and Harpers Ferry. Up until that time a variety of muskets had been used during and after the revolution. The main patterns in use were either captured British weapons or French made arms supplied when French troops arrived in North America in 1778. German muskets and bayonets also featured in the new army, these being mainly weapons captured from German mercenaries employed by the British. After the revolution, the American army was supplied with 1763 and 1777 muskets and bayonets but in 1795, the American made muskets and bayonets were adopted. For the first few years, the bayonet was a permanent fixture to the barrel but in 1801, they were removed and replaced with a socket bayonet with zig-zag slot and 15 in. triangular sectioned blade. This style of bayonet, with minor variations in blade length continued until 1812, when a bridge at the end of the socket was introduced to strengthen it. This pattern, again with variations remained standard issue until 1840, when a socket bayonet with 18 in. blade of triangular section and a locking ring on the socket was adopted. This pattern with a slight change in the shape of the top of the blade was retained with the 1855 musket until 1873, when the socket was bushed and the bayonet redesignated Pattern 1873 to fit the breech loading Springfield rifle adopted in that year. In 1884, experiments were tried with a ramrod bayonet, which when not in use was pushed back in a channel in the stock like a ramrod but was withdrawn and locked into place when required. This pattern ousted the socket bayonet but was itself made obsolete by the adoption of a knife bayonet with the Krag Jørgensen rifle approved in 1892.

Another type of bayonet which employed a socket was the trowel bayonet adopted on a limited scale for the 1873 Springfield. The bayonet combined entrenching tool and socket bayonet in one. The socket had an internal groove in the top half which swung over to one side to allow the barrel to be put in, then closed to lock the bayonet in position. Less than 10,000 of them were made and it is doubtful whether very many were ever issued.

As in a number of armies, there were a great many variations in sword bayonets, a large proportion of which were experimental of only trial issues. The first pattern of sword bayonet adopted was that to fit the 1841 musket. As this musket was not originally issued with any form of bayonet, various modifications were made to adapt it to take a socket and a sword bayonet. Two types of bayonet were decided upon by the Ordnance; one for rifles already made and another for those being manufactured, and where a bar could be fitted to the barrel. Other than fit a bar, a special band with stud was designed to clamp on the barrel but this method was less common. The first bayonet had two rings to the hilt, one on the normal muzzle ring position and another at the pommel end which could be folded down when the bayonet was used as a short sword. The muzzle ring, which was oval in outside shape, was fitted with a spring loaded catch that held it in position on the barrel. The grip of the bayonet was in brass and ribbed with the cross piece being 'S' shaped and cast as an integral part. The blade was 'yatagan' in form and the scabbard black leather with two brass mounts. The sword bayonet for the new rifles with band and rifles fitted with the adaptor had a brass hilt with large muzzle ring and forward curving quillon. The blade was again 'yatagan' in form and the scabbard the same as the previous bayonet.

Another sword bayonet with a strange fitting arrangement was the Sappers and Miners model of 1841 whose overall appearance was like a Roman short sword with brass hilt engraved with scales and a leaf shaped blade similar in form to the Brunswick rifle bayonet blade. The grip had a slot in the pommel to take the sword bar on the musketoon but also had a muzzle ring on the cross piece which had a locking ring incorporated into it. The bayonet locked on the barrel in two places, the slot in the pommel and the muzzle ring.

In 1855, a further pattern of sword bayonet was adopted for the rifle approved in that year. The bayonet's overall appearance was similar to the bayonet just described except that the slot in the pommel of the hilt was shorter. The bayonets used on the 1861 Navy rifle were a sword bayonet similar to the 1855 model but without the finial on the top of the muzzle ring and the Dahlgren knife bayonet. Admiral Dahlgren described the sword bayonet as 'similar to that of the French' (French pattern 1842) and the knife bayonet as 'a short, broad and stout knife of the well-known Bowie pattern'. The hilt had a cross piece, which was 'S' shaped, a back piece and flat pommel cast in one which enclosed a wood grip. The spring was fitted to the right side of the back piece worked by a stud on the opposite side. The blade was 12 in. long with spear point and single cutting edge.

During the American Civil war period, a large number of sword bayonets were adopted by the Confederate States; some to the design of American manufacturers. The bayonets fitted the Boyle, Gamble and Macfee rifle, and had brass hilts and various blade forms, which fitted to this rifle and various others apparently using an adaptor band. Another type was the bayonet for the Fayette Armoury rifle which except for the scaled grip looked like the French pattern of 1842. Various European arms and bayonets were imported by both sides, the most popular being the British Enfield of 1853 with socket and sword bayonets.

In 1862, a sword bayonet very similar again in style to the French pattern of 1842 was adopted on the Remington 'Zouave' rifle but with a straightish blade with only a gentle curve. In 1870, the Remington breech loader was adopted which for the Navy was issued with a sword bayonet, which had a curious brass hilt, with a raised section at the top which took the bayonet bar and incorporated the spring. The grip was scaled and the pommel decorated with the badge of the Navy Bureau of Ordnance. The blades found on various examples were either yatagan or straight.

In 1892, the American Army adopted the Krag rifle and with it a short knife bayonet similar in appearance to the Swiss Schmidt Rubin bayonet of 1889. It had a blade length of 11¾ in. with a single cutting edge and deep fuller. The pommel and crosspiece were steel and the grips wood held by rivets to the tang. The scabbard was blued steel with a metal belt attachment fitted to it. A shorter bayonet was issued with the cadet rifle and another version with a wide Bowie blade with a clipped point which could be used as a knife for clearing brush.

In 1895, the Navy adopted on a limited scale the Lee rifle with a bayonet nearly the same as the Mannlicher 1895 adopted by Austria but without the rivets in the cross piece. This pattern of bayonet, but with a down sweeping quillon was used on the Remington rifle sold to Mexico in 1899, the reason being that both patterns were made by the Remington Arms Company.

1905 was the year when the sword bayonet was adopted for the 1903 Springfield rifle, which had for two years been equipped with a ramrod bayonet. The new bayonet had a 16 in. blade with single cutting edge and deep central fuller. The cross piece and pommel were in steel with the locking catch in a slot in the pommel but activated by a catch just behind the cross guard. The grips were wood held to the tang with a single screw and nut. This bayonet was used throughout World War One together with the Pattern 1917 bayonet used on the American version of the P.14 rifle with which the British were experimenting when the War broke out. The bayonet for this pattern is the same as the British version except for the oil drain hole in the pommel and American markings.

Except for two instances, Canadian troops were equipped with British pattern bayonets. The first pattern peculiar to Canada was approved in 1893 for use on a special batch of Martini-Metford rifles purchased in England in an attempt to find a suitable replacement for the Snider-Enfield. The bayonet of which only one thousand were made was manufactured by Wilkinson's. The Martini-Metford bought by Canada was basically a Martini-Henry rifle but in .303 calibre instead of .45/577. The new Metford barrel fitted had the same outside dimensions as the Henry barrel and therefore could take a Martini-Henry bayonet which was the case with those Martini-Metford Mk VIs manufactured. The majority of Martini-Metfords, however, were fitted with the nose cap of the Lee-Metford rifle and therefore took the 1888 bayonet. The new bayonet had the pommel and shortened cross guard of the 1887 Mk III bayonet but the blade and grips of the pattern 1888. Shortly after issue, the rifles were found to be too heavy and incorrectly sighted and so were withdrawn.

The second type of bayonet peculiar to Canada was the Ross. the first batch of new rifles were received in 1905 but the bayonets were not issued until 1908. Modelled on the British pattern of 1903, the Ross bayonet had a wide blade with rounded point, a cross guard with slightly set back muzzle ring and a square pommel. In 1910, a new pattern was issued which differed in having no set back muzzle ring and a large diameter to the ring to fit over the heavier barrel adopted in that year. On the outbreak of the First World War, the bayonets had the rounded points ground to give them more of a spear point with increased penetration. In 1916, the Ross rifle which had had numerous troubles since the beginning of its life was withdrawn from service as it was totally unsuitable in the mud of the trenches. It was replaced by the SMLE with pattern 1907 bayonet.

Besides the Remington rolling block rifle, which was adopted by Mexico, Argentina in 1871, and number of other South American countries, the Mauser rifle, introduced at the time when German influence on South American uniforms and tactics became noticeable, was the favoured weapon. Mexico, after having abandoned the Swiss made Mondragon rifle used both the Remington and the Mauser 98, the latter eventually replacing the American made arm. The bayonet for the Mexican Mauser was similar in design to the Spanish pattern of 1893 with a single edged blade of 11 in. and steel pommel and cross piece. Peru also adopted the Mauser in the 1890s using the pattern 91, then the 98 with the standard long bladed German pattern used on the Kar 98. Costa Rica used the Gew 98 rifle but with 95 Mauser fore-end fitting so that there was no need to change bayonet patterns, which was the same design as the Spanish Mauser pattern of 1893. Argentine having used a sword bayonet with brass hilt and 'S' shaped guard on the Remington rifle adopted the Mauser in 1891. The bayonet used with this rifle was unusual in having brass or white metal grips. The pommel and cross piece with down sweeping quillon were in steel and the blade, which was straight and single edged with a deep fuller measured 15¾ in. All these bayonets were made in Germany and some can be found with the Argentine Coat of Arms on although these are normally removed by the authorities prior to disposal. In 1909, the bayonet lost the metal grips which were replaced by ones in wood held by two screws and rivets. Again, these were German made and the scabbard for both patterns was all steel.

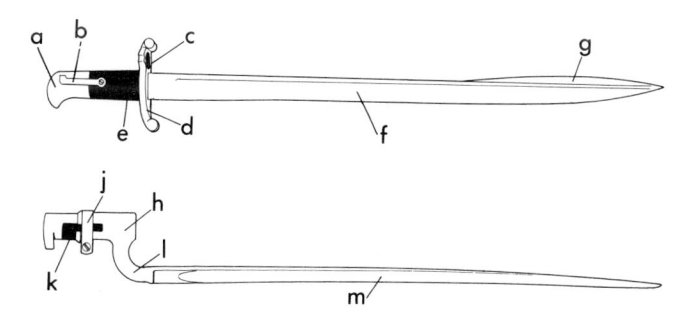

Fig. 8. Parts of a Bayonet. a) Pommel. b) locking spring. c) muzzle ring. d) cross guard or cross piece. e) grip. f) blade. g) Pipe back or falchion. h) socket. j) locking ring. k) zig zag or slot. l) shoulder m) blade with fullers.

7   *Native Weapons*

Abyssinia

The swords called *shotels* used in this country had a curved sickle style of blade with the cutting edge on the inner side. The grips consisted of horn shaped crudely, and placed on the tang or riveted to it if it was made wide. The grip swelled out towards the top which was finished by having an ornamented plate put on it before the tang was burred over. Straight bladed swords were also used and the great variety of blade shape and size is due to the importation of European made blades during the nineteenth century. These 'Trade' blades usually of bad or indifferent quality were crudely decorated with various standard designs. During the 1930s The Wilkinson Sword Company produced a series of blades for the Abyssinian market (plate 100). These blades, slightly curved, very curved, thin and thick were highly decorated with blue and gilt and etched with foliage, inscriptions and the Lion of Juda. A special pattern 'Flame' blade etched and inlaid with brass, copper, blue and gilt gave the impression of a flame. The blades were fitted with a wood hilt and used to arm Haile Selassie's bodyguards.

Barong

This was the traditional weapon of the Moros of the Philippines. The blade was broad and slightly curved and simply etched. It was crudely made by the Moros of pieces of iron and was fitted with a rough wood grip, the top of which was decorated with a tuft of human hair.

Dha

The *dha* was a weapon peculiar to Burma and had a slightly curved single edged blade and a long hilt without a cross guard. The hilt was topped by a metal cap and the grip was in wood bound in fish skin, bands of metal or other materials. The scabbard was also made of wood and the two halves held together with bands of metal or thongs. Some scabbards of superior weapons were completely covered in metal. A thick cord was bound around the top of the scabbard and tied to form a loop which was passed over the shoulder, suspending the sword at the hip. Smaller versions, dagger size, but exactly as described were also used.

Japan

Japanese swords have hardly changed in basic style for hundreds of years, but the style of fittings to hilt and scabbard are many and various according to fashion and cost. The most valuable part of the Japanese sword was the blade which was passed down through the family for many generations, a new hilt, furniture and scabbard being put on when required.

The blades fall into certain periods, those forged before 1537 were from the *Koto* period, those between 1537 and 1876 were from the *Shinto* period and those manufactured after 1876 are termed as of the *Showato* period. Up until the ninth century the blades were straight, the same as the Chinese but after that date they became slightly curved.

Japanese swords and daggers fall into the following types:
    a) *nodachi*. A long sword anything up to six feet in length and carried slung across the back.
    b) *tachi*. A long sword shorter than (a) and slung from the belt.
    c) *katana*. A long sword carried by being pushed through the wait sash of the wearer. Scabbard with companion knife and tool for putting up hair.
    d) *wakishashi*. The smallest sword with length between one

and two feet. Scabbard had companion knife and hair implement.

e) *tanto*. Small dagger with handguard as used on swords.

f) *aikutchi*. Similar to *tanto* but with no hand guard.

The *Samurai*, the warriors of Japan had the privilege of carrying more than one sword. In pairs they were called *daisho*, which could be a long and short sword or a sword and dagger.

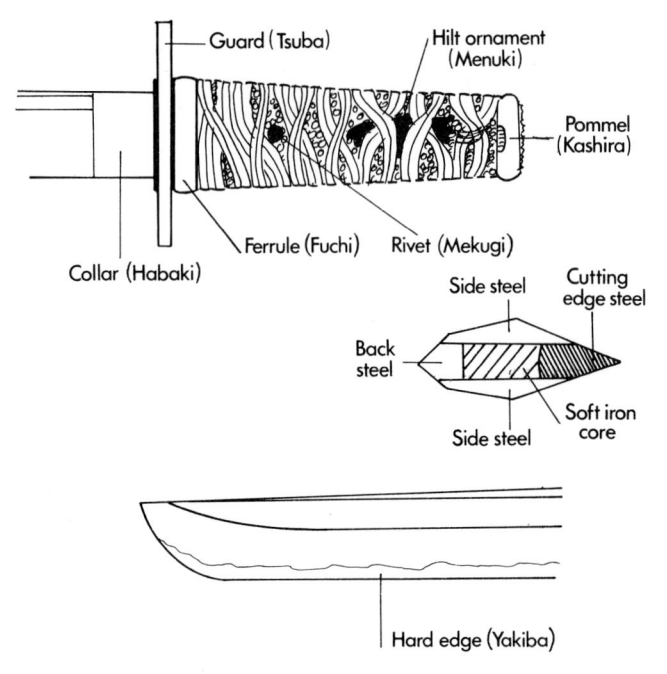

Fig. 9. Japanese sword parts.

The Japanese sword or dagger consisted of the following component parts. The grip was made in two parts, grooved on the inside to fit the tang and glued together. Over the wood, rayskin, called the *same*, was stuck, over which was put a criss-cross of braid holding two small ornaments in metal, one each side called

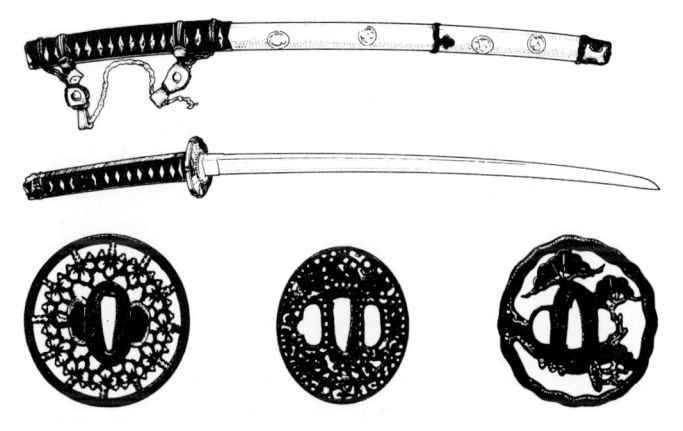

Fig. 10. Japanese sword and scabbard with various designs of Tsuba.

the *menuki*. The grip was drilled to take a wood peg which passed through a corresponding hole in the tang and held the grip to the blade. On top of the grip was a cap called a *kashira* and at the base was a ferrule known as a *fuchi*. Before the grip was slid on to the tang a copper washer *(seppa)* was placed between the *fuchi* and the hand guard *(tsuba)* and between the *tsuba* and the shoulder of the blade. All the metal fittings were made as a set with the same basic designs in chisel and inlay. *Tsubas* with three holes were for the small sword where companion implements were carried. Metal fittings to the lacquered wood scabbard matched the hilt mounts in design.

Japanese sword blades can be found with plain wood grips and plain scabbard but these were never intended for wear, being purely a storage case.

In 1876, the Emperor forbade the wearing of swords by all except the military and the traditional art of the sword maker suffered considerably because of the massed produced Western style of military sword. This period of mass produced weapons was termed the *Shin-Shinto* period but in 1937 the traditional sword was reinstated. This was the *Shin-Gunto* period which lasted until the end of the Second World War. Mass produced military weapons appeared during the Second World War having brown leather covers to the scabbard. Nco's had a sword in the traditional style but with a steel scabbard and alloy cast grip incorporating the braid work which was painted brown. Ancestral swords were used by officers who had new scabbards with leather covers or covered the ornamental scabbard in this way.

Firangi

The *firangi* was an Indian sword akin to the *tulwar* but was a two handed weapon. The blade of the *firangi* unlike the *tulwar* was straight, but the hilt was similar except that the cross guard was replaced with a bowl guard with knuckle bow and a flat top to the grip with a projecting spike. The grip was held in one hand and the spike in the other. Some examples had two separate guards and in this case there was no spike. In both varieties, the bowlguard was padded to protect the knuckles.

Jambiya

This was one of the most common style of dagger which could be found because of its widespread use. It was the weapon of the Arabs mainly but was also used by the Indians and Persians. The Arab model had a blade that was double edged with a central strengthening rib with the end of the blade sharply curving away to the left when viewed. The grip with a rudimentary ferrule which closed over the mouthpiece of the scabbard when sheathed went from the width of the blade, tapered in the centre then swelled out at the top. The Indian and Persian version had a more gentle curve to the blade and different grip. The scabbard of the Arab version did not follow the contours of the blade but turned almost at right angles to the left when viewed. The grips and scabbards of these weapons were often highly decorated with gold, silver and precious stones and carried on a special belt that fastened to loops on the scabbard. The weapon was not worn at the side like a normal dagger but on the front. In the Indian,

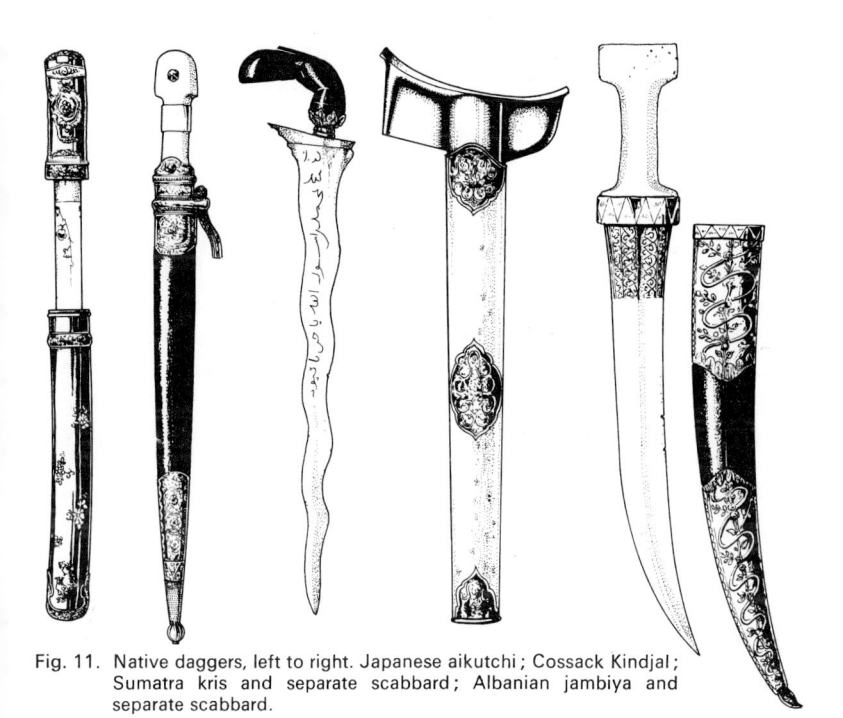

Fig. 11. Native daggers, left to right. Japanese aikutchi; Cossack Kindjal; Sumatra kris and separate scabbard; Albanian jambiya and separate scabbard.

Caucasian and Balkan versions the scabbard followed the contours of the blade and was in wood covered in velvet or other cloth with decorative locket and chape. The Indian version usually had the grip made from bone riveted to the widened tang, and in some examples the top of the blade was pierced with decorative work.

Kard

The Kard was an Indian knife with a single edged blade with the appearance of a kitchen knife. The blade on occasions had a thickened point for piercing armour of chain mail. The grip was in bone or horn fitted to a widened and shaped tang. The unusual feature of the kard was that the leather covered wood scabbard appeared too large for the knife. This is because, when sheathed, the scabbard accommodated most of the grip, leaving a small portion showing.

Khouttar or Katar

This knife from India was used in the way a boxer might deliver a straight punch. The dagger consisted of a double edged tapering blade with thickened point for piercing armour or mail and no grip. The blade had two continuing pieces of metal at each side of the shoulder which were joined a little way up with a cross bar giving the appearance of a letter 'H'. The cross bar was gripped in the fist and the weapon used in a jabbing motion. Usually the cross bar and shoulder of the blade were decorated with chiselling and piercing work. The scabbard in wood covered in velvet or other cloth conformed to the blade and had only a small decorative shape.

Kindjahl

The *kindjhal* had a long double edged blade with a central fuller and a most distinctive hilt shape. The *kindjhal* was used in various countries including Persia, the Balkans and Russia, the Russian style being predominant. The grip was wide at the shoulder and abruptly tapered to form the holding portion and then broadened out at the top to form a hand stop. The top of the grip was usually rounded and the sides held to the tang by two large dome headed rivets at the shoulder and top of the grip. The scabbard was made in wood and covered in leather but examples are quite common that have the scabbard covered in silver which is highly decorated with engraving and chiselling work. In these cases this work is extended to the grip. The weapon was suspended by a single band around the scabbard with a loop to take a suspension strap or cord.

Kris

The *kris* was a dagger peculiar to South-east Asia, being found in Bali, Java, Malaya and other islands. The blade of the *kris* came in two versions; the straight blade from Java and other islands and the wavy blade from Malaya. The blade form was distinctive in that in both patterns, the blade widened out at the shoulder to form a guard to the simple grip. The grip was either round and straight or more often cocked back at right angles like a walking stick handle. The grips were often ornately carved as were the scabbards which conformed to the outward shape of the shoulder and then descended parallel for both patterns of blade. The blade itself was usually left rough, showing the various layers of metal from which it was made. Some examples were painted on the sheath and grip with jungle scenes depicting animals etc. while other grips were carved in various ways, the so called 'Kingfisher' grip being quite rare. Larger versions of the *kris* are known but these *Sundangs* as they were named were for ceremonial use only.

Kukri

The *kukri* was and is the native knife of Nepal and was made in differing blade sizes from 14 to 24 inches. The blade was curved widening from the shoulder with the cutting edge on the inner curve of the blade. The grip, either hollowed to take a narrow tang or two side pieces to fit to the shaped tang were in wood and had a distinctive shape. The grip swelled from the shoulder to a small hand stop about ¼ in. wide and then swelled out to a flat oval sectioned pommel surmounted by a plate with a tang button. The government issue *kukri* for Gurkha troops had a black leather scabbard made in wood covered in leather with no mouth pieces but a small metal chape. The blade is plain and the grip in black polished wood. In the scabbard two small replicas of the *kukri* were carried, one a knife, the other a sharpening steel. There were also decorative versions with the scabbard decorated with pierced and engraved silver mounts over a velvet covered wood scabbard. Larger versions of the *kukri* were used for ceremonial. The *kukri* shown on plate 127 is the government issue version.

Kyber knife

The Kyber knife had a single edged tapering blade of 'T' cross section with a bone grip rivetted to the shaped tang. This grip was wide at the shoulder, tapered in on the cutting edge side and curved round at the top to form a handstop. The scabbard was similar to the *kard* in that it was longer than the blade but unlike the scabbard of the *kard* swelled out on the portion which covered just the lower part of the grip.

Mandau

The *mandau* was the sword of the head-hunters of Borneo. The blade widened from the shoulder to the rounded point rather like a machete and was concave in section, decorated and chiselled with designs. The hilt was a simple grip carved from bone or horn, occasionally in the shape of an animal's head. To the grip were attached tufts of hair which legend has it were human but were more probably animal. The scabbard was made from two pieces of wood, carved out on the inside to take the blade and then bound together with thongs made from grass or creeper. The smaller sheath was attached to the scabbard which housed a knife and the whole scabbard was decorated with tufts of hair and users' good luck beads or charms.

Pata

The *pata,* or 'gauntlet' sword was a thrusting weapon to be found in India. The blade was straight and usually double edged and the cross grip similar to the *khouttar* was encased in an armoured gauntlet. The gauntlet and the top of blade were usually decorated with engraving and chiselling.

Pesh Kabz

The *pesh kabz* was similar to the kyber knife previously described, but had a shorter blade and usually an armoured point for piercing chain mail. The grip was usually made from bone or carved jade.

Shamshir

This curved bladed sword was to be found in India and neighbouring countries. The blade ranged from slightly curved to almost the curve of a sickle blade, in which case the scabbard had a special slot at the back to allow for this. The hilt was the 'mameluke' shape later adopted by many countries for high ranking officers' swords and presentation weapons. The cross guard which terminated in acorn like finials had down pointing langets each side, a ferrule and then the grip of ivory, bone or horn. The projection at the top of the hilt was usually bound in the same metal as the ferrule and not left the same as the grip. The scabbards were made in wood covered in cloth with a long locket incorporating a band and ring and a long chape, usually at least half the length of the scabbard.

Sudan

The sword of the Sudanese warrior was called the *kashara* and had a straight double edged blade terminating in a rounded point. The hilt consisted of a faceted iron cross piece with down pointing langets, a leather bound grip and a flat leather disc for a pommel. The legend has it that the blades on the Sudanese swords were made from swords left behind during the Crusades, but although the odd sword may have an old blade the majority were manufactured in Germany or England and sold or bartered with the Sudanese. To enhance their value, the blades were often marked with old sword makers' marks, suns and moons being particularly popular as well as the names of famous makers. The

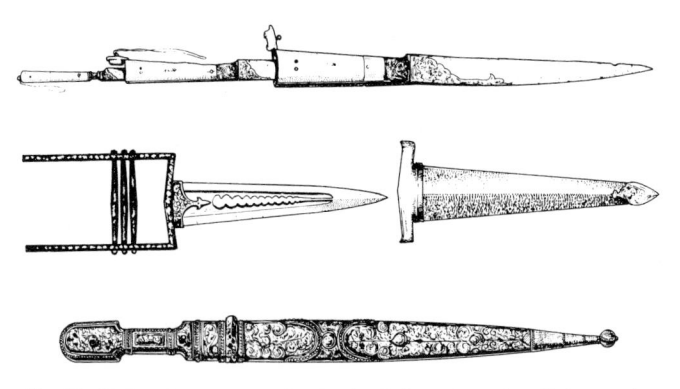

Fig. 12. Native daggers. top. Persian kards in various sizes fitting one into the other. centre. Indian Katar. below. Caucasian kindjal.

blades can also be found with long carved inscriptions on them taken from the Koran. The scabbards were made in leather which followed the contours of the blade but broadened out to a spear shaped point at the end. Just below the opening for the blade a leather band was sewn beneath the covering which was decorated with tooling in lines, cross-cross and designs to take the rings for suspension.

Tulwar

The *tulwar* was the predominant style of sword used in India, although in detail there are a huge number of variations. All *tulwar,* however, have a curved sharp blade and an all metal hilt, with a distinctive disc pommel. The grip cast with the cross guard which had down pointing langets narrowed from the cross guard, then widened before narrowing again under the disc pommel. This pommel was held to the tang with a top nut which did not hold the grip and cross piece to the blade as this was usually either hammered tight on or stuck on with a form of glue. Some *tulwar* had a knuckle bow included in the design while others had a more elaborate version of the normal cross hilted design. Most *tulwar* were plain with minimal decoration of engraving and chisel work but a large number were more ornate with inlaid silver work. Others had inlaid silver and gold and these designs were reflected in the scabbard mounts. The scabbard was in wood covered in velvet with a single mount, the chape, the weapon tucked into a sash for carrying. Larger sacrificial *tulwar* with normal hilts but exceptionally wide blades are also to be found. While most of the blades were of native workmanship and decorated with Indian symbols and legends, *tulwar* can be found with old French and British cavalry sword blades with Indian symbols chiselled over the original markings. These date from the mid 1700s.

In Africa there was a great variety of daggers used by the various tribes, many crudely made weapons with badly made blades or blades made from broken swords with wood grips usually bound with leather or brass wire. Some of the daggers and swords from central Africa have leaf shaped blades, some spear shaped blades.

There are also a great variety of spears to be found in Africa ranging from the broad leaf shaped blades of the Sudanese spear to the narrow leaf shaped bladed weapon of the Zulus. While most spears to be found were intended for throwing, the short shafted weapon of the Zulus from about 1820 were intended as thrusting weapons not to be thrown. Spears with long tapering heads similar to a sword blade, short shafts and long ferrule were the weapons of the Masai and seem to be the most effective of spears. Other weapons to be found with barbs and the like were more often than not, not weapons of war but fishing spears or hunting spears. Many of the weapons intended for throwing will be found with coil of iron at the tip for balance and some have even been found with a British Martini-Henry Rifle cartridge case partially filled with lead as a weight.

Makers' Marks

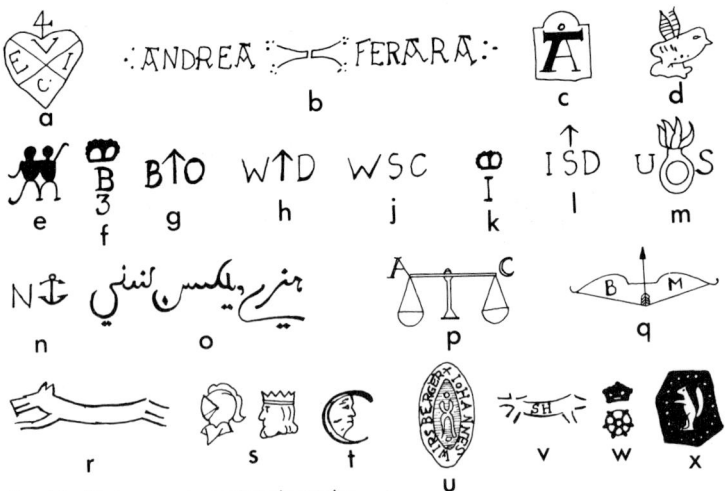

Fig. 13. Makers marks and trade marks.

a) Honourable East India Company. b) Andrea Ferara, Italian swordsmith 1555–93. c) Anthonio de Baena, Spanish bladesmith. d) Toledo mark, Spain seventeenth century. e) Peter Henkel, Solingen *c.* 1620. f) Inspector's Mark, British, Birmingham *c.* 1820 to *c.* 1939. Other letters denoted various areas or manufacturers as follows: 'BR' Birmingham Repair; 'E' Enfield; 'S' Solingen and 'W' Wilkinson. The number denoted a particular viewer or inspector. g) Ownership mark of the Board of Ordnance up to 1855. h) Ownership mark of the War Department 1855. j) Mark on the Wilkinson Sword Company found on bayonets and swords 1939–1945 and on contract sword to present time. Earlier naming was in full. k) Inspector's mark of the India Stores Depot, London. l) Acceptance mark of the India Stores Depot to denote ownership. m) Acceptance mark, United States of America. n) Royal Navy ownership mark. o) Henry Wilkinson, London, inscription on Persian military sword. p) Alex Coppel, Solingen 1860–1945. q) J. E. Bleckmann, Solingen 1860–1918. r) Running wolf mark of

140

Solingen and Passau. s) Weyersburg Kirschbaum and Co. 1883. The King's head was used alone by Weyersburg prior to 1883 and the Knight's head with WKC beneath used *c.* 1920. t) Half moon mark, Solingen. Used during the nineteenth century on African trade blades. u) Iohannes Wirsberger, Solingen *c.* 1620. v) Samuel Harvey, Birmingham 1748. w) Crown and Rose mark of James II. x) Squirrel mark of Friedrich Eickhorn, Solingen seventeenth century. This mark continued to be used by the firm of Eichhorn until recent months when they ceased trading.

Retailers and Manufacturers Locket Shields

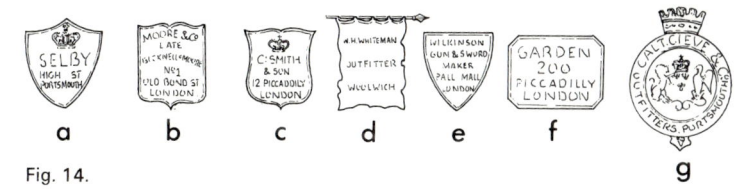

Fig. 14.

a) Selby Portmouth 1830–62. b) Moore and Co. 1838–50. c) Charles Smith 1836–59. d) Whiteman, Woolwich *c.* 1860. e) Wilkinson, Pall Mall, London. 1860–88. f) Garden, 1862–88. g) Galt Gieve and Co 1863–80.

THE COLOUR PLATES

1. Bronze Age sword blades.
2. Bronze Age dagger blades.
3. Bronze Age spear heads.
4. Bronze Age arrow heads.

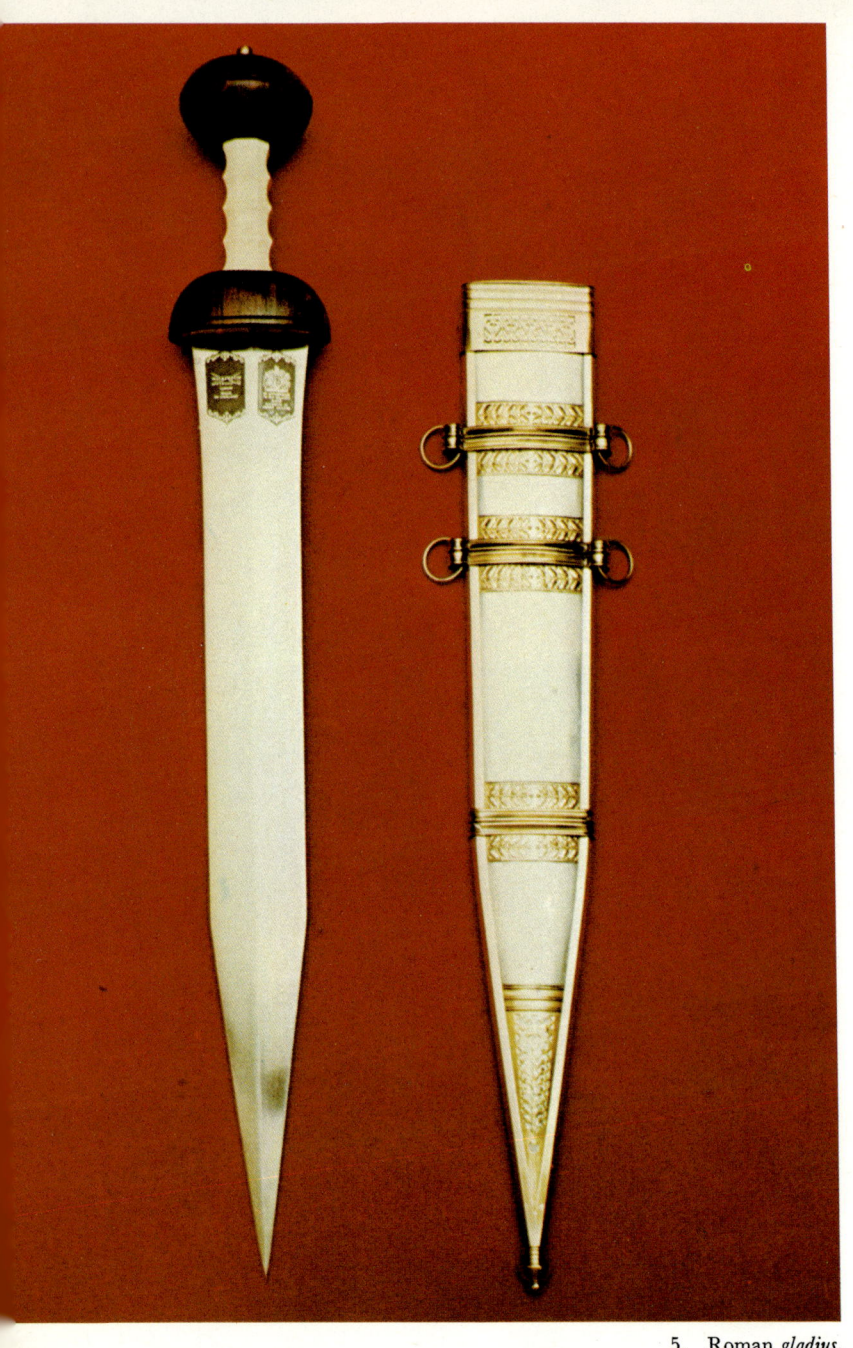

5. Roman *gladius*.

Viking, Saxon, Norman and medieval swords.

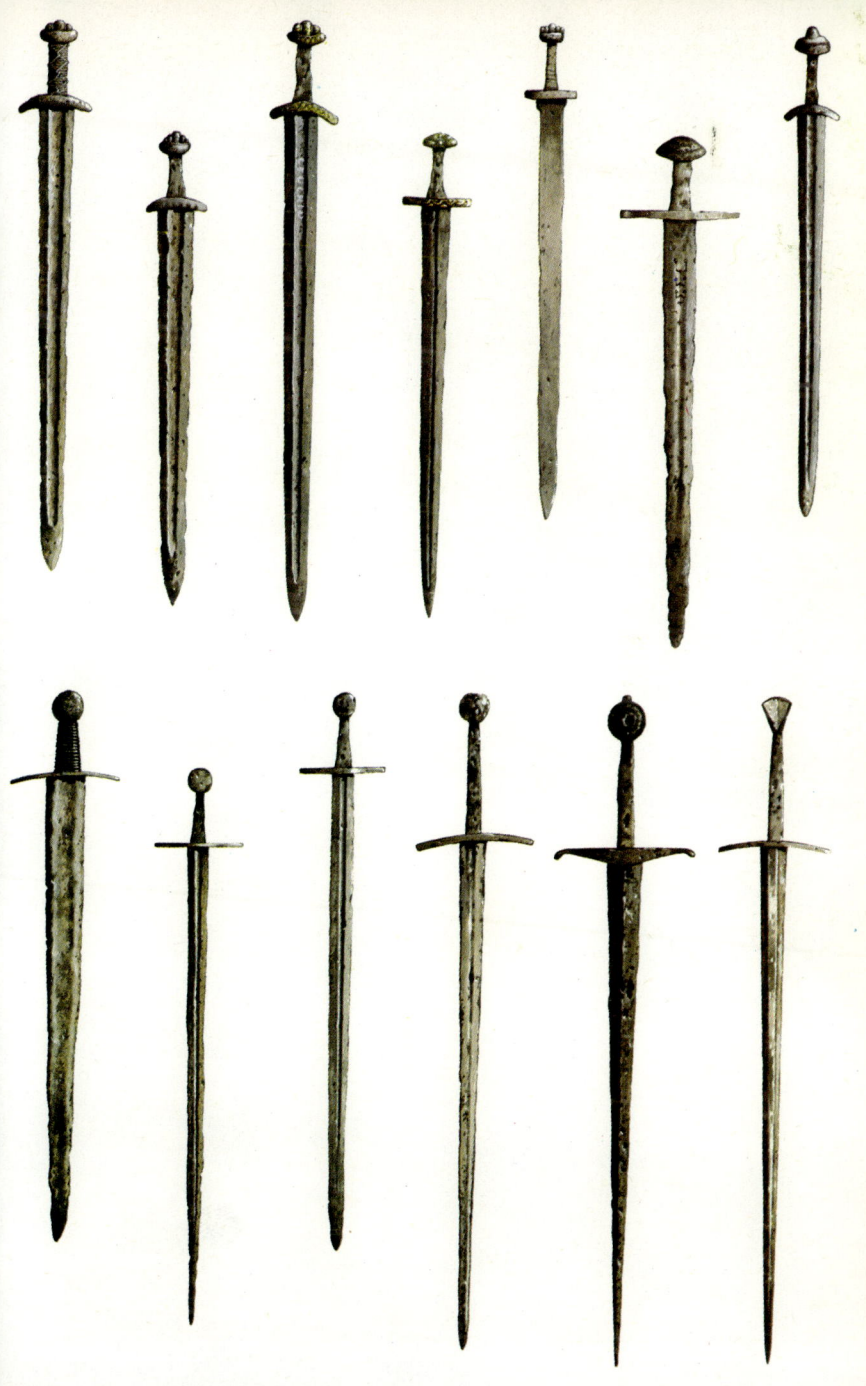

7. Two handed sword.

8. Two handed sword.

9. Fencing

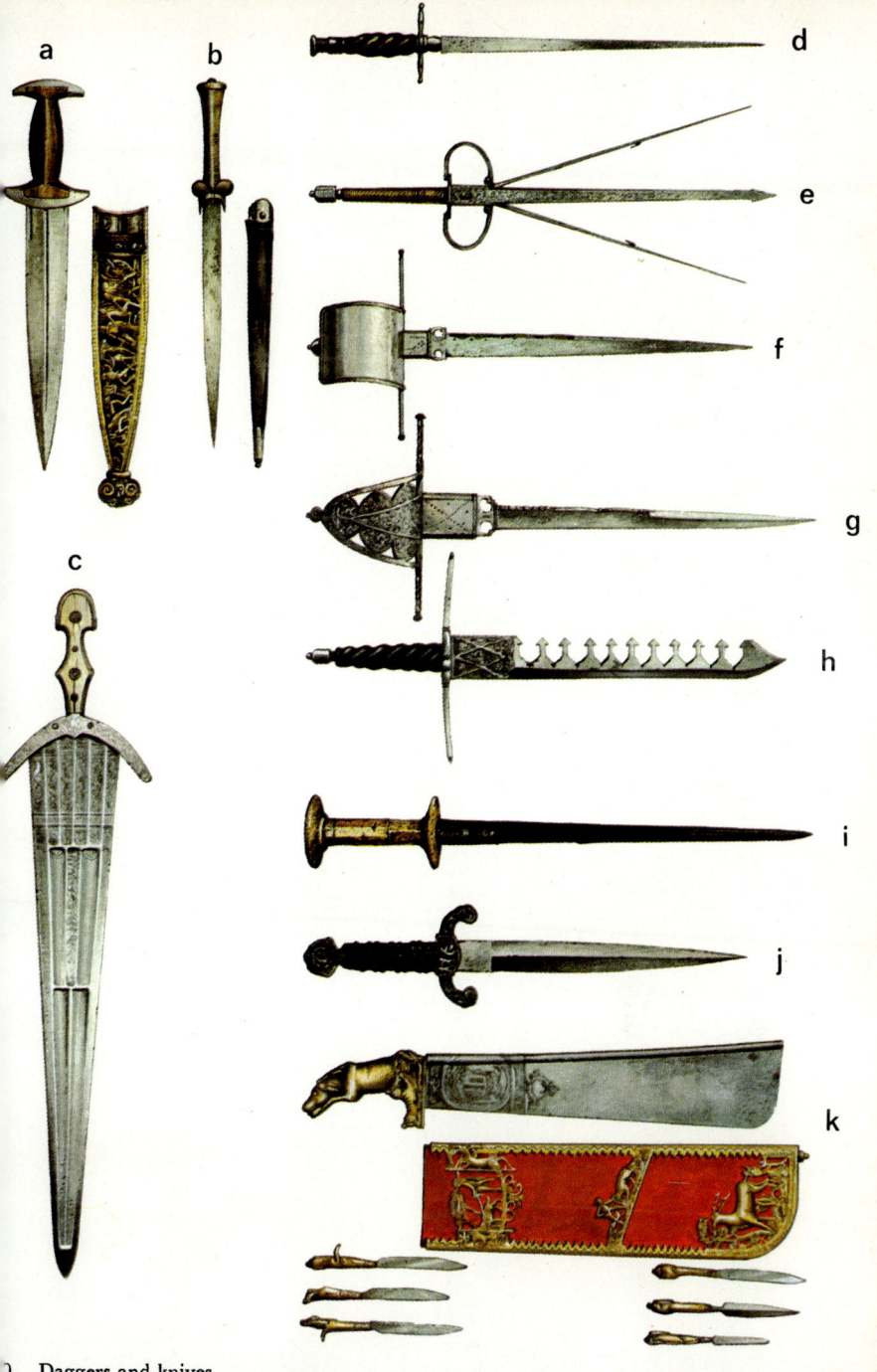

Daggers and knives.

11. Rapiers. 12. Rapiers.

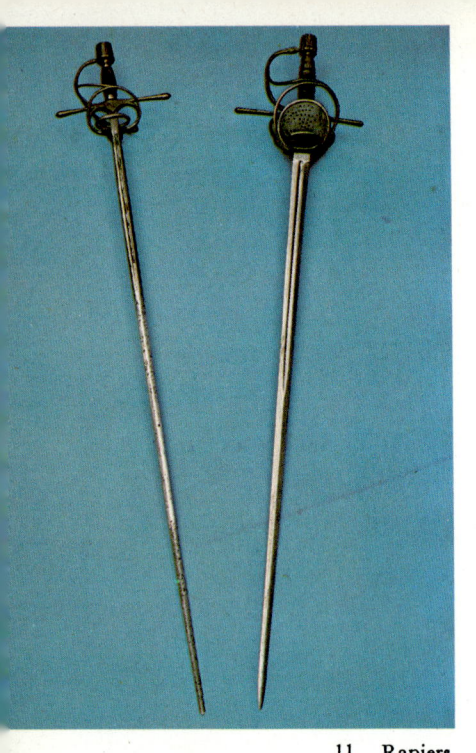

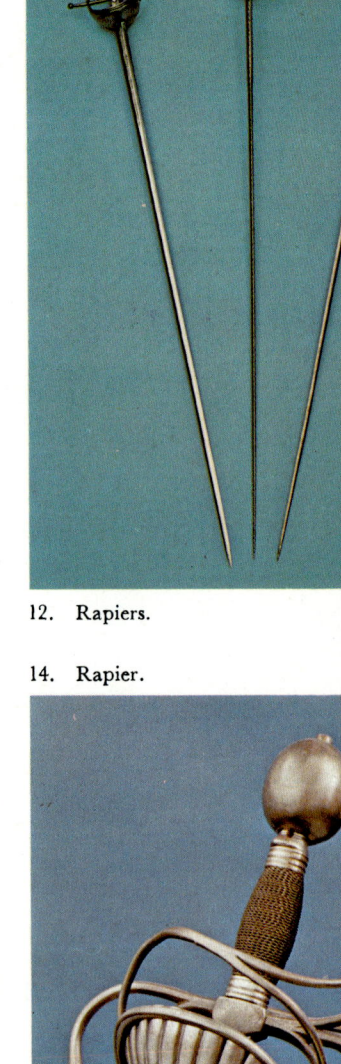

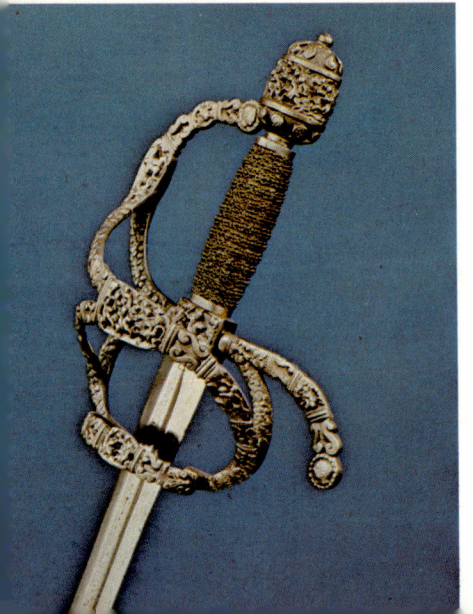

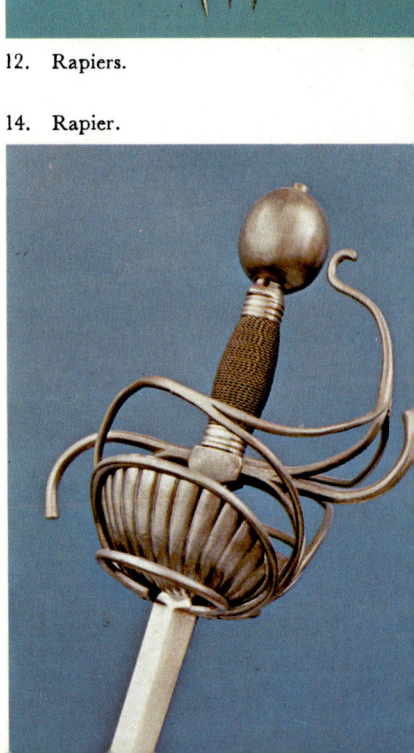

13. Rapier. 14. Rapier.

15. Rapier.

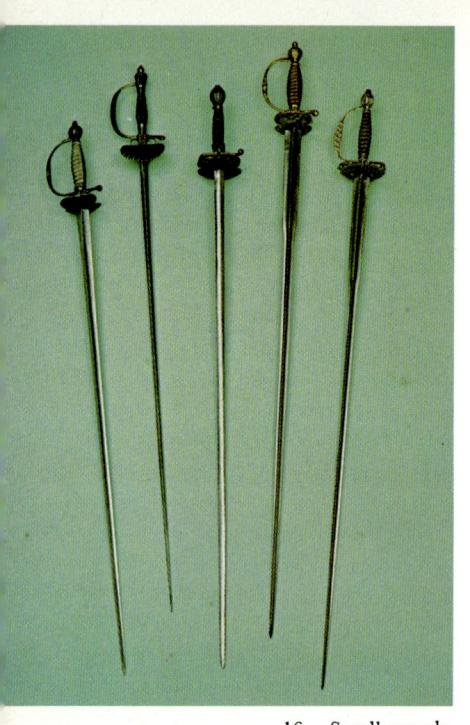

16. Small-swords. 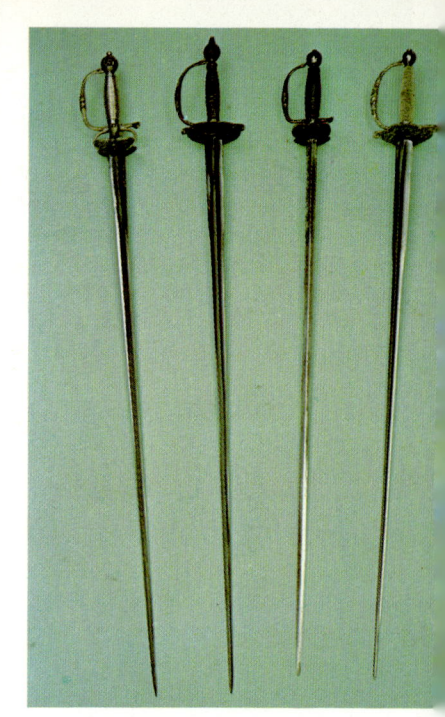 17. Small-swords.

18. Small-sword. 19. Small-sword.

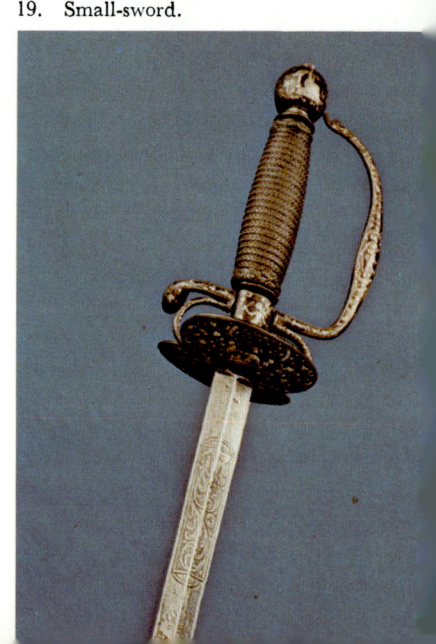

20. Small-sword.   21. Small-sword.

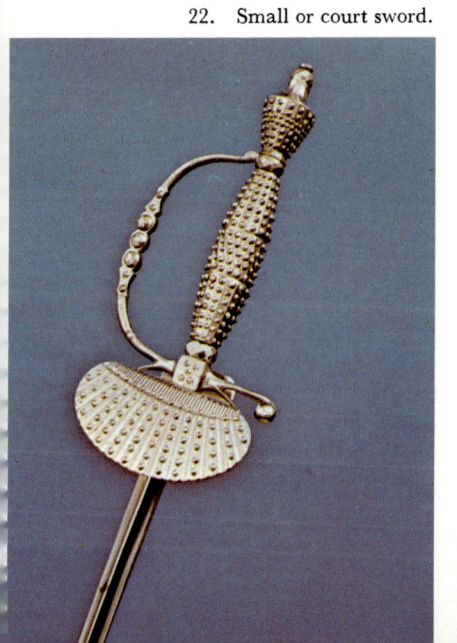

22. Small or court sword.   23. Presentation small-sword.

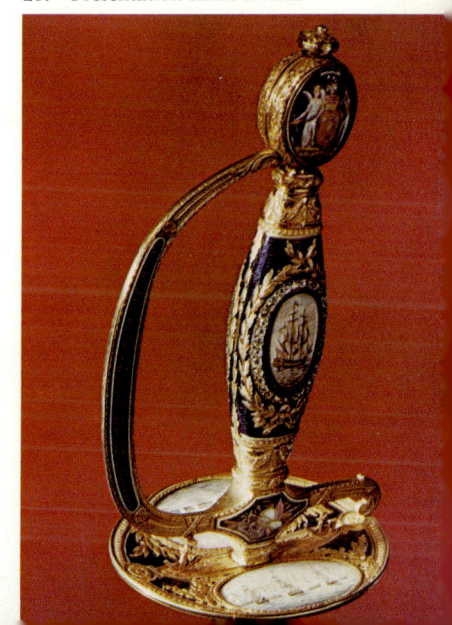

24. Presentation small-sword.
25. Presentation small-sword.

26. Court sword.
27. Court sword.

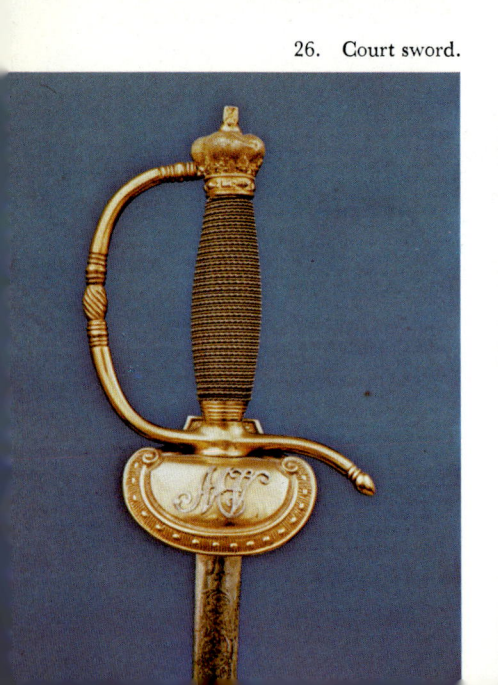

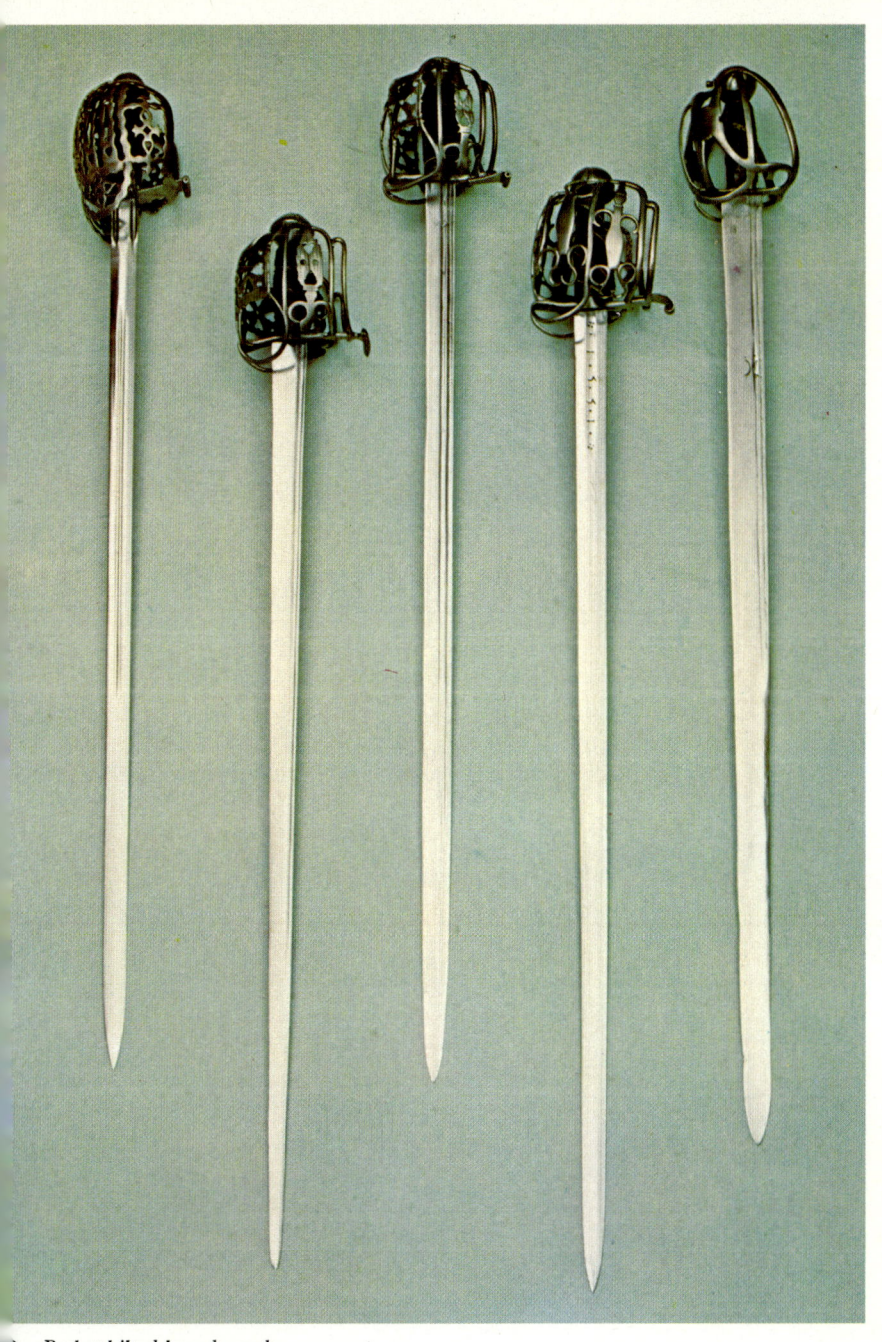

Basket hilted broadswords.

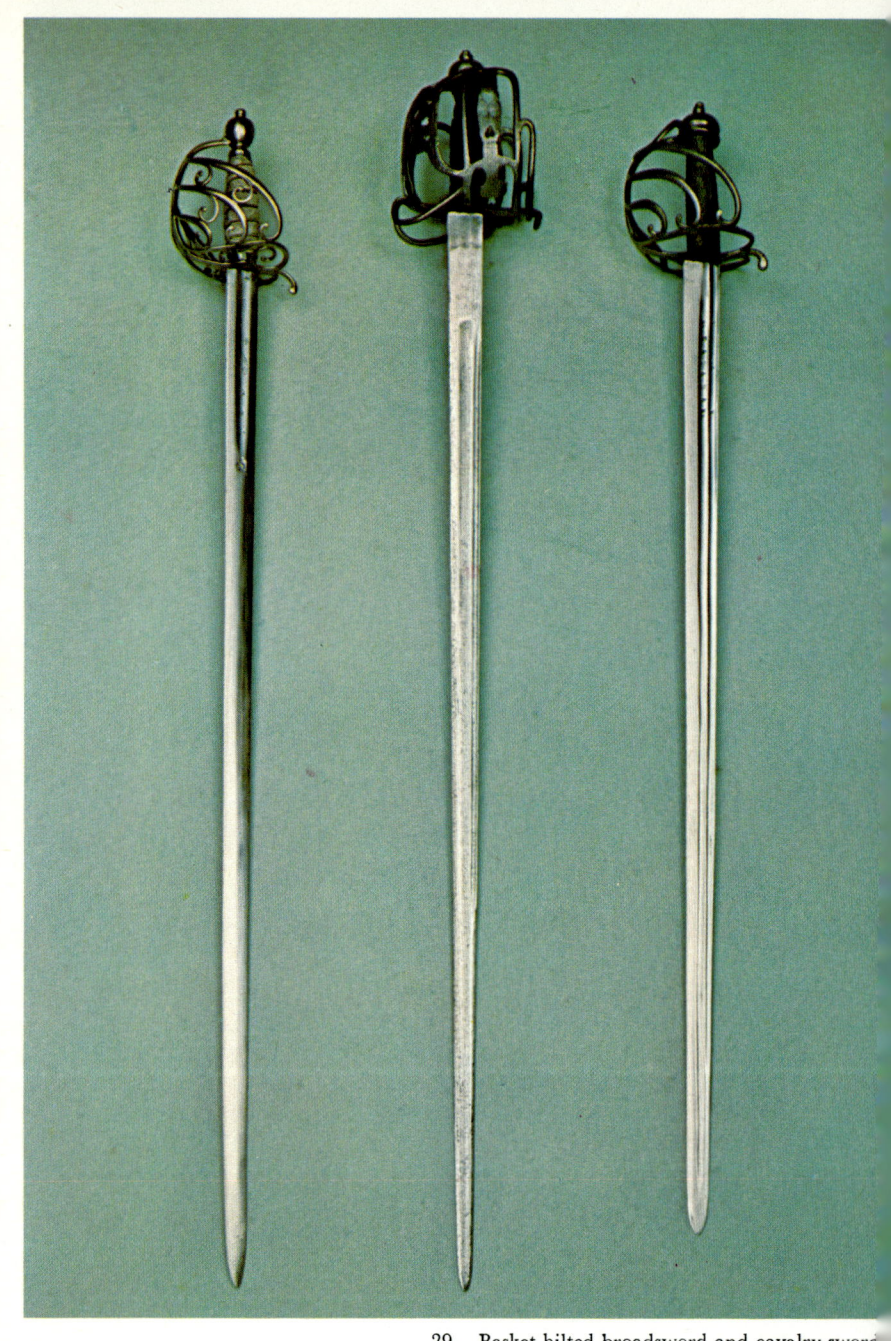

29. Basket hilted broadsword and cavalry sword

30. Basket hilted cavalry sword.

31. British. Horse Grenadier sword.

32. British. Heavy Cavalry officer's sword 1788.

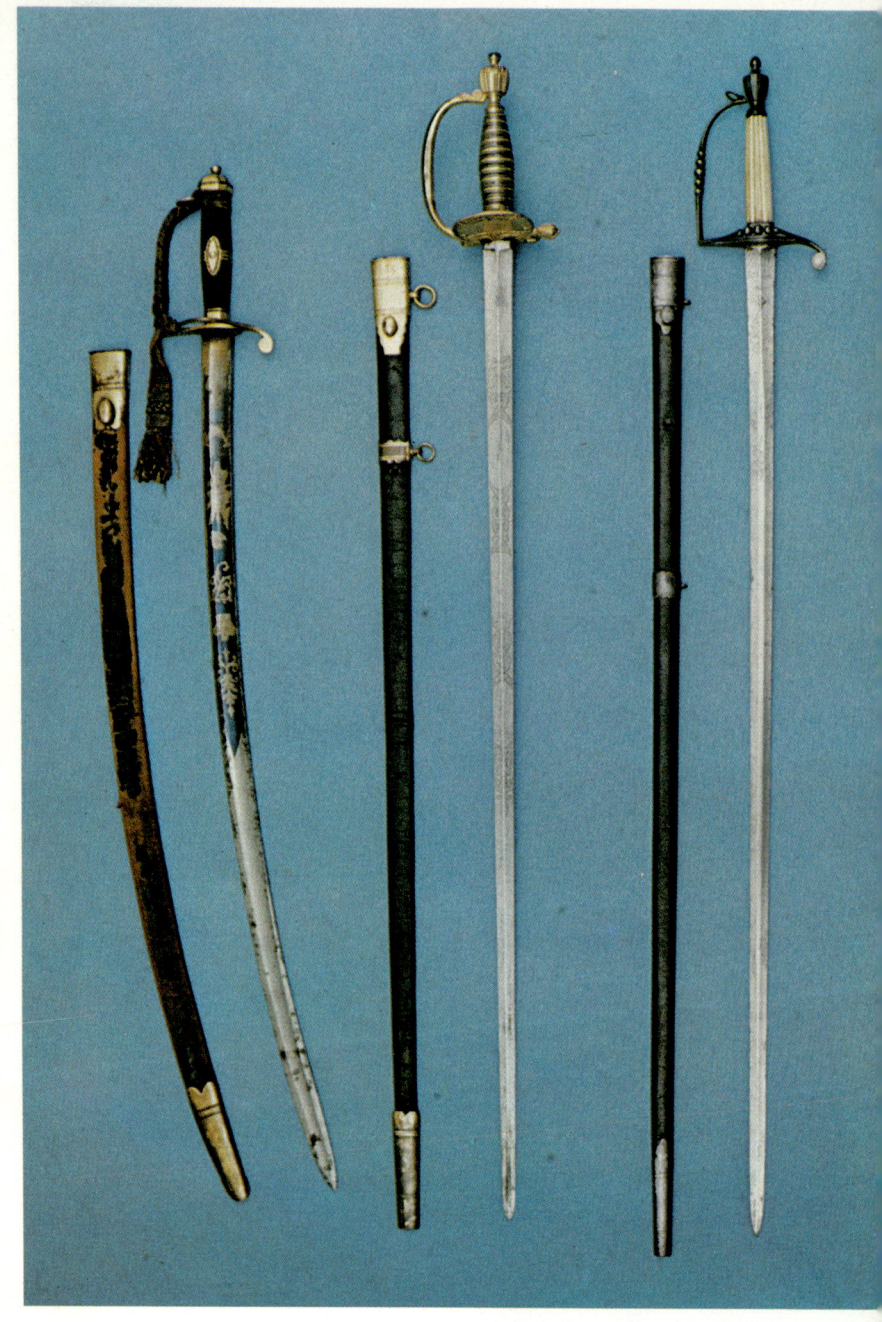

33. British. Officers' sword

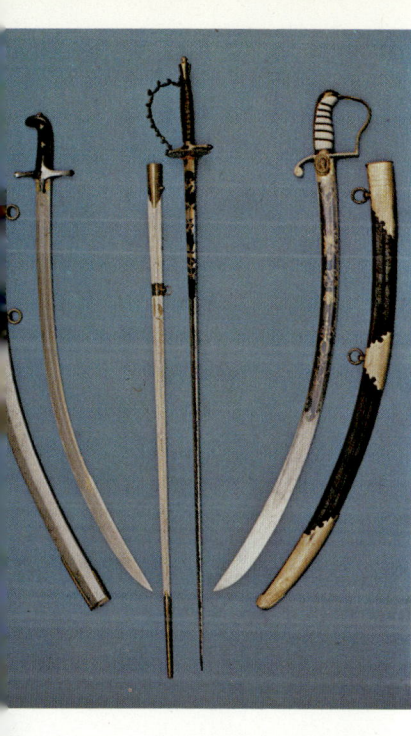

34. British. Officers' swords and small sword.

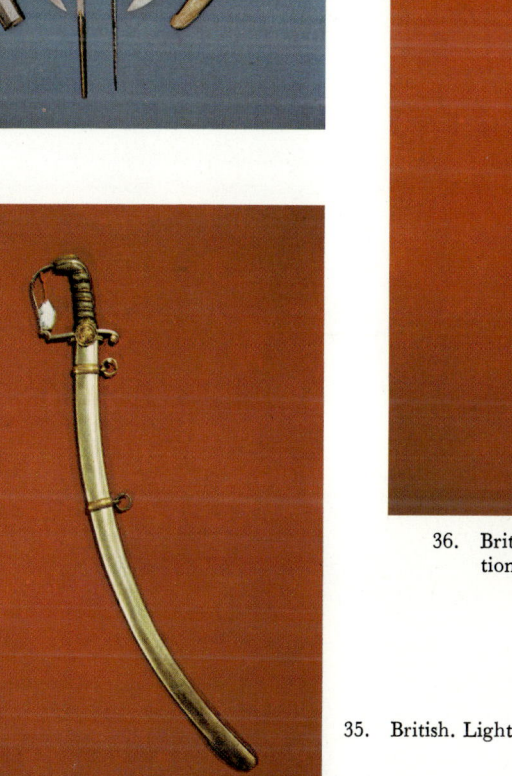

36. British. Light Cavalry presentation sword.

35. British. Light Cavalry sword.

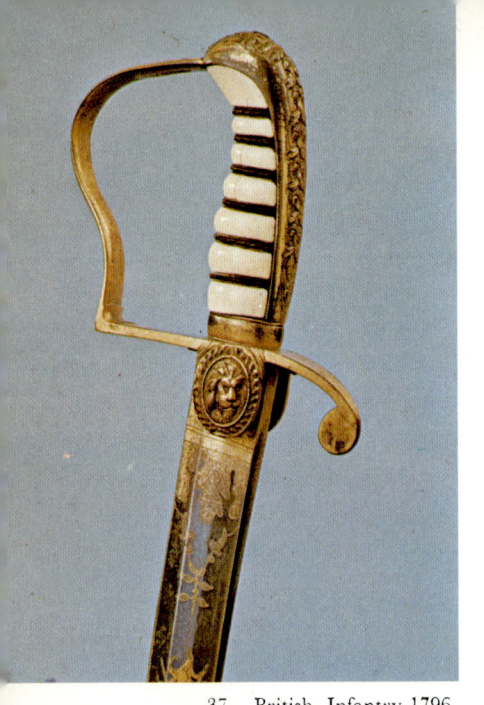

37. British. Infantry 1796.   38. British. Infantry 1786.

39. British. Naval sword 1795.   40. British. Officer's sword.

41. Fencing.    42. Fencing.

43. British. 15th Hussars sword.   44. British. Infantry 1796.

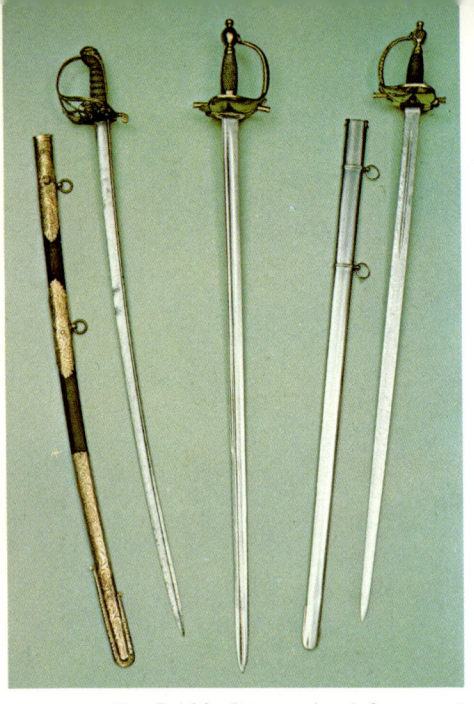

45. British. Presentation infantry and cavalry swords.

46. British. Heavy Cavalry 1796.

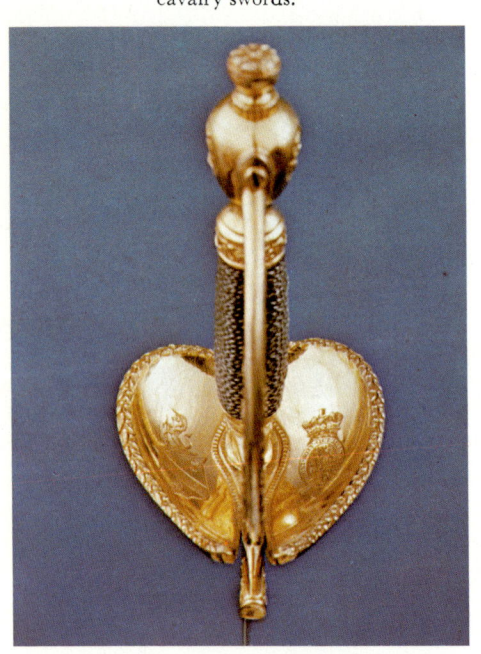

47. British. Heavy Cavalry 1796.

48. British. Presentation Infantry 182°

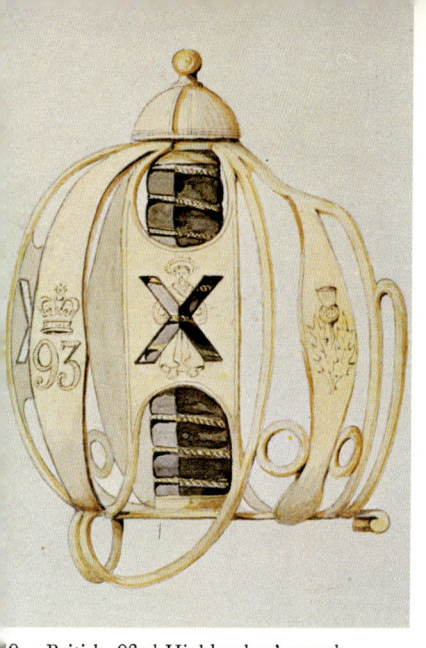

49. British. 93rd Highlanders' sword.

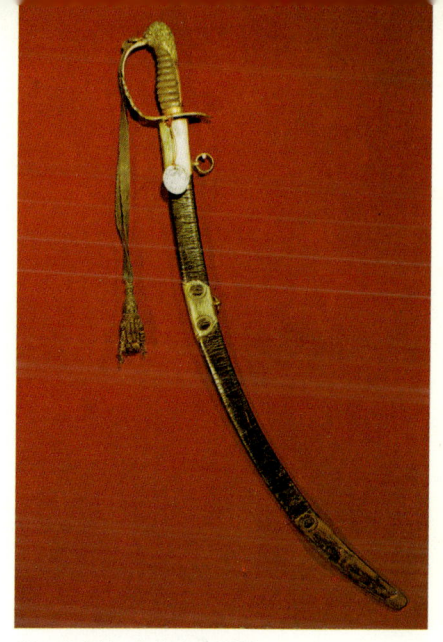

50. British. Infantry 1803.

51. British. Yeoman warder's sword.

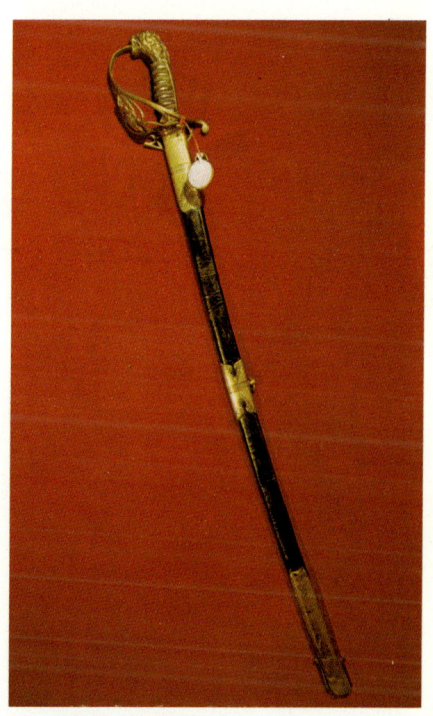

52. British. East India Company Infantry sword.

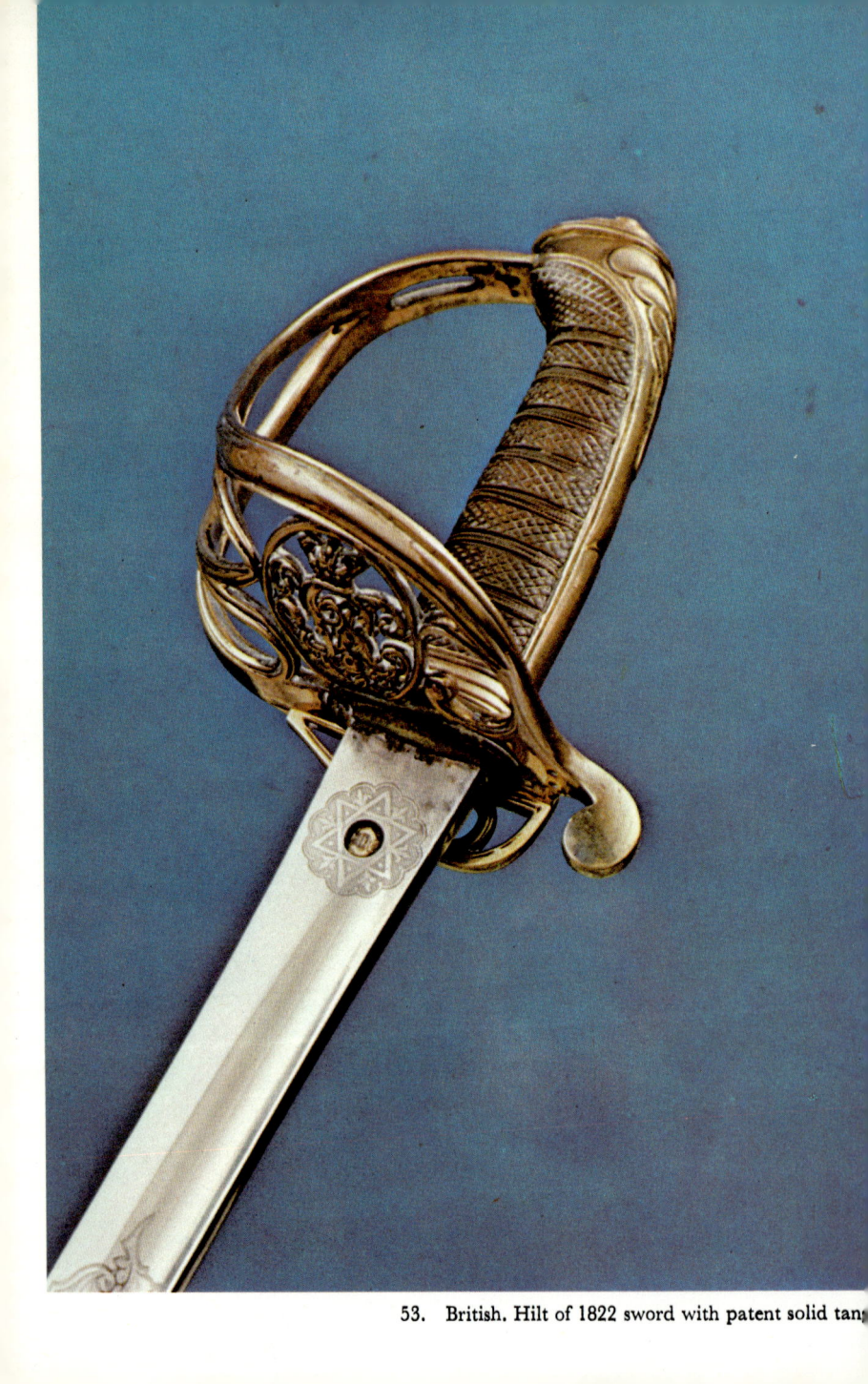

53. British. Hilt of 1822 sword with patent solid tang

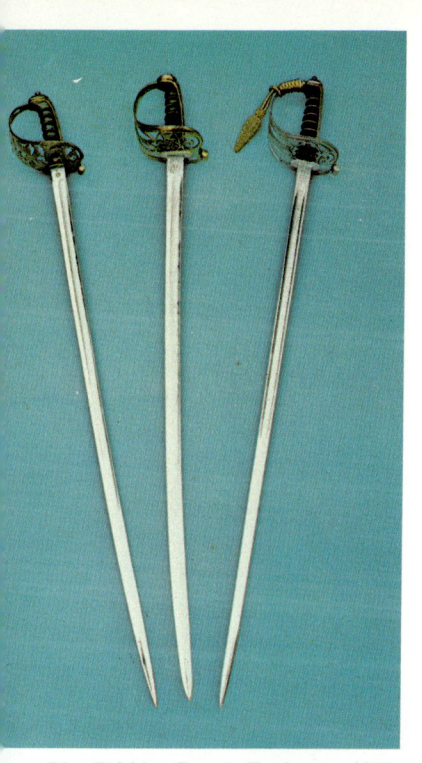

54. British. Royal Engineers 1856; Infantry 1822, Guards 1854.

55. British. Royal Engineers 1856.

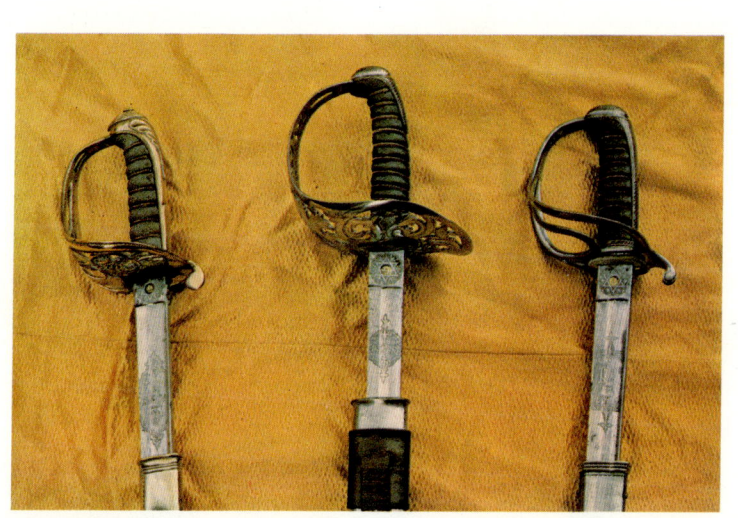

56. British. Infantry 1822; Heavy Cavalry variation 1856; Light Cavalry 1822.

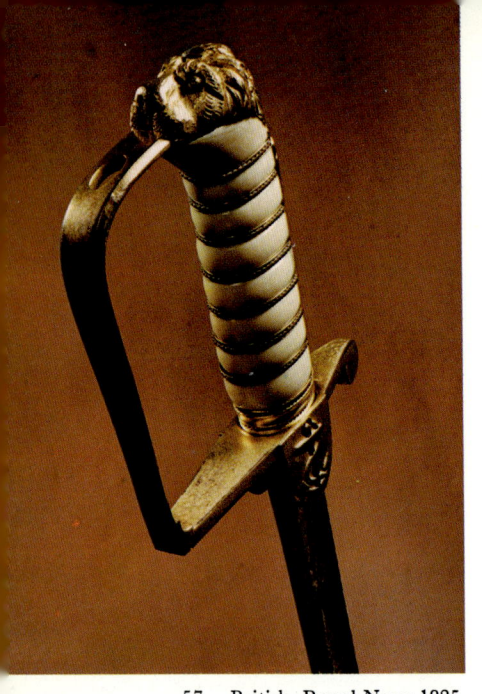

57. British. Royal Navy 1825.

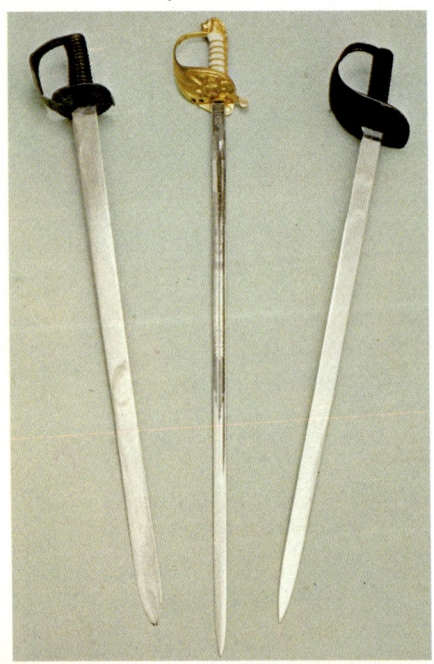

58. British. Royal Navy 1829.

59. British. Cutlass 1800; Royal Navy 1926; cutlass 1889.

60. British. Regimental pattern 6th Dragoon Guards 1877.

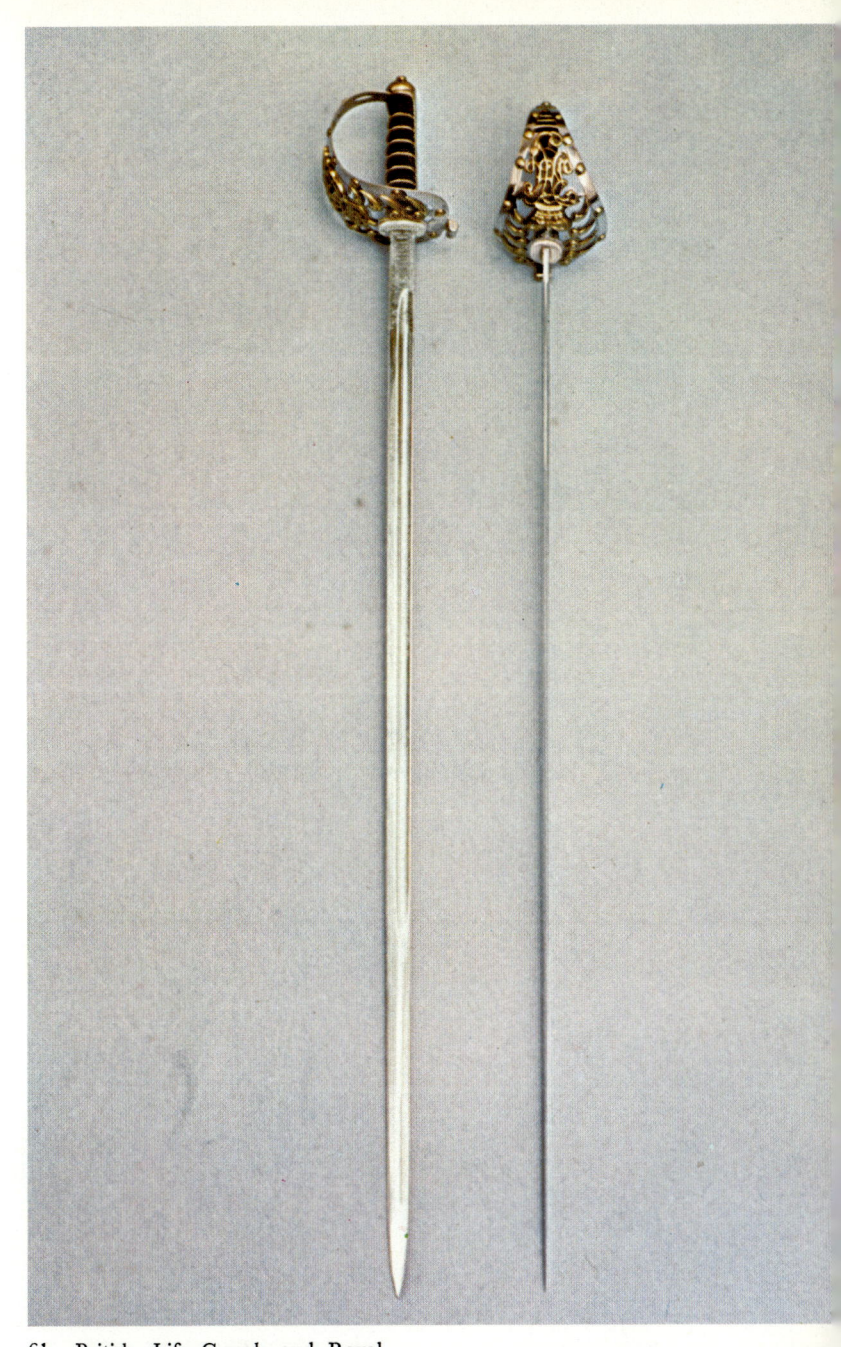

61. British. Life Guards and Royal
    Horse Guards c. 1860.

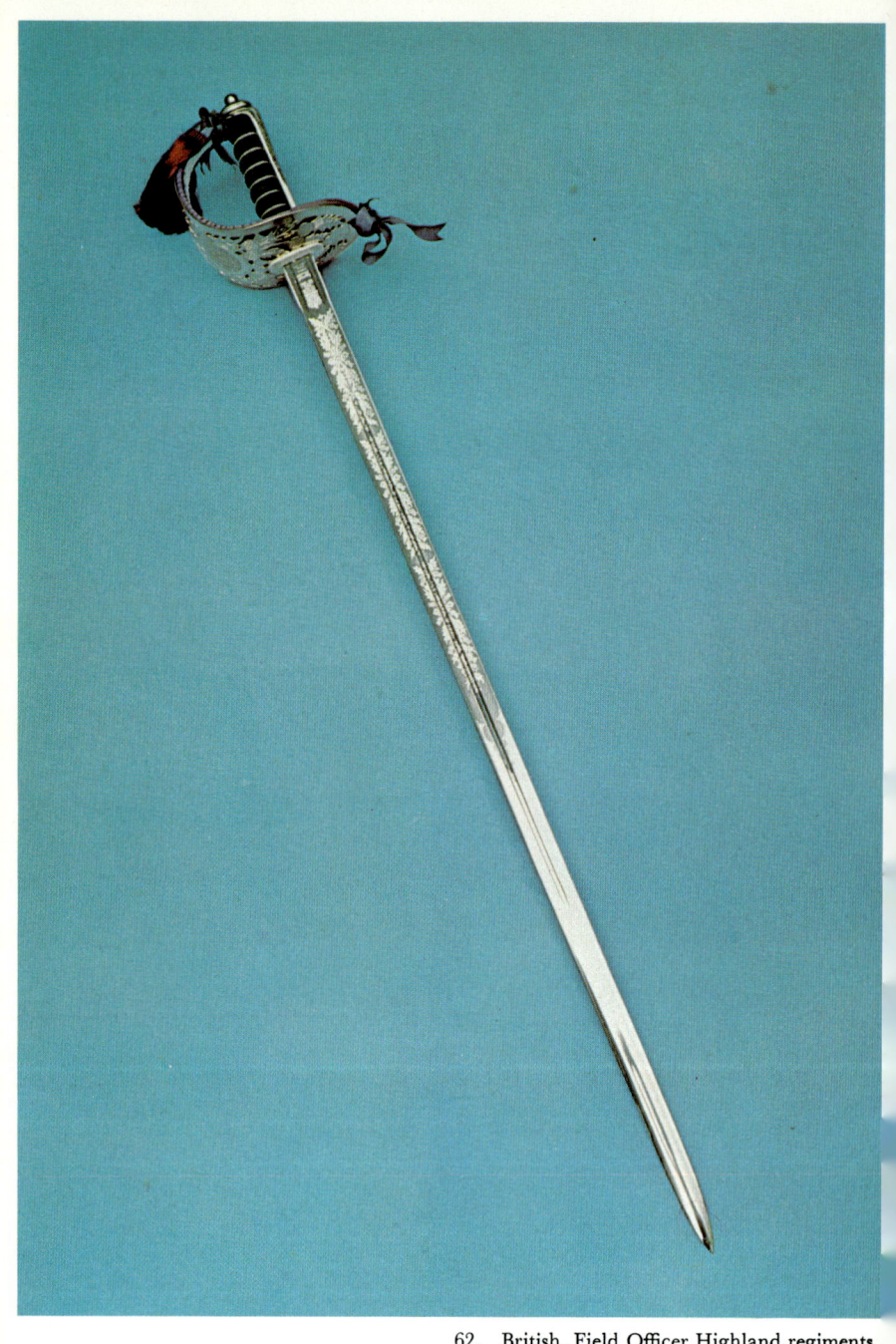

62. British. Field Officer Highland regiments.

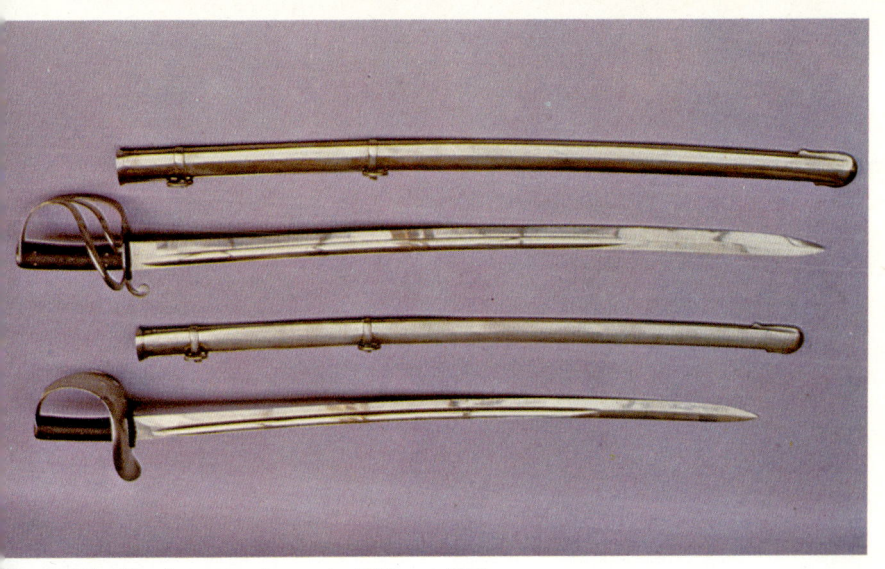

63. British. Cavalry trooper's swords, 1853 and 1864.

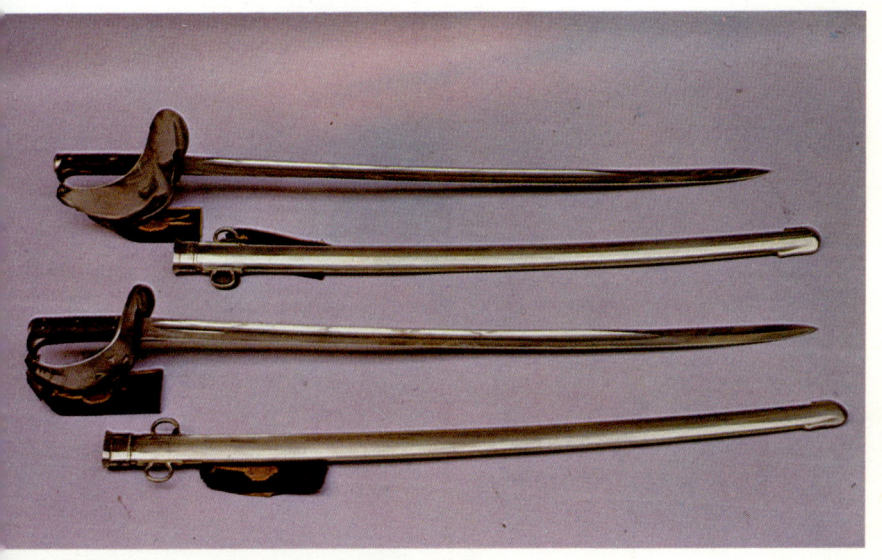

64. British. Cavalry trooper's swords 1899 and 1885.

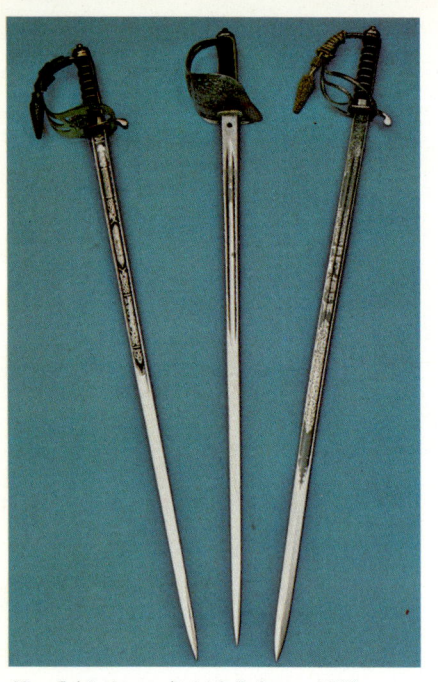

65. Irish Army; British Infantry 1897; Royal Artillery 1822.

66. British. Various patterns of scimitars.

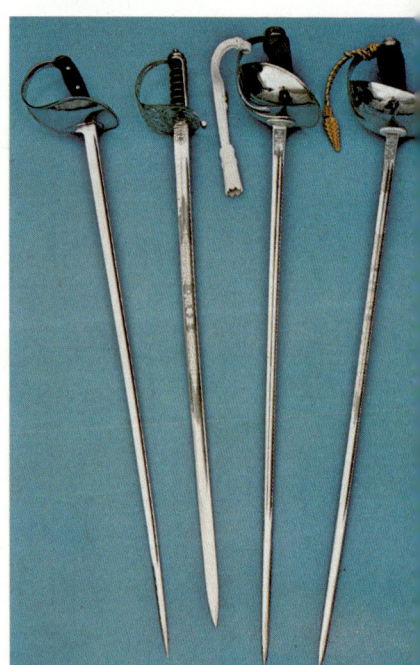

67. British. Cavalry swords. 1904, 1896, 1908, 1912.

68. British. Cavalry swords 1908, 1912.

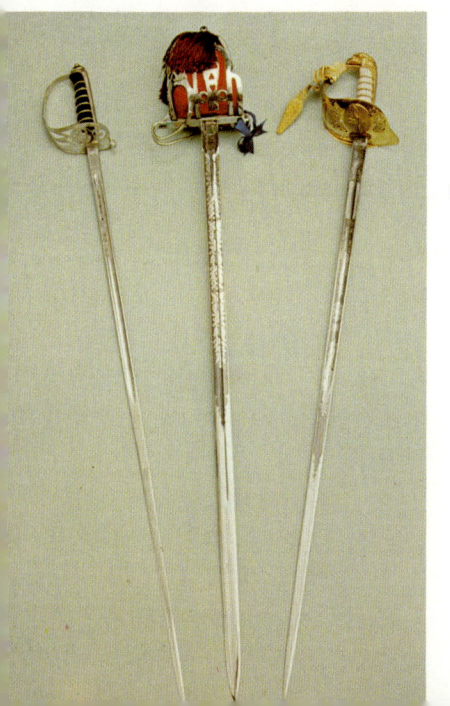

69. British. Rifles 1827; claymore; Royal Air Force 1920.

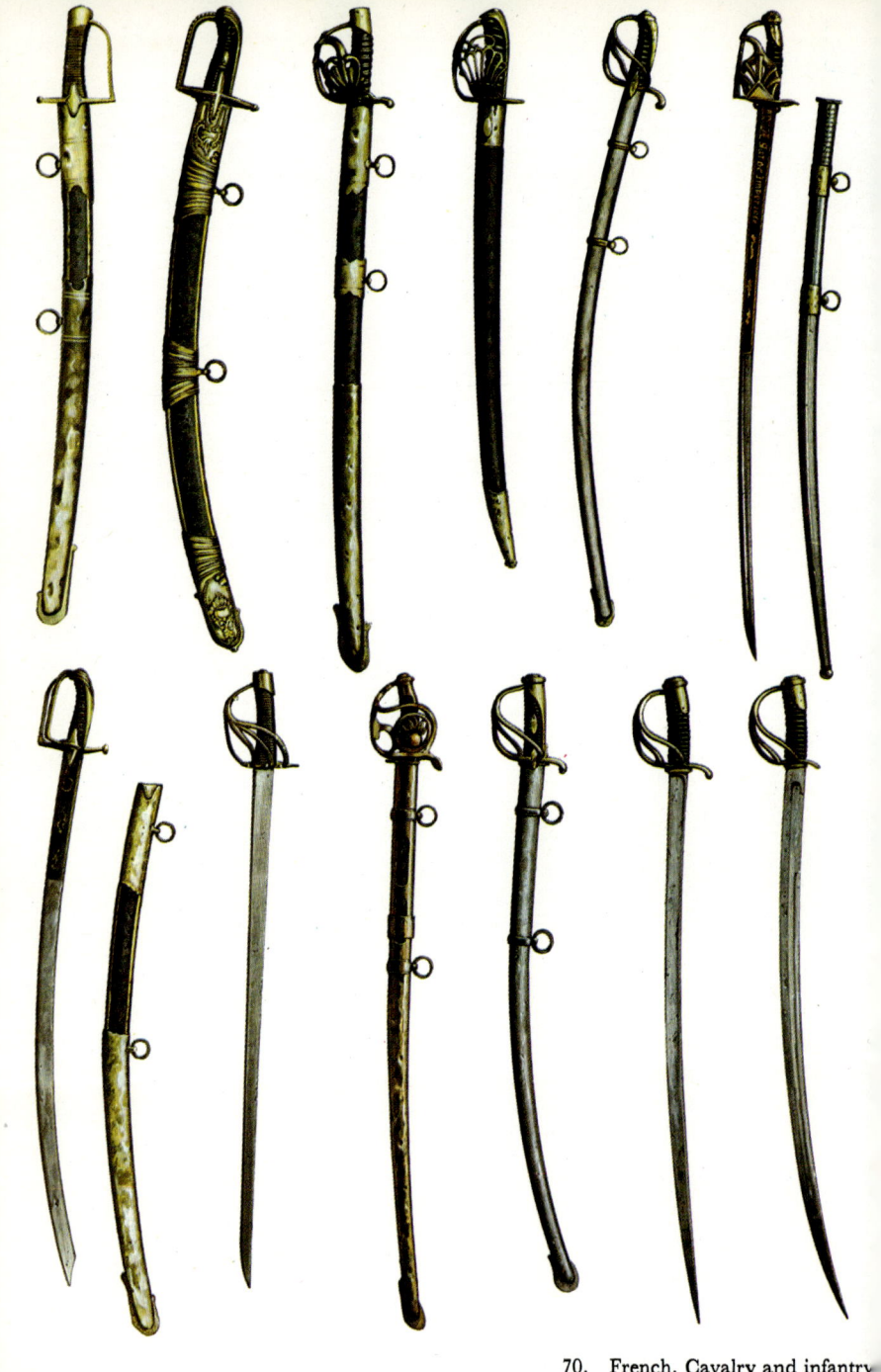

70. French. Cavalry and infantry

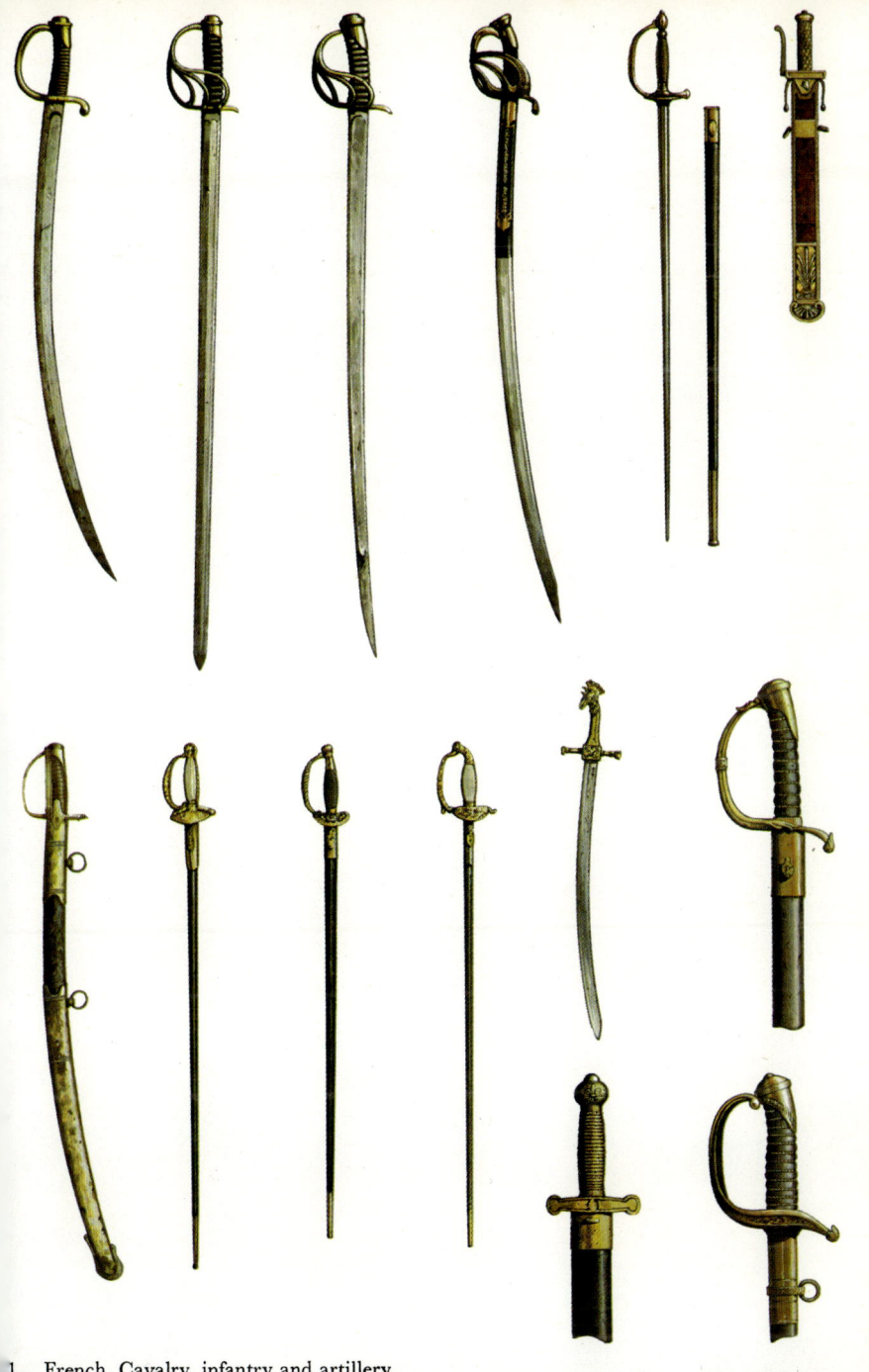

1. French. Cavalry, infantry and artillery.

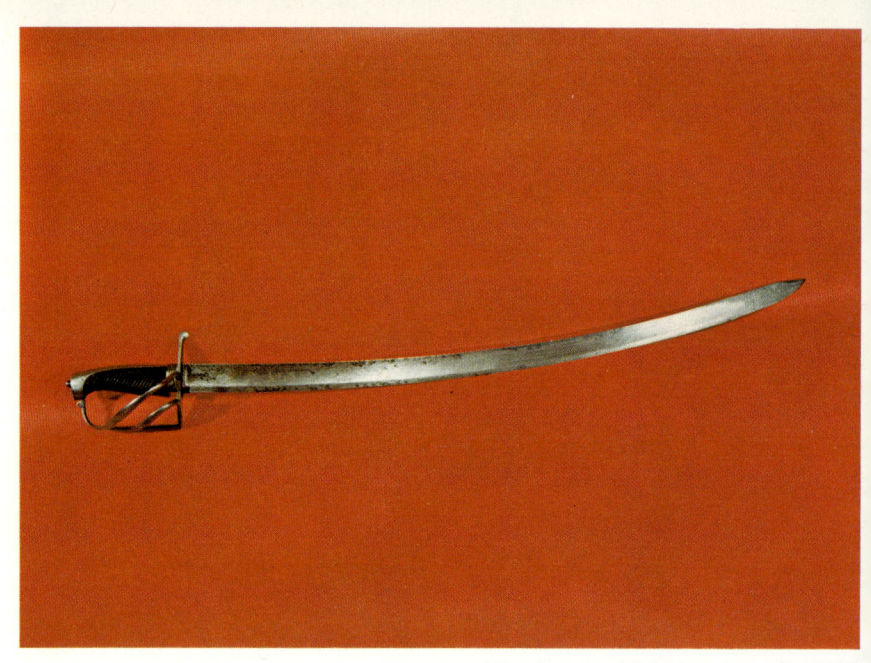

72. German. Light Cavalry sword 1806.

73. German. Prussian cuirassier's sword 1819.

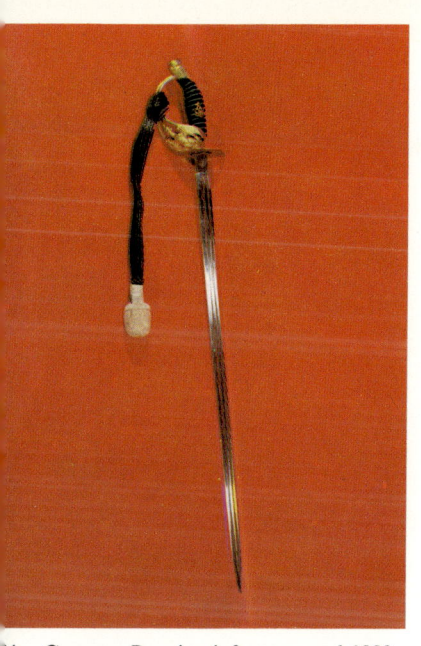

74. German. Prussian infantry sword 1889.

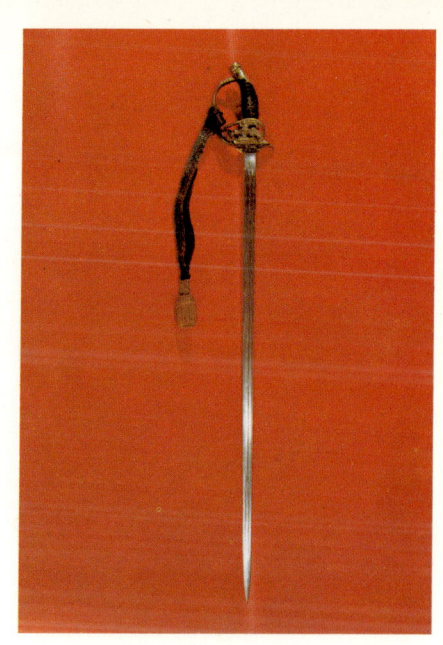

75. German. Infantry sword 1911.

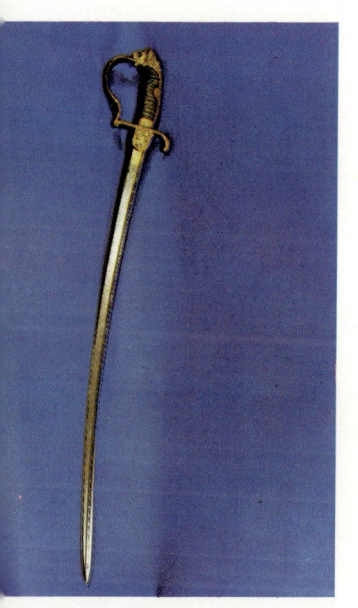

76. German. Cavalry officer's sword 1889.

77. German. Infantry sword 1911, presented to Von Hindenburg 1916.

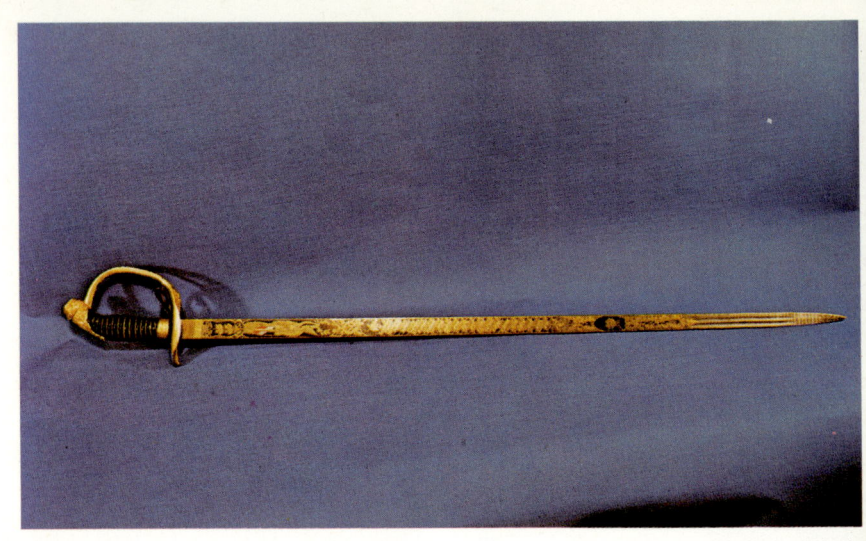

78. German. Reverse of blade.

80. German. Blade inscription

9. German. Close up of hilt.

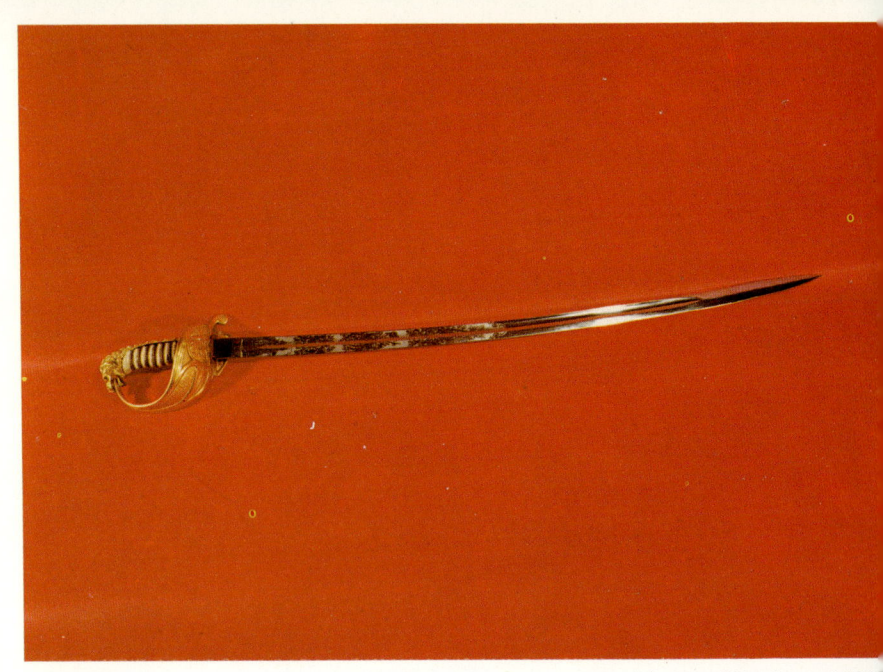

81. German. Naval sword 1889

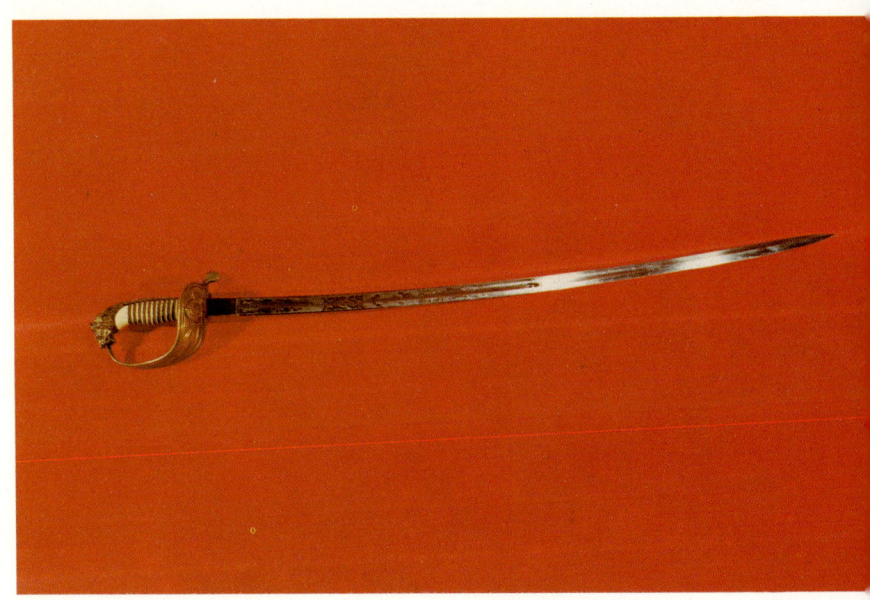

82. German. Naval sword 1889 variatio

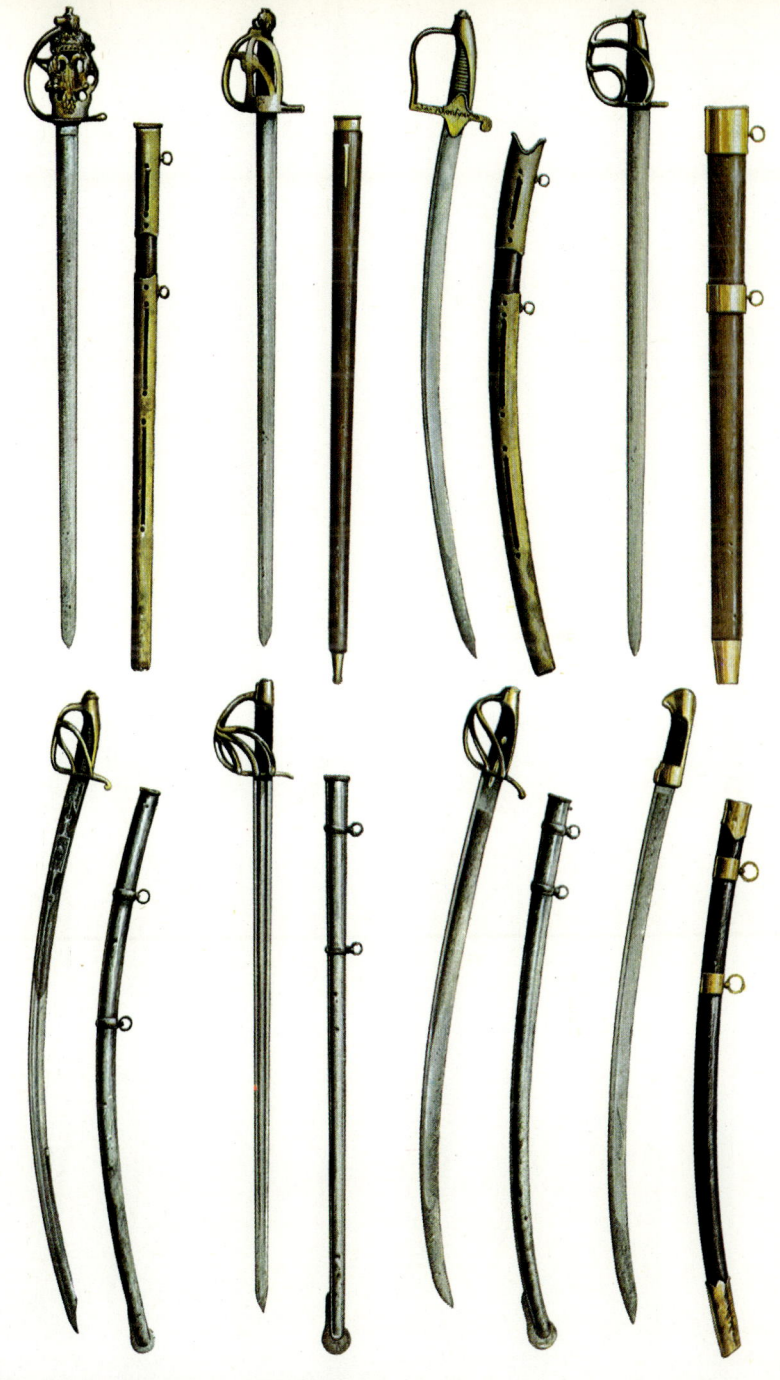

3. Russian. Guard cuirassier and other cavalry.

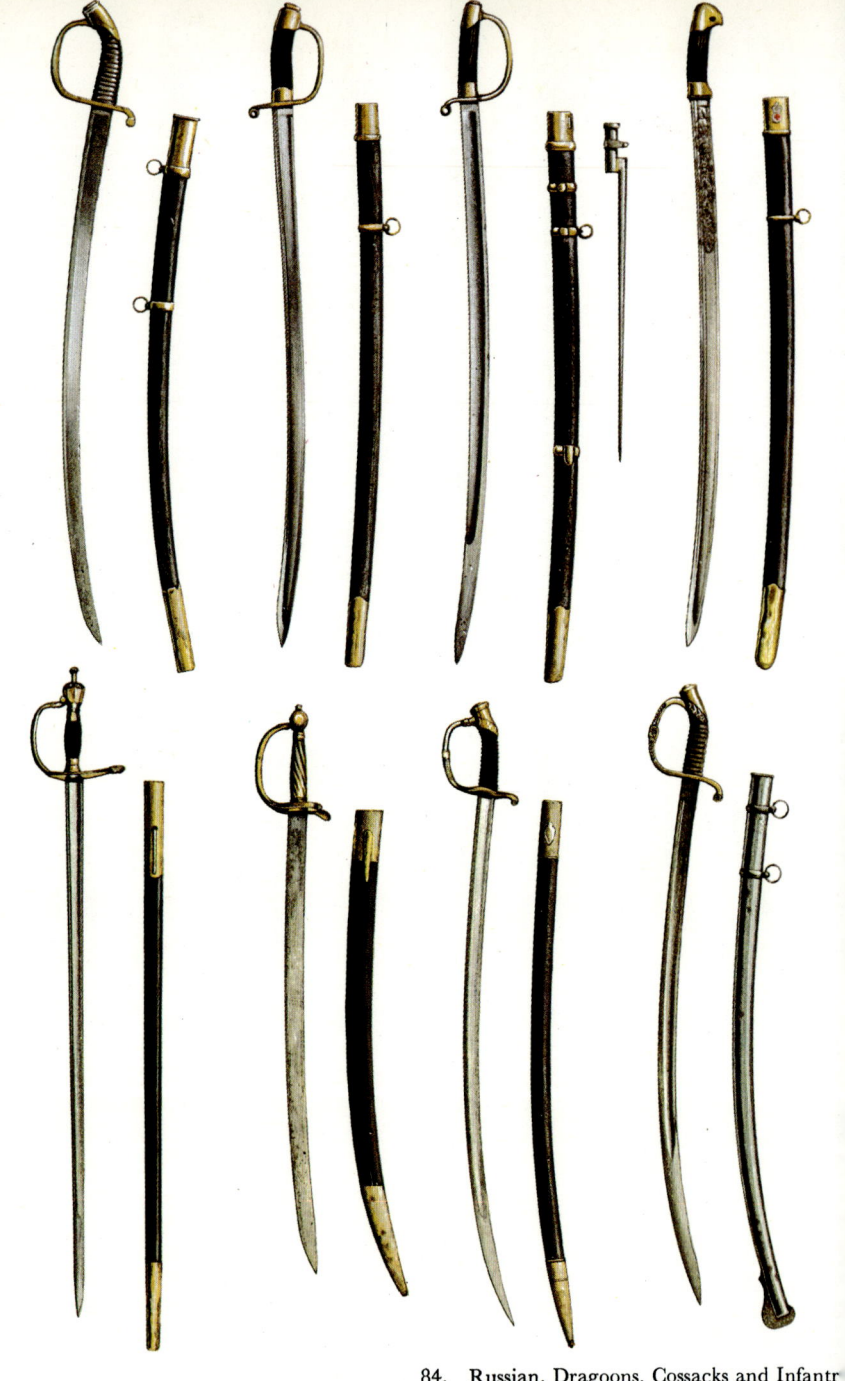

84. Russian. Dragoons, Cossacks and Infantr

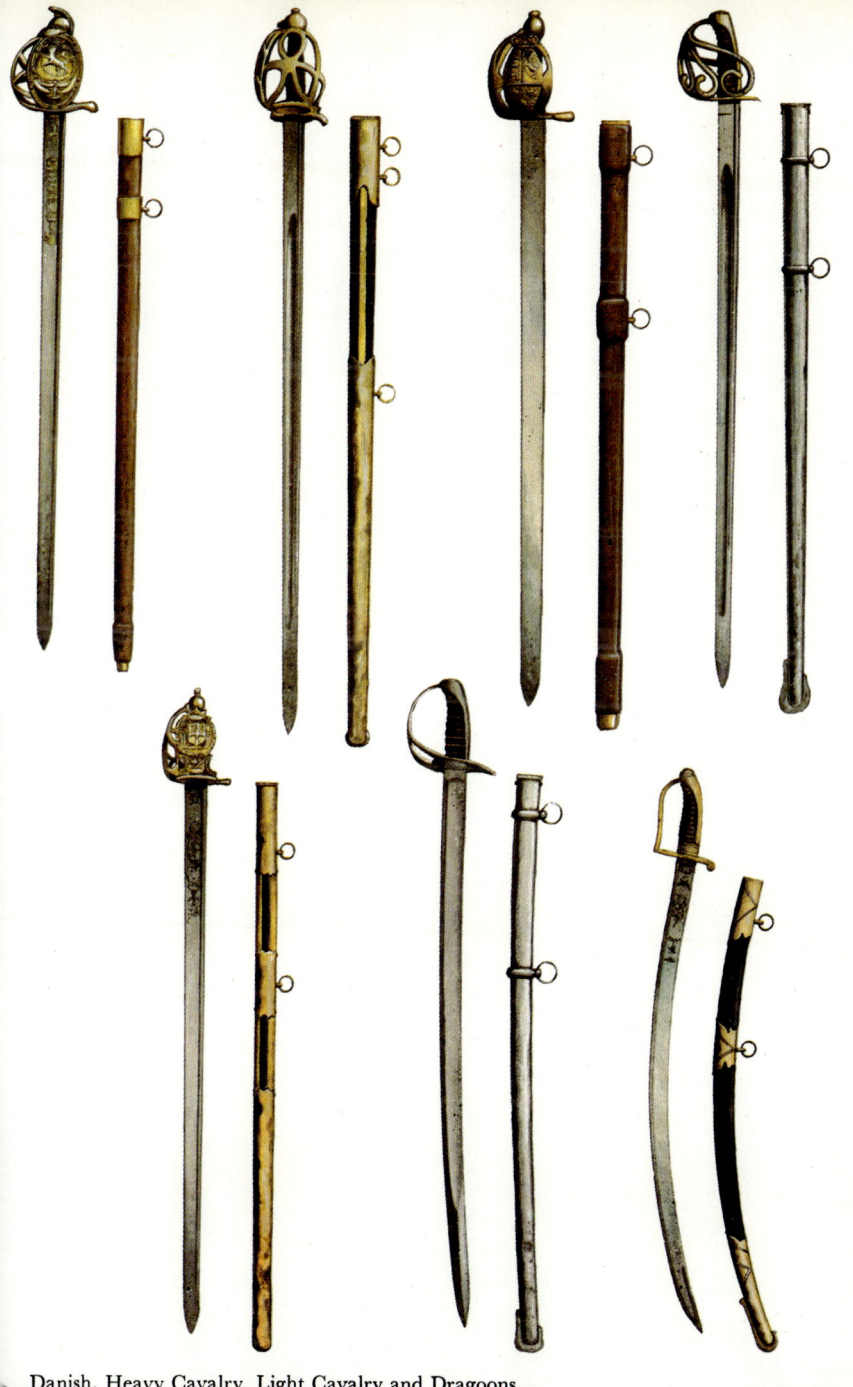

Danish. Heavy Cavalry, Light Cavalry and Dragoons.

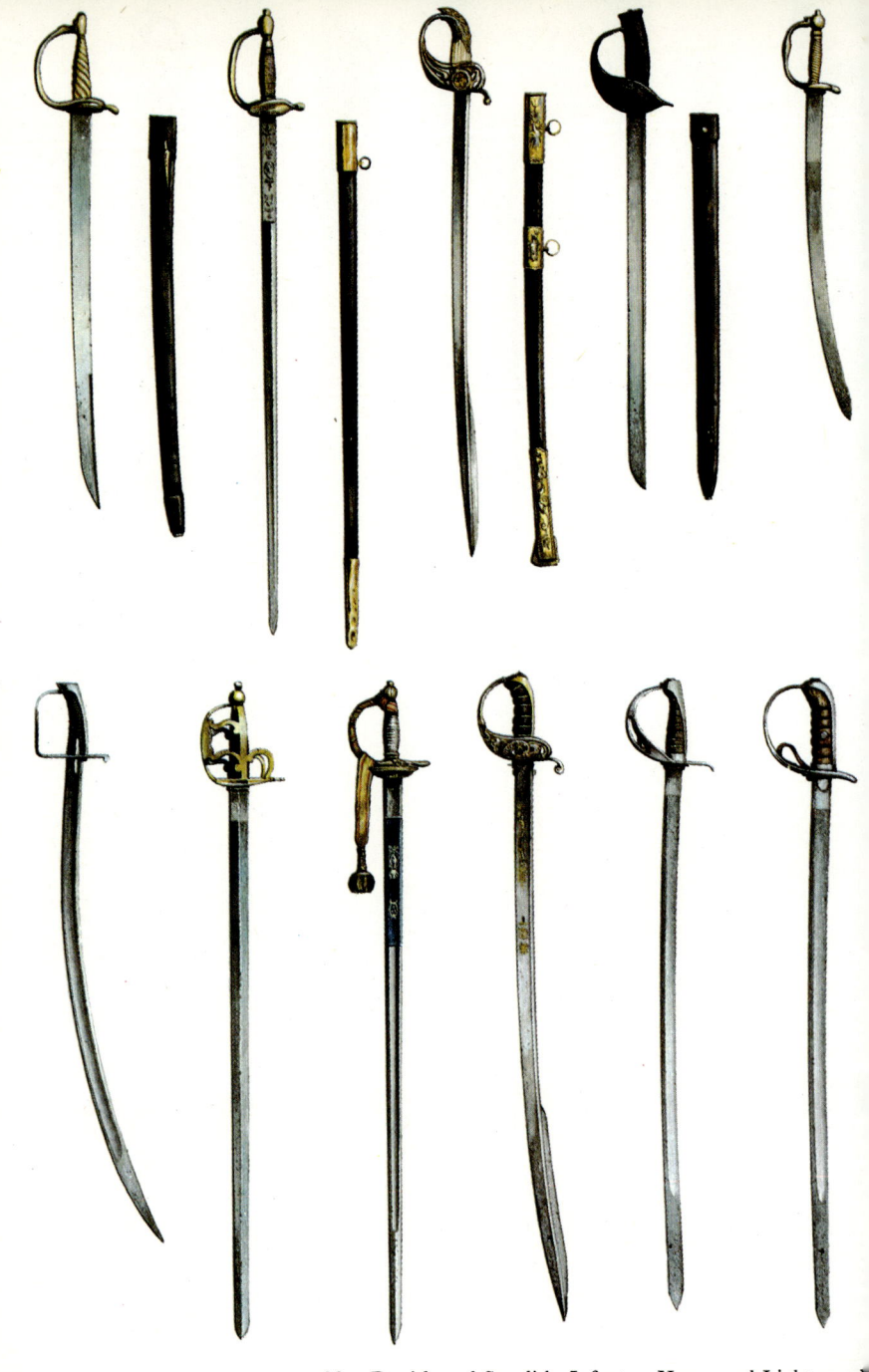

86. Danish and Swedish. Infantry, Heavy and Light caval

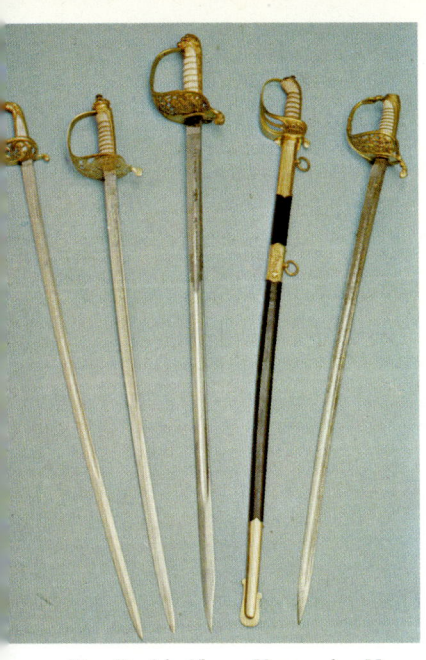

87. Danish, Navy; Venezuelan Navy; Burmese Navy; Danish Marine; Argentinian Navy.

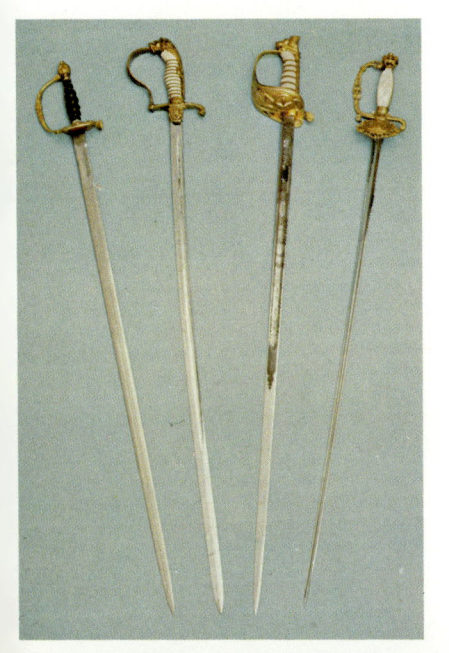

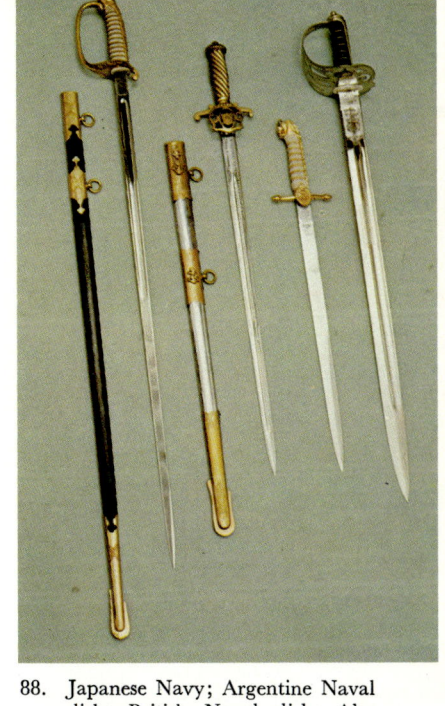

88. Japanese Navy; Argentine Naval dirk; British Naval dirk; Abu Dhabi cutlass.

89. Argentinian diplomatic; Venezuelan; Burmese Navy; Danish diplomatic.

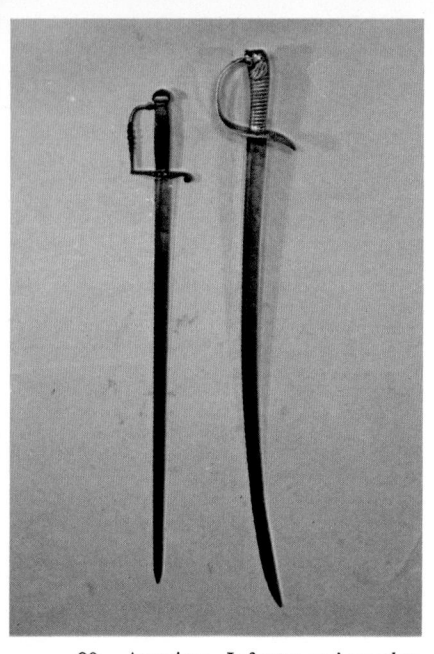

90. American. Infantry and cavalry.

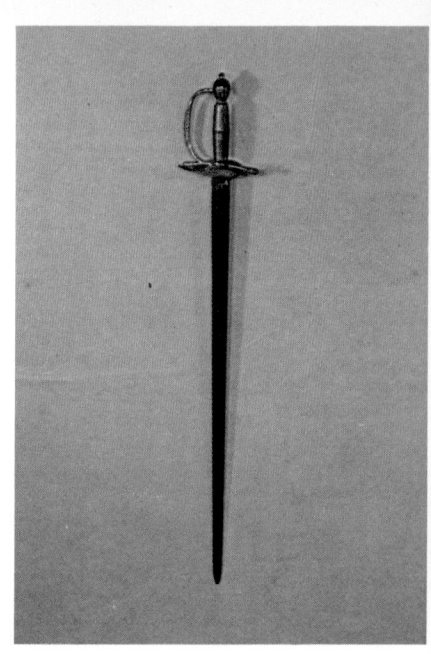

91. American. General and staff.

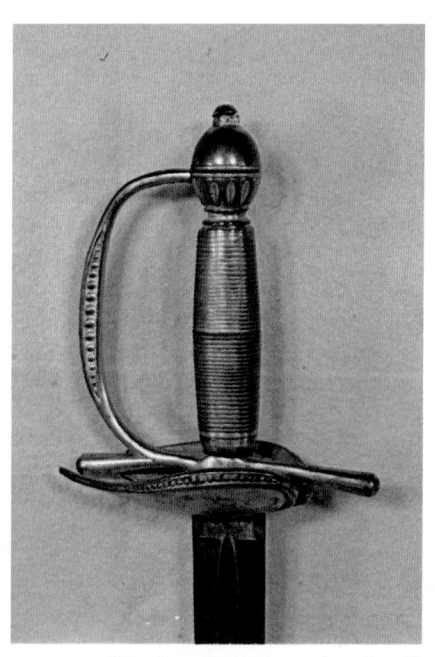

92. American. General and staff.

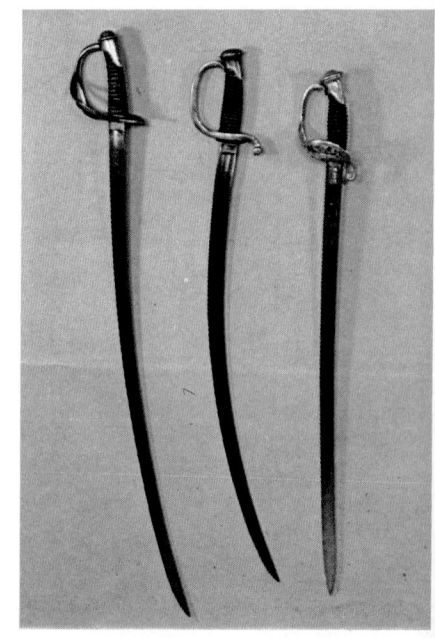

93. American. Dragoon, light artillery and infantry.

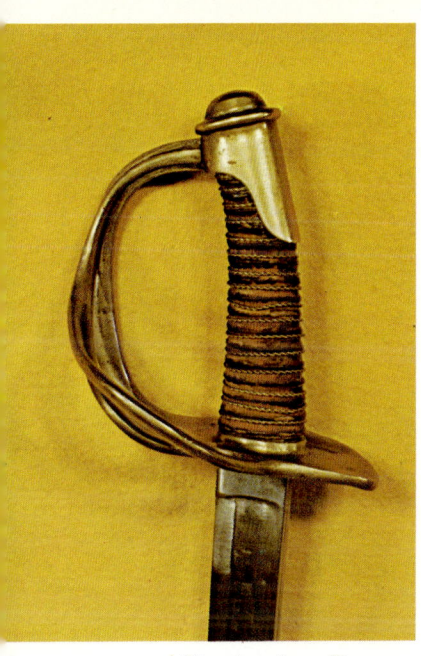

94. American. Dragoon.

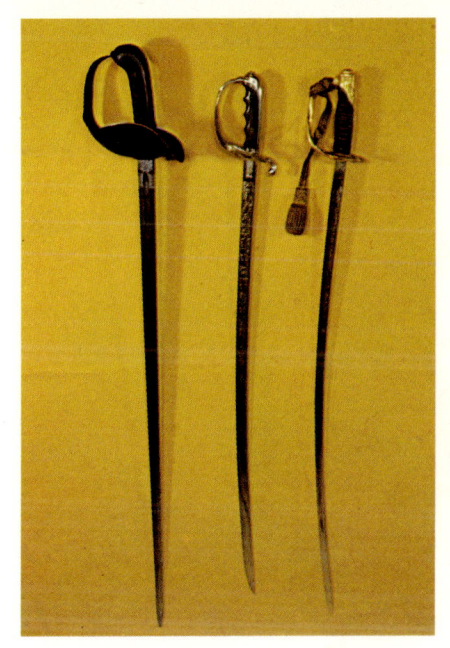

95. American. Cavalry, cavalry and universal army.

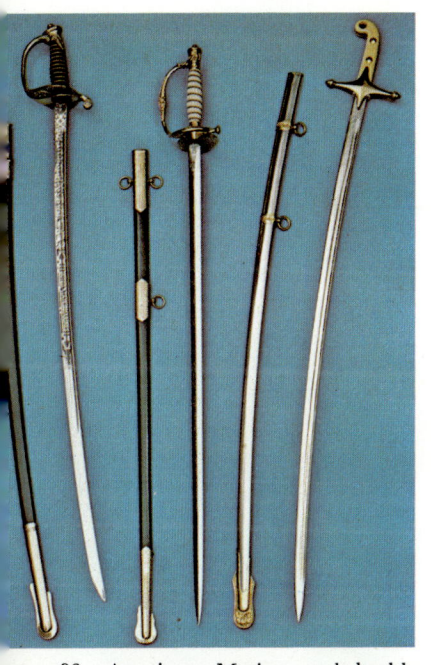

96. American. Marines and health officials.

97. American. Cavalry troopers.

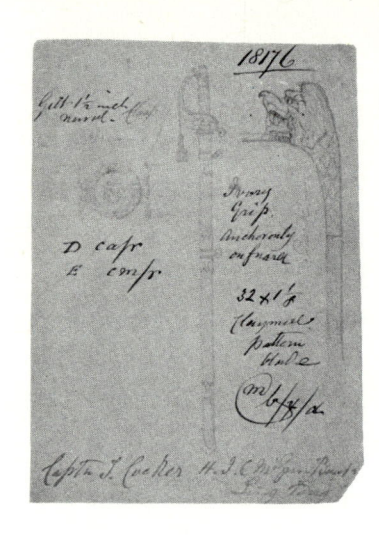

98. Siamese. Cavalry.   99. Chinese. Maritime Customs.

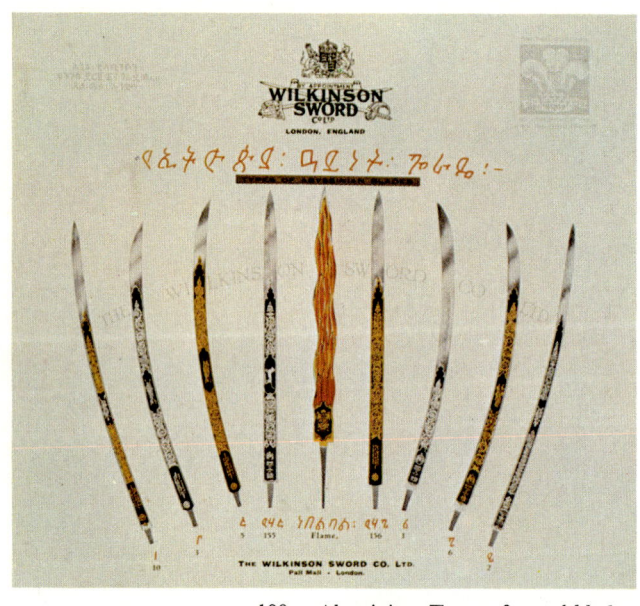

100. Abyssinian. Types of sword blades.

101. Arab sword and jambiya.

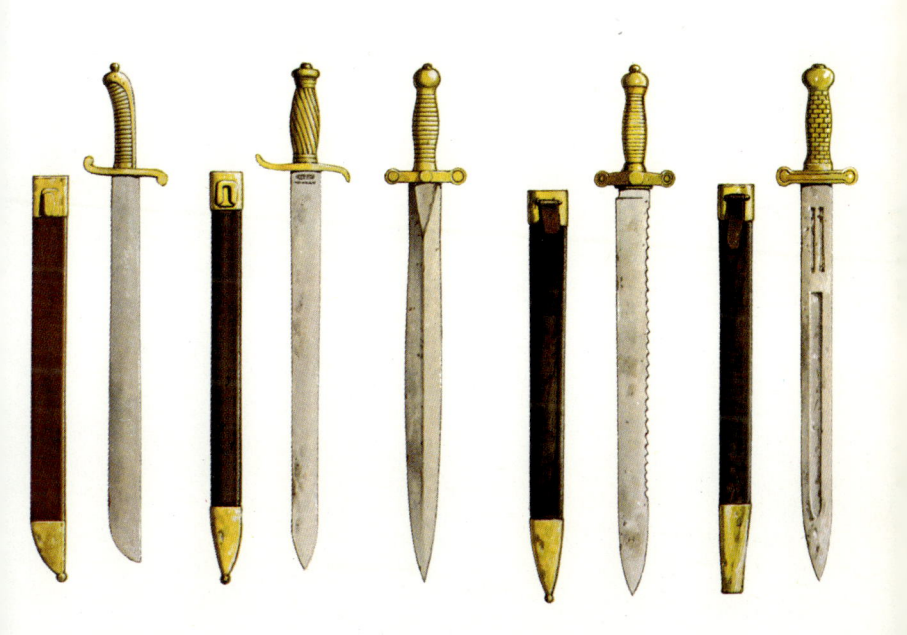

102. Sidearms. American; Swiss; French; German.

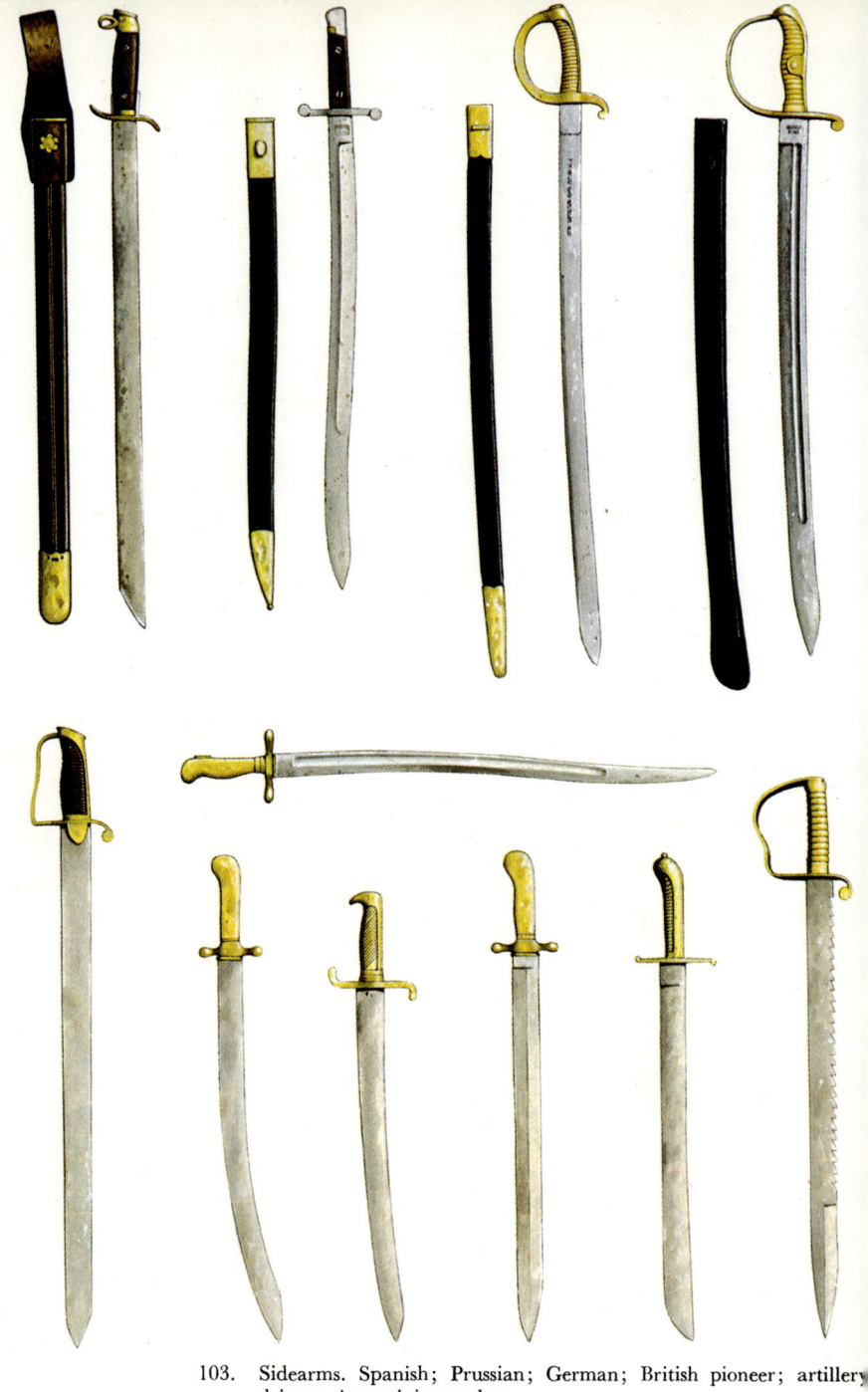

103. Sidearms. Spanish; Prussian; German; British pioneer; artillery drivers; Argentinian cutlass.

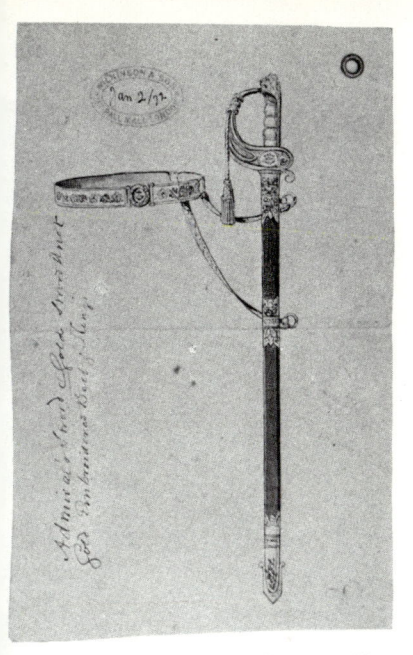

104. Japanese. Navy.   105. Japanese. Navy buckle.

106. British. Lloyds presentation swords.

107. British. Presentation swords.

108. British. Presentation swords.

109. British. Prince of Wales presentation sword.

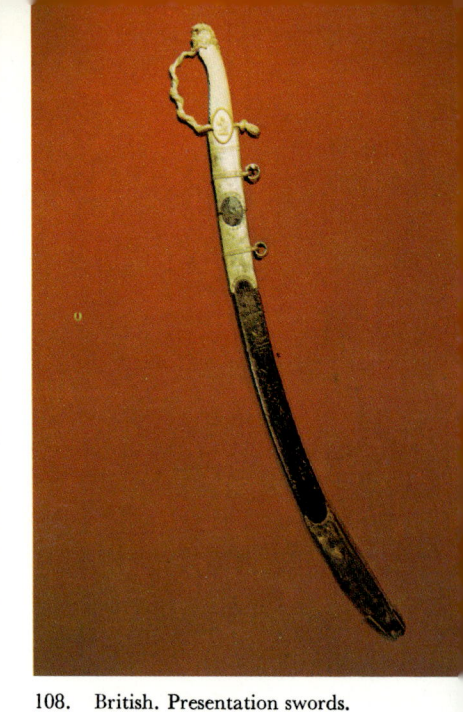

110. British. Hilt of presentation sword (109)

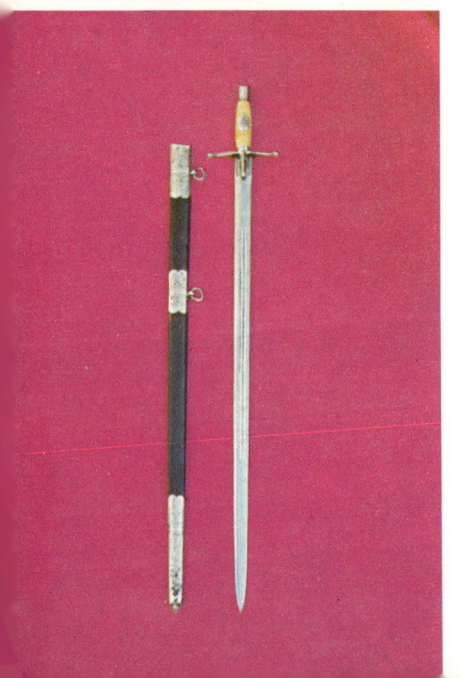

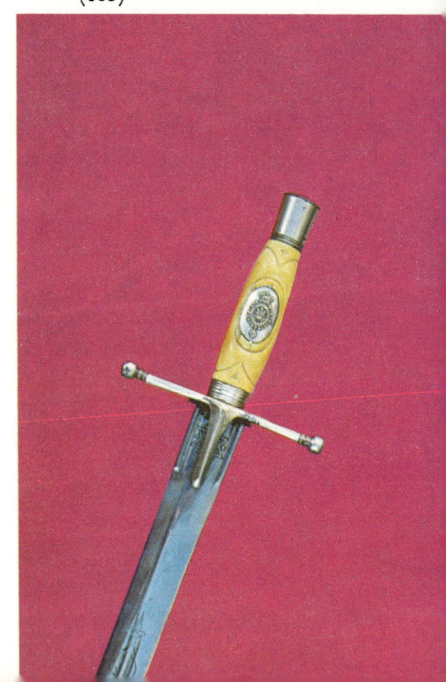

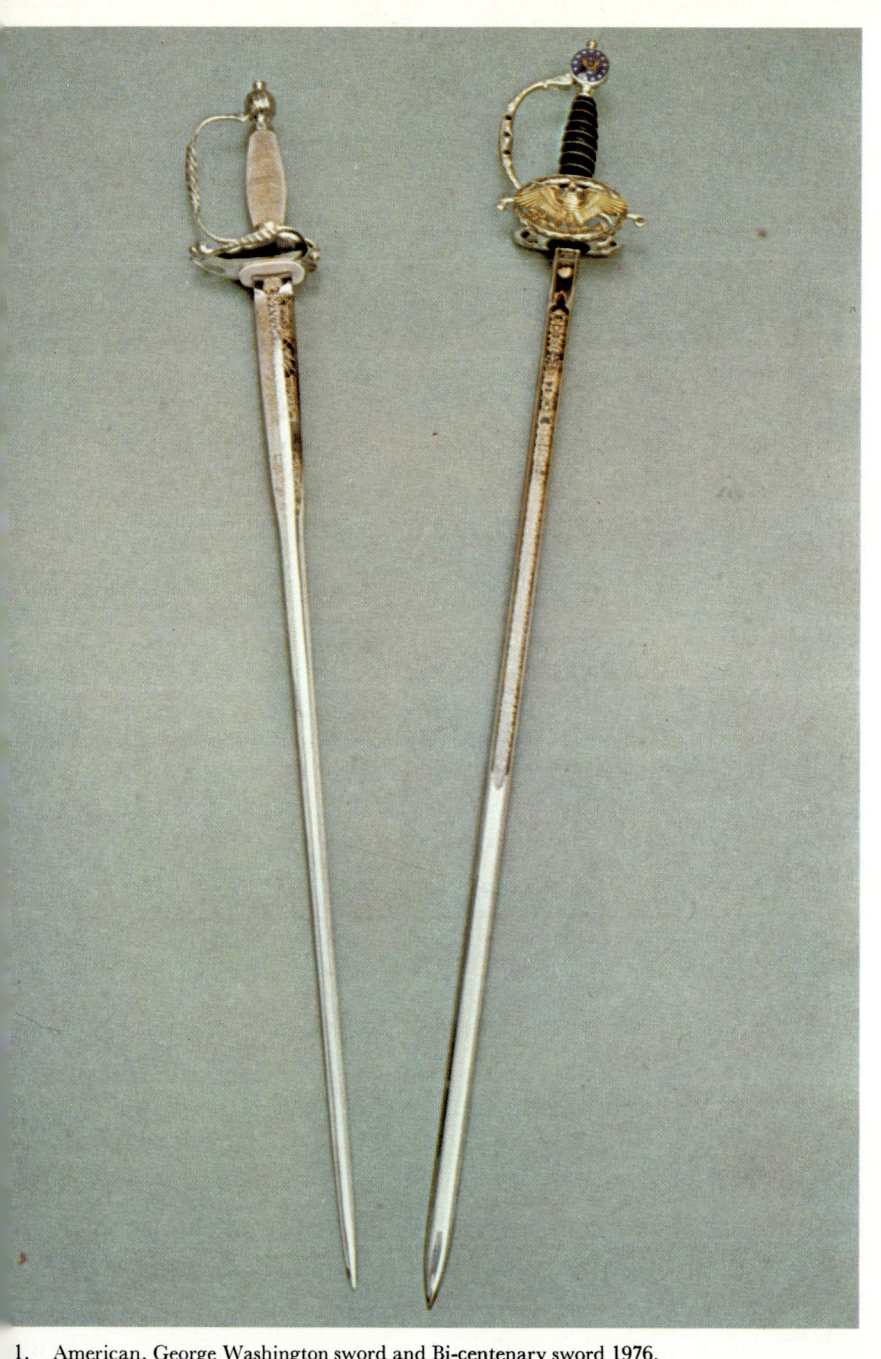

1. American. George Washington sword and Bi-centenary sword 1976.

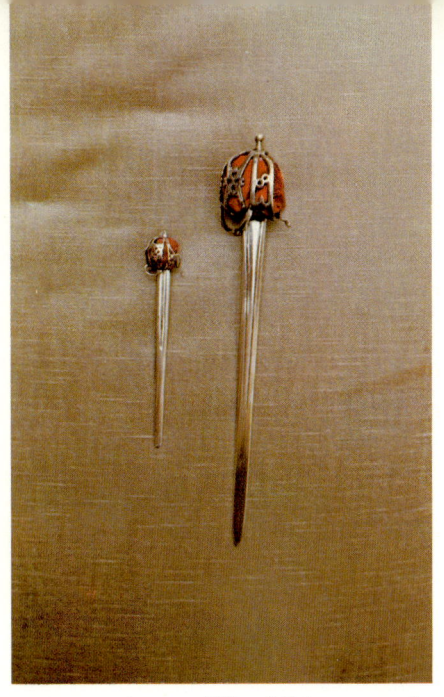

112. Miniature swords. 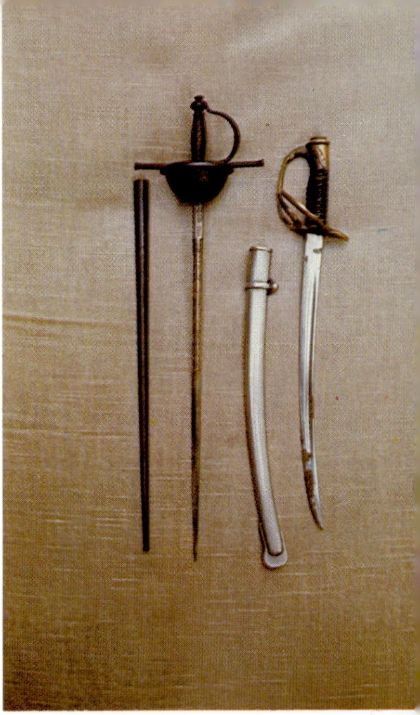 113. Miniature swords.

114. Miniature swords. 115. Miniature swords.

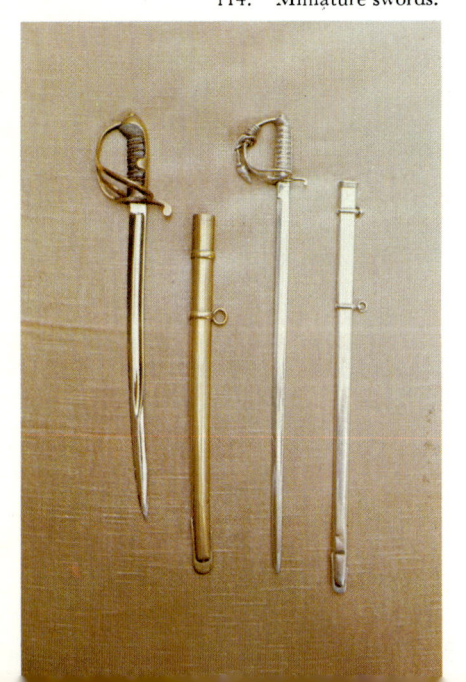

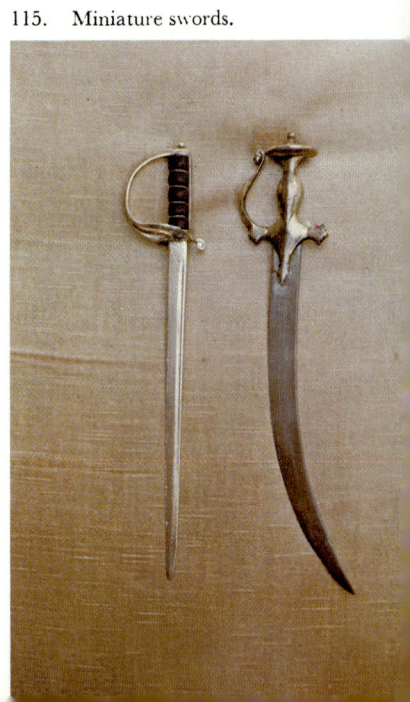

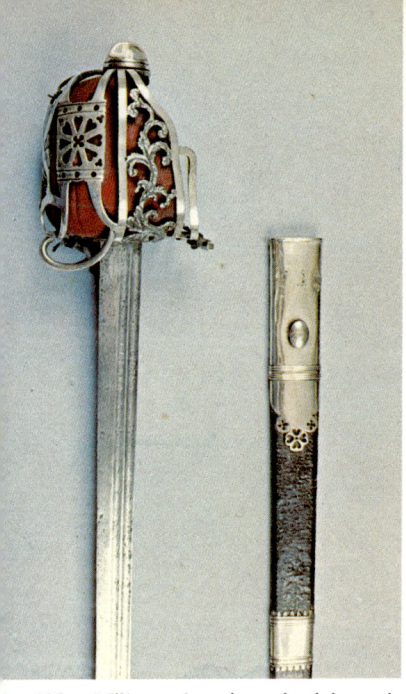

116. Military broadsword eighteenth century.

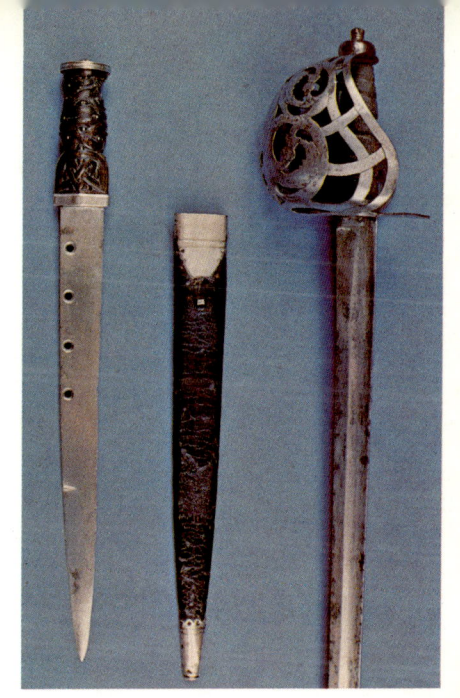

117. Military broadsword and dirk eighteenth century.

118. Military dirks.

119. Presentation sword for Seringapatam 1799.

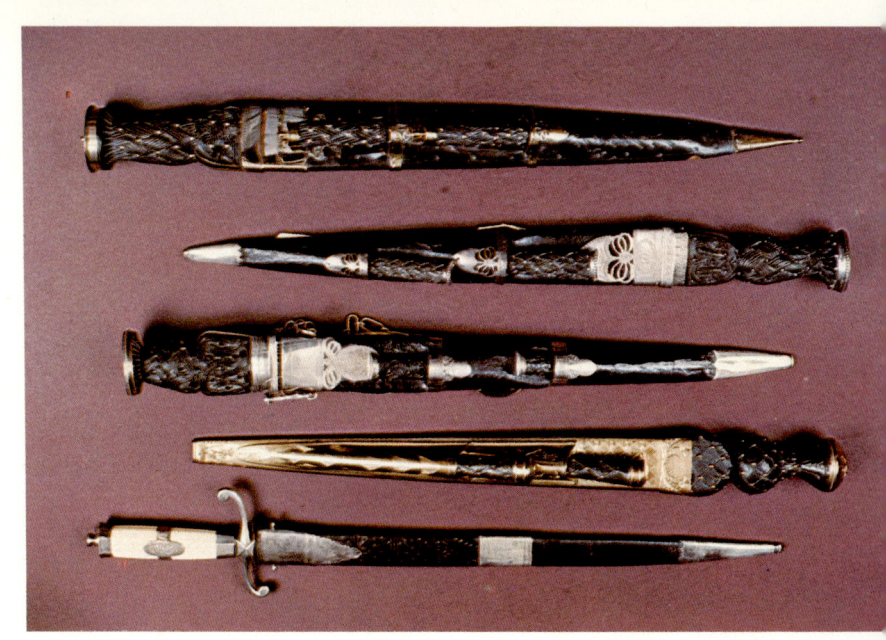

120. Officers' dirks pre-188[8]

121. Officers' and civilian dirks eighteenth centur[y]

2. Staff weapons.

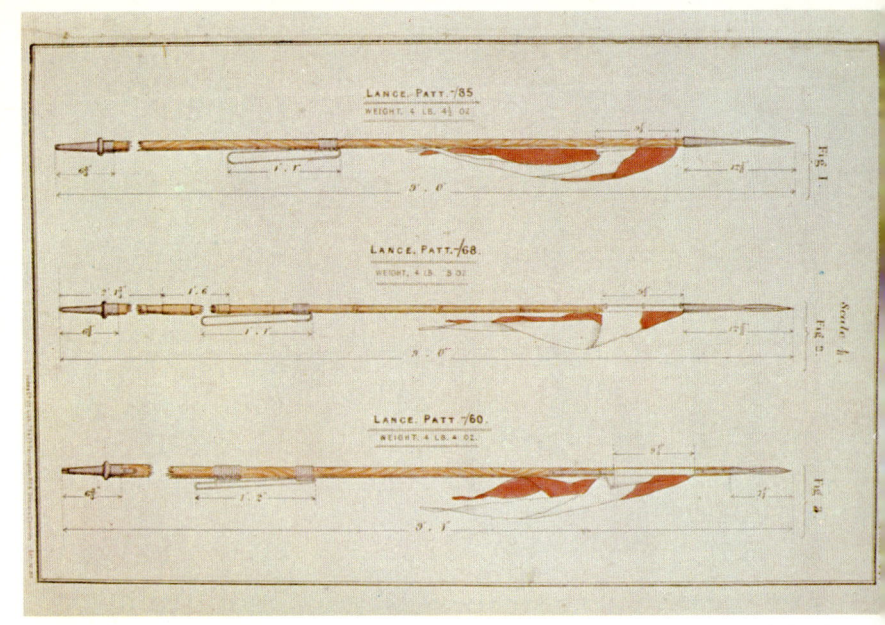

123. Lance

124. Halberd.   125. Partisan.

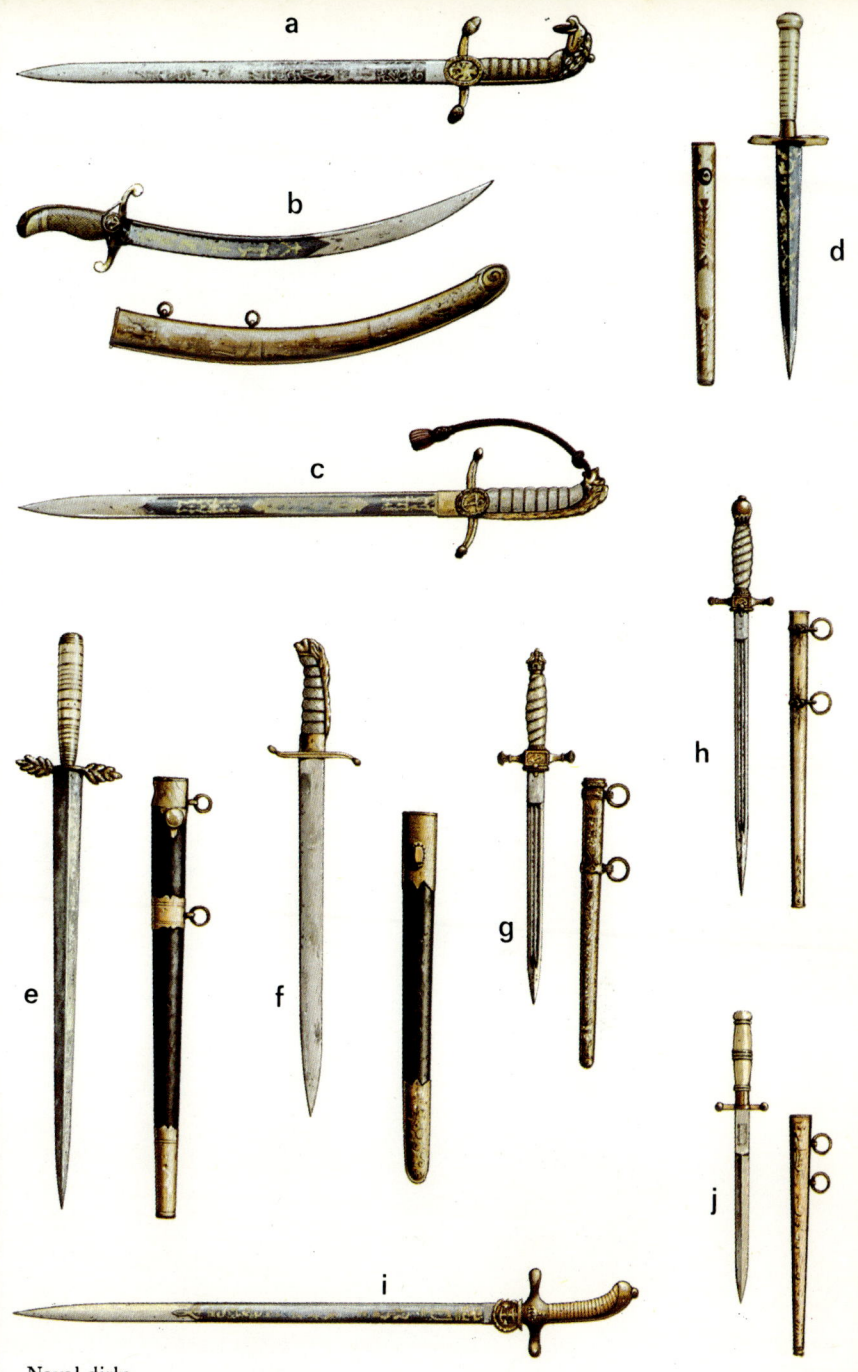

6. Naval dirks.

127. Kukr

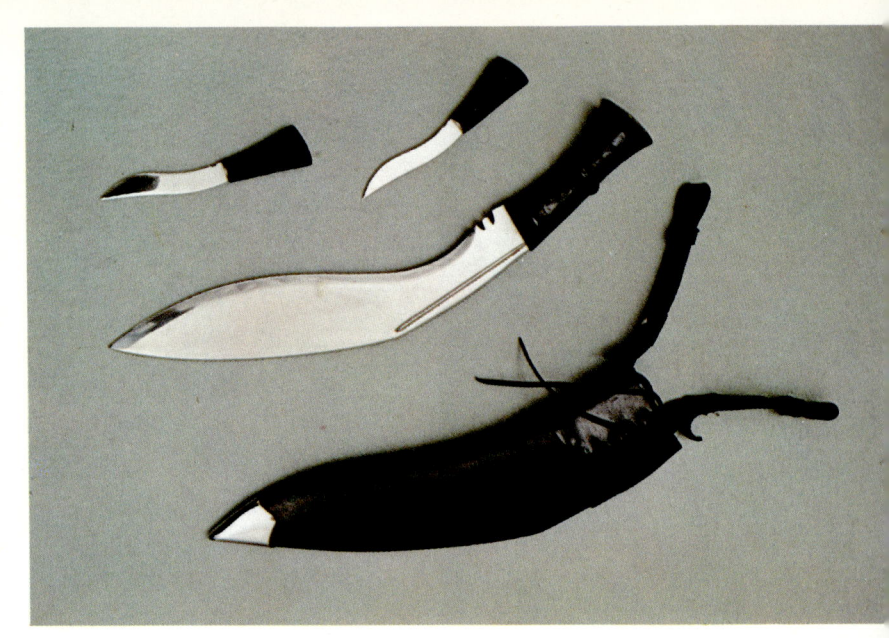

128. Commando kniv

129. Hunting knives and Bowie knives.

130. Bayonets. British.

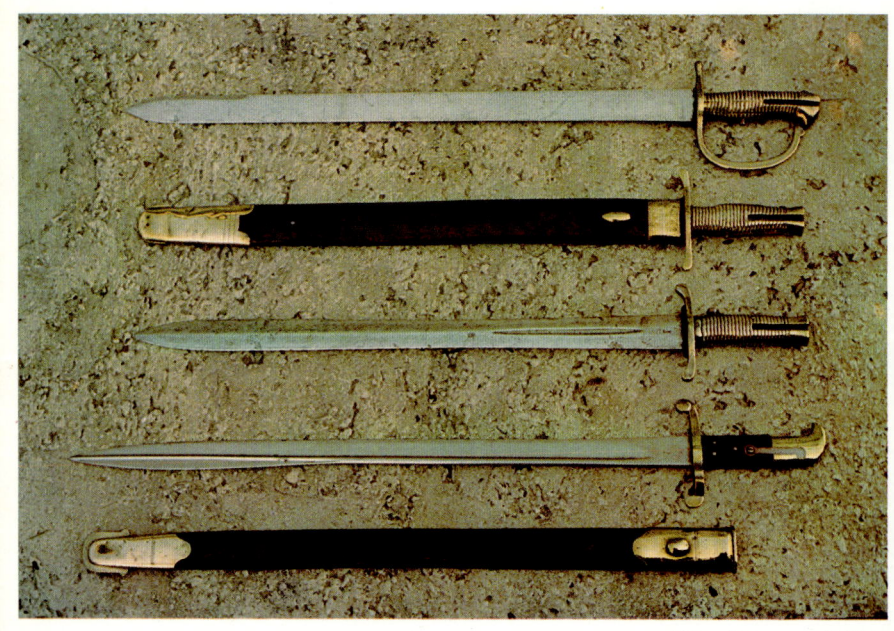

131. Bayonets. British.

132. Bayonets. British.

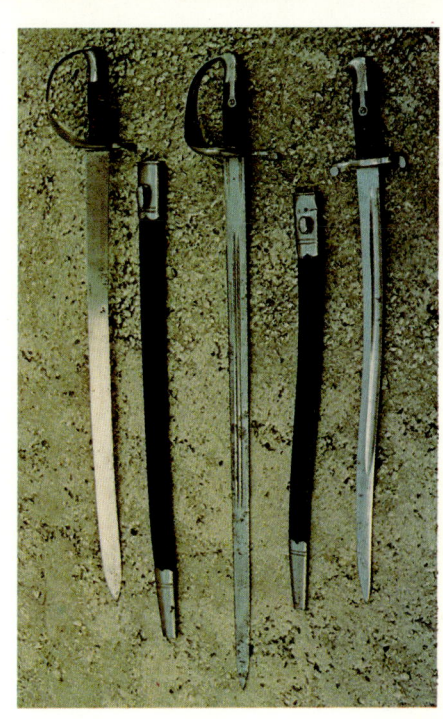

133. Bayonets. British.

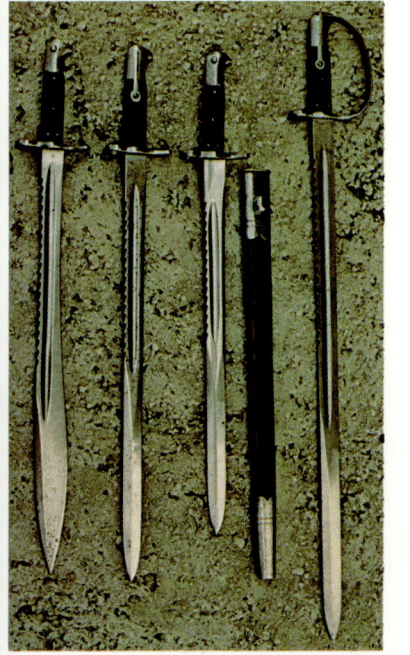

134. Bayonets. British.

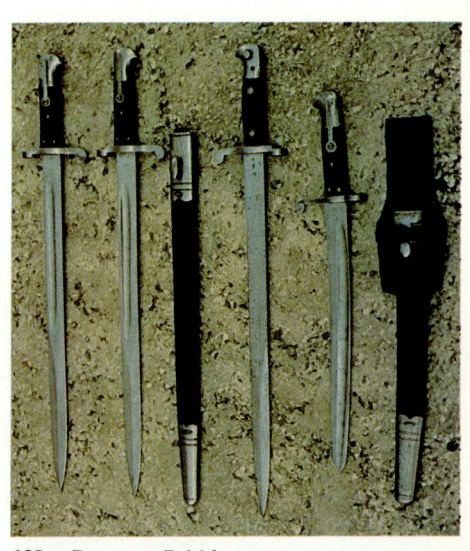

135. Bayonets. British.

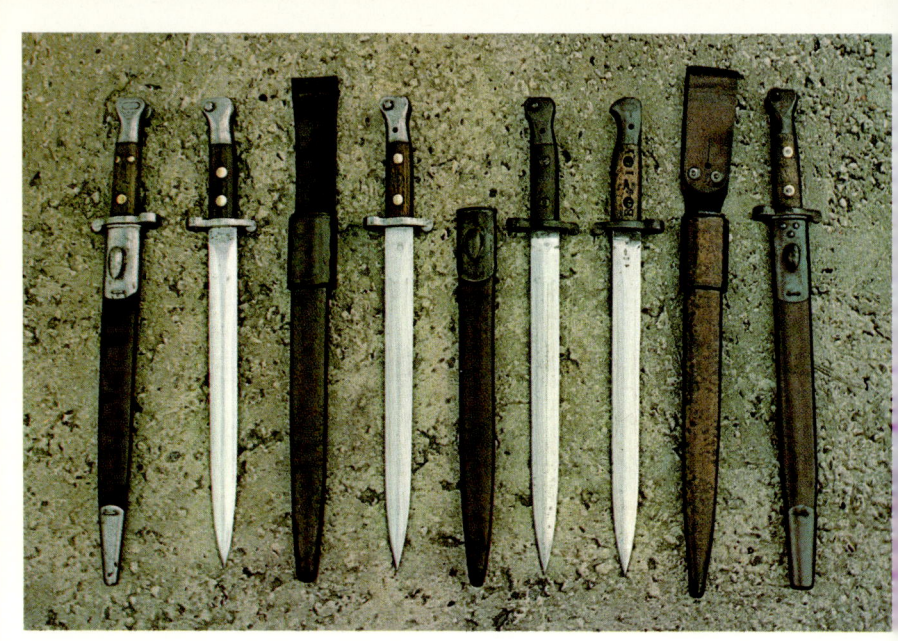

136. Bayonets. British.

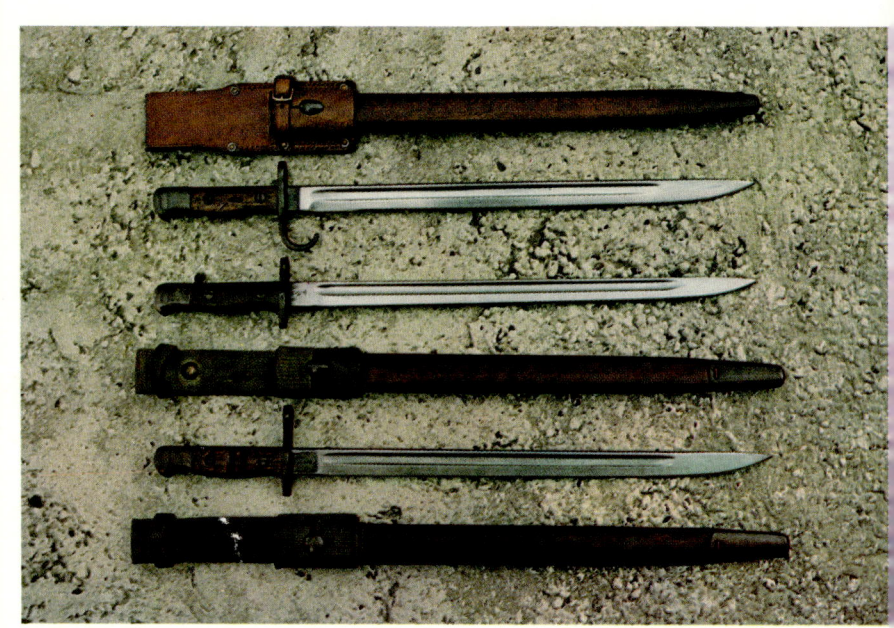

137. Bayonets. British.

138. Bayonets. Prussian and German.

139. Bayonets. German.

140. Bayonets. German.

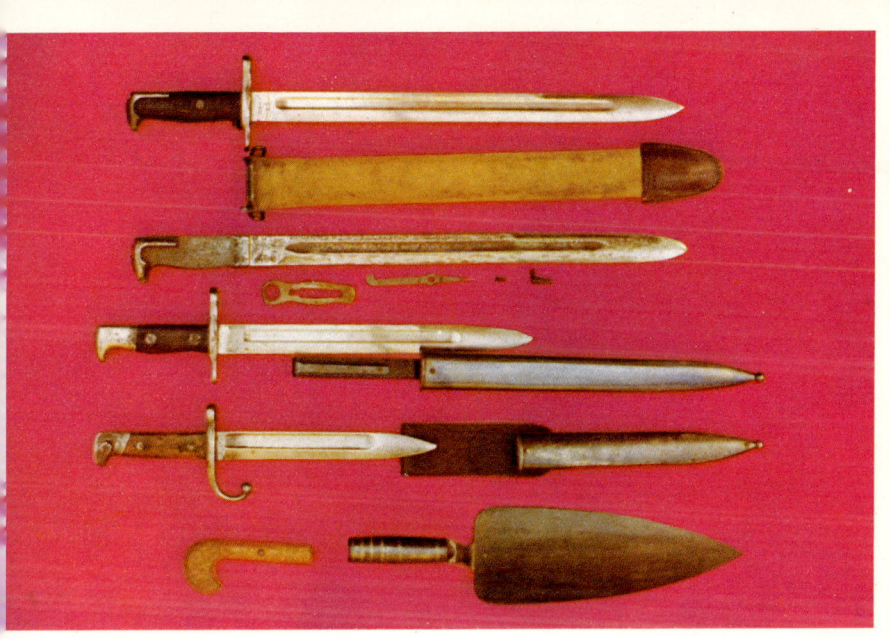

141. Bayonets. American.

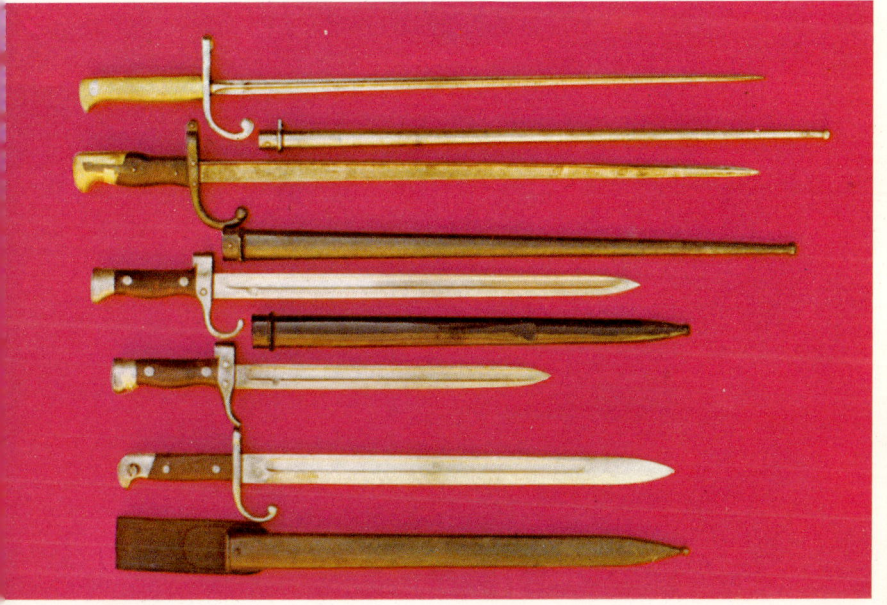

142. Bayonets. French.

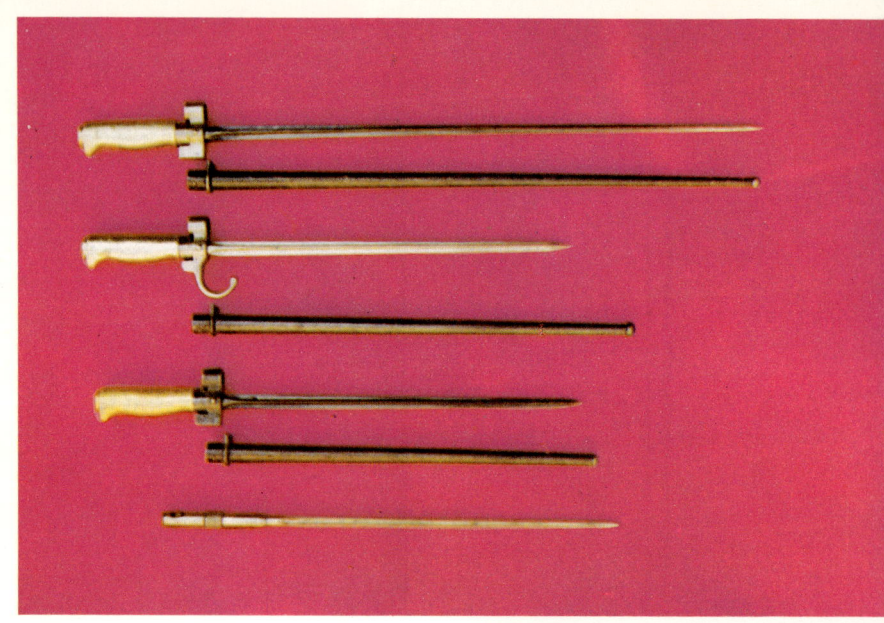

143. Bayonets. French.

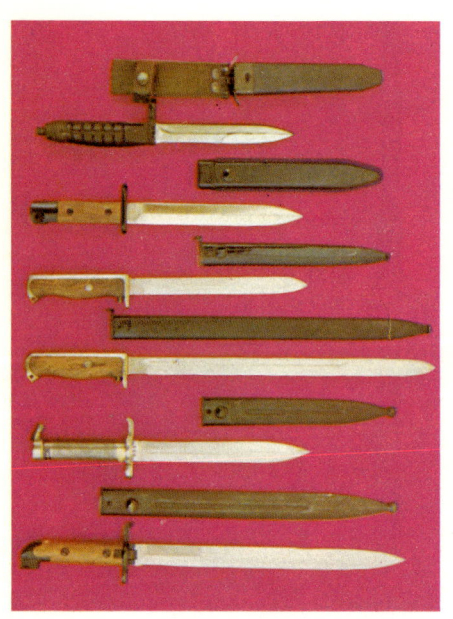

144. Bayonets. Scandinavian. 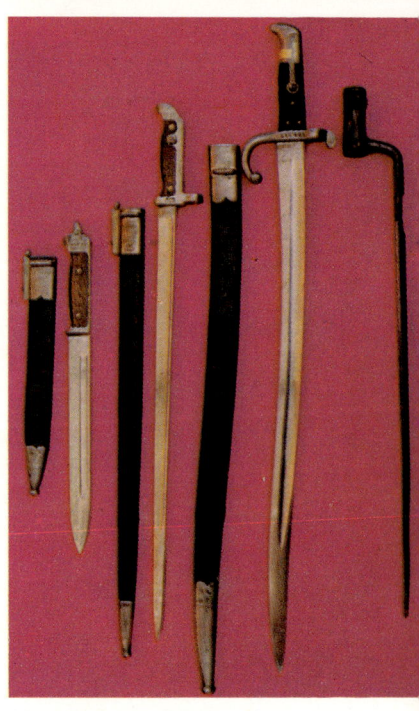   145. Bayonets. Scandinavian.

THE PLATE DESCRIPTIONS

Plate 1 – Bronze Age sword blades. Persian 2nd/3rd Millenium BC; 1200 BC; 1200–800 BC.

Plate 2 – Bronze Age dagger blades. Persian 900 BC; 2nd/3rd Millenium BC.

Plate 3 – Bronze Age spear heads. Persian *c.* 1500 BC.

Plate 4 – Bronze Age arrow heads.

Plate 5 – Roman *gladius,* reproduction made by Wilkinson Sword Ltd.

Plate 6 – Viking, Saxon, Medieval and late Medieval swords from ninth to fourteenth century.

Plate 7 – Two handed sword, German fifteenth century.

Plate 8 – Two handed sword, German early sixteenth century.

Plate 9 – Fencing. A print depicting left the 'Spanish guard' and right the 'Italian guard'.

Plate 10 – Daggers and knives. a) Swiss dagger with scabbard chased representing Holbein's 'Dance of Death' 1573. b) Flemish kidney or ballock dagger 1450–60. c) Italian *cinquedea* (the name deriving from 'five fingers', the width of the blade) *c.* 1490. d) Stiletto *c.* 1630. e) German triple bladed left hand dagger (main-gauche) *c.* 1600. f) Main-gauche dagger, companion to cup hilt rapier, Spanish first half seventeenth century. g) Main-gauche dagger, Spanish first half seventeenth century. h) Italian combined dagger and sword breaker *c.* 1600. i) Rondel dagger *c.* 1440–50. j) Italian left hand or main-gauche dagger with downpointing quillons late sixteenth early seventeenth century. k) German. Set of eviscerating instruments. *Trousse de Chasse* consisting of large knife and six smaller knives and instruments. *c.* 1732.

Plate 11 – Swept hilt rapiers. Left German *c.* 1590; right Flemish second quarter seventeenth century.

Plate 12 – Cup hilt rapiers. Left Spanish eighteenth century, centre Spanish *c.* 1660; right Spanish *c.* 1680.

Plate 13 – Italian swept hilt rapier with chiselled hilt *c.* 1580.

Plate 14 – German(?) so called 'Pappenheimer' rapier showing the combination of swept hilt with shell guard. *c.* 1620.

Plate 15 – Spanish cup hilt rapier with long quillons. Late seventeenth century.

Plate 16 – Small-swords. Seventeenth and eighteenth centuries with in centre a transitional small-sword without knuckle guard *c.* 1660.

Plate 17 – Small-swords. Eighteenth century showing hilts both in silver and steel.

Plate 18 – Italian transitional small-sword *c.* 1660.

Plate 19 – French gilt and russet hilt of a small-sword *c.* 1700.

Plate 20 – English. Pierced silver hilted small-sword *c.* 1750.

Plate 21 – English. Gilt hilt with steel facets and urn pommel small sword with faceted bead and chain knuckle guard. Late eighteenth century.

Plate 22 – English nineteenth century cut steel hilted small sword, with faceted knuckle guard, pommel, grip and shell.

Plate 23 – English. Gold, jewelled and enamelled small sword presented to Admiral Viscount Duncan by the City of London 1797.

Plate 24 – English. Gold hilted small sword presented by Nelson to Captain Cockburn 1796.

Plate 25 – English. Gold, jewelled and enamelled small sword presented to Admiral Lord St Vincent 1797.

Plate 26 – British. Gilt hilted small sword worn in full dress by officers of the Duke of Manchester's Light Horse *c.* 1870.

Plate 27 – British. Gilt hilted small sword worn by the Royal Company of Archer's, the Queen's Body Guard for Scotland.

Plate 28 – British. Basket hilted broadswords, cavalry and highland seventeenth and eighteenth century.

Plate 29 – British. Heavy Cavalry officer's sword 1788; Highland broadsword *c.* 1740; Horse Grenadier Guard's sword (2nd Troop) *c.* 1780.

Plate 30 – Basket hilted cavalry sword of the style used in many countries c. 1740.

Plate 31 - British. Hilt of Horse Grenadier Guard's Sword (2nd Troop) c. 1780.

Plate 32 - British. Hilt of Heavy Cavalry officer's sword 1788.

Plate 33 - British. Officer's sword Percy Tenentry Militia 1780; Infantry officer's sword 1796 pattern; Infantry officer's sword 1786 pattern.

Plate 34 - British. Mounted officer's sword 1796 pattern; Town or Walking sword (see plate 21 above); Mameluke hilted sabre, 15th Hussars c. 1790.

Plate 35 - British. Volunteer light cavalry sabre with very curved blade 1796. Note gilt mounts to scabbard and langet to guard.

Plate 36 - British. Presentation volunteer light cavalry sword with horse head pommel and backpiece. c. 1801.

Plate 37 - British. Hilt of Infantry mounted officer's sword 1796.

Plate 38 - British. Hilt of Infantry officer's sword pattern 1786.

Plate 39 - British. Royal Naval officer's sword with beads or 'five ball' guard 1795.

Plate 40 - British. Spadroon type hilt of the sword of the Percy Tenentry Militia 1780.

Plate 41 - Fencing. A print depicting left the 'Outside guard' and right the 'Inside guard'.

Plate 42 - Fencing. A print depicting left the 'Half circle guard' right 'St George's guard'.

Plate 43 - British. Hilt of the 15th Hussar sabre c. 1790.

Plate 44 - British. Hilt of the Infantry officer's sword 1796 pattern.

Plate 45 - British. Presentation version of the Infantry officer's sword pattern 1822; Heavy Cavalry officer's sword 1796 pattern; Presentation version of the Heavy Cavalry officer's sword 1796 pattern.

Plate 46 - British. Hilt of Heavy Cavalry officer's sword

1796 pattern.

Plate 47 – British. Inside of guard of Heavy Cavalry officer's sword pattern 1796 (plates 45 and 46) showing presentation engraving to the Groom of the Bedchamber of the Duke of Clarence 1815.

Plate 48 – British. Hilt of the presentation version of the 1822 Infantry officer's sword to the Duke of Wellington on becoming Commander-in-Chief 1838 with 'VR' in the cartouche, embossed bars to hilt and pipe backed blade.

Plate 49 – British. Drawing of the regimental pattern hilt of the broadsword of the 93rd Highlanders *c.* 1820.

Plate 50 – British. Infantry and Flank Company officer's sword pattern 1803. Grenadier Company officers had the grenade above the badge and Light Company officers a stringed bugle horn. Regimental variations are known with super imposed badge on the Royal cypher.

Plate 51 – British. Sword of the Yeoman Warder's *c.* 1820 with on the shell guard the 'Horse of Hanover'. The sword was later altered to have a crown pommel and had the Royal Crest on the shell after 1837.

Plate 52 – British. East India Company variation on the 1822 Infantry officer's sword with their arms in the cartouche and a lion head pommel and backpiece.

Plate 53 – British. Hilt of the 1822 Infantry officer's sword with the Wilkinson pattern blade of 1846 and the Wilkinson patent solid tang which had two side pieces wired to the tang rather than the thin tang passing through a hollowed out wood grip.

Plate 54 – British. Royal Engineers officer's sword 1856 pattern with gun metal hilt; Infantry officer's sword pattern 1822 with 1846 pattern blade; Guards officer's sword 1854 pattern.

Plate 55 – British. Hilt of the 1856 Royal Engineers officer's sword in gun metal. This pattern in steel was adopted in the same year by officers of Heavy Cavalry.

Plate 56 – British. Infantry officer's sword of 1822 with wide curved Wilkinson pattern blade; Heavy Cavalry officer's sword of 1856 with non regulation grip and pommel but incorporating a 'French' style cap pommel 1856; Light Cavalry officer's sword 1822 pattern made in 1860. All these swords show the indented brass proof mark introduced by Henry Wilkinson and John Latham, which was to be copied by other cutlers and retailers.

Plate 57 – British. Naval officer's sword.

Plate 58 – British. Naval officer's sword pattern 1829. Following closely the infantry pattern of 1822 this sword hilt did not have open work bars although a number of examples with open bars in the infantry fashion are known and are due to the misinterpretation of the specifications by cutlers.

Plate 59 – British. Cutlass *c.* 1800; Naval officer's sword pattern 1829 but with straight blade as ordered in 1926; Cutlass pattern 1889.

Plate 60 – British. Pattern drawing of special regimental pattern hilt for officer's sword of the 1856 pattern for the 6th Dragoon Guards approved in December 1877.

Plate 61 – British. Officer's swords of the Life Guards and Royal Horse Guards of the pattern adopted *c.* 1860.

Plate 62 – British. Field officer's sword with thistle hilt of certain Highland Regiments, *c.* 1860.

Plate 63 – British. Above. 1853 Cavalry trooper's sword universal issue; below 1864 Cavalry trooper's sword, with Maltese Cross pierced out in hilt.

Plate 64 – British. 1885 (below) and 1899 Cavalry trooper's sword. These examples are sealed patterns to guide manufacture.

Plate 65 – Irish Free State Army sword pattern 1922; British Infantry officer's sword 1897 pattern; Royal Artillery officer's sword 1822 pattern.

Plate 66 – British. City of London Marshal's sword; Lord Lieutenant's sword; Royal Fusiliers Band sword of special pattern with long blade presented to the regiment by the Duke of Kent *c.* 1820; Presentation scimitar; General's sword, Johore State.

Plate 67 – British. 1904 Experimental Cavalry trooper's sword; Heavy Cavalry officer's sword 1896 pattern; Cavalry trooper's sword 1908 pattern; Cavalry officer's sword 1912 pattern. The two last mentioned swords are considered the most perfect cavalry swords ever designed and although the 1908 pattern was disliked by Edward VII he nevertheless approved the design.

Plate 68 – British. 1908 cavalry trooper's sword and 1912 cavalry officer's sword with in the background 1868 pattern lances. Note the buff knot for the trooper's sword and the crimson and gold cord and acorn knot for the officer's sword. Some regiments had their own pattern of knot such as the Royal Scots Greys who substituted the thistle for the acorn and had the silk in green.

Plate 69 – British. Rifle pattern sword 1827 but with 1892 pattern blade; Scottish broadsword or as known in Regulations, the Claymore; Royal Air Force officer's sword pattern 1920.

Plate 70 – France. Top row left to right; Hussar officer late eighteenth century; Hussar officer Louis XVI; Infantry sword with shell guard with 'Montmorency' pattern blade late eighteenth century; Marechaussée infantry sword late eighteenth century; Light Cavalry sword, Restoration period; Honour sword given in AnX (1801/2) to Citizen Compagnon, Sergeant-Major of the *Gendarmerie d'Élite* for his conduct at the battle of Marengo. Before the creation of the Legion of Honour in 1802, only forty-four of these swords were awarded. Bottom row, left to right; Hussars officer with folding guard, 1st Empire; *Grenadier à Cheval* (Horse Grenadier)Imperial Guard, pattern AnIX (1800); Officer *Gendarmerie d'Élite* 1813–15; Light Cavalry AnXIII (1804–05) many of which were used by the Russians after large supplies were captured after 1812; Light Cavalry 1816; Light Cavalry 1822.

Plate 71 – France. Top row left to right; Mounted Artillery 1829; Heavy Cavalry AnXIII (1804–05); Heavy Cavalry 1822; *Gendarmerie départmentale,* superior officer 1830; Dress, junior officer *Gendarmerie* and Army 1855; *à l'antique* of a pupil of the *École de Mars* (Revolutionary military academy) which lasted for only 1794. Designed by the artist Jacques David it was in imitation of Roman *gladius*. Bottom row left to right; Light Cavalry officer with folding guard Louis XVI; Officers of the *État-Major* (General Staff) !st Empire, three variations; Sapper or pioneer !st Empire; Senior officer, Army 1845 (beneath) Foot Artillery sidearm 1816; Infantry officer 1821.

Plate 72 – German. Light cavalry officer's sword with blade inscribed *Für den Vater des Vaterlands* 1806–1813.

Plate 73 – German. Prussian cuirassier officer's sword 1819 pattern copied from the Russian pattern in use in 1808.

Plate 74 – German. Prussian infantry officer's sword pattern 1889 also carried by engineer officers. The guard has the crowned eagle and the grip has the badge of the monogram WR II with crown above.

Plate 75 – German. Infantry officer's sword pattern 1911. This closely follows the pattern of 1889 but has a hinged guard with the eagle.

Plate 76 – German. Cavalry officer's sword pattern 1889 carried in the Prussian Dragoon regiments in particular. Carried by sergeants and standard bearers who had passed the officer test in the 3rd, 4th and 5th Dragoons.

Plate 77 – German. Presentation infantry pattern 1911 made in 1916 by Weyersberg Kirschbaum of Solingen presented to General and Field Marshal Von Hindenburg on the occasion of his 50th year in military service.

Plate 78 – German. Reverse side of blade showing blue and gilt work.

Plate 79 – German. Hilt of 77 showing the fine workmanship and the gilt and enamel star beneath the Kaiser's monogram.

Plate 80 – German. Close up of the blade showing the presentation inscription and the fine etching and blue and gilt work.

Plate 81 – German. Imperial Naval officer's sword pattern 1889 with wire wound ivorine grip.

Plate 82 – German. Imperial Naval officer's sword pattern 1889. This variation has a more British style hilt and a fish skin covered grip.

Plate 83 – Russia. Top row left to right; Guard Cuirassier c. 1800; Dragoon c. 1800; Light Cavalry c. 1800; Dragoon 1806 pattern. Bottom row left to right; Cavalry 1809 pattern; Cuirassier 1809 pattern; Cavalry pattern 1826; Cossack *shashka* 1838 pattern.

Plate 84 – Russia. Top row left to right. Dragoon 1841 pattern; Officer's 'System of 1881'; Dragoon trooper 'System of 1881' with bayonet carried in scabbard; Cossack *shashka* 'System of 1881', this example with the badge of the Order of St Anne, fourth class was presented for bravery. Bottom row left to right. Infantry officer c. 1800; Infantry hanger c. 1800; Infantry 1826 pattern; Infantry 1865 pattern.

Plate 85 – Denmark. Top row left to right; Officer Heavy Cavalry 1780; Trooper Heavy Cavalry 1774; Dragoon 1785; Heavy Cavalry 1831. Bottom row left to right; Officer Horse Guard 1772; Universal issue cavalry trooper 1843; Hussar officer 1790.

Plate 86 – Denmark and Sweden. Top row left to right Denmark; Infantry private 1838; Infantry officer 1766; Naval officer 1849; Cutlass c. 1840; Sweden; Infantry private 1748. Bottom row left to right; Hussar 1759; Heavy Cavalry 1777; Infantry officer c. 1820; Infantry officer 1859; Universal issue cavalry 1854; Universal issue cavalry 1867.

Plate 87 – Danish Navy; Venezuela Navy; Burma Navy (old pattern); Danish Marine; Argentine Navy. All late nineteenth early twentieth century.

Plate 88 – Japanese Navy late nineteenth century; Argentine Naval dirk; British Naval dirk, presentation version; Navy cutlass. Abu Dhabi Navy. (Only six were made.)

Plate 89 – Argentine diplomatic; Venezuela Army; Burma Navy (new pattern 1962); Danish diplomatic.

Plate 90 – United States. Infantry officer 1790–1810; Cavalry c. 1785–1800 with blade marked 'American Light Horse'.

Plate 91 – United States. General and Staff officer 1832 pattern.

Plate 92 – Detail of hilt of 95.

Plate 93 – United States. Dragoon trooper 1840 pattern; Light Artillery other ranks 1840 pattern; Infantry officer 1850 pattern.

Plate 94 – Detail of hilt of Dragoon trooper 1840 pattern.

Plate 95 – United States. Cavalry troopers sword pattern 1913 (a); all Army officer's pattern 1902 (b); Cavalry officer pattern 1872 (c); derived from the British pattern of 1908 (see plate 67 and 68).

Plate 96 – United States. US Marine 'enlisted man' following the pattern of sword adopted by Infantry officers; Public Health officials' sword; US Marine officers' sword pattern 1825–59 and 1875 onwards.

Plate 97 – Detail of hilt of 99.

Plate 98 – Siam. Pattern drawing of cavalry sword hilt showing the arms in gilt and the guard in steel.

Plate 99 – China. Pattern drawing of the sword and belt buckle of the Chinese Maritime Customs supplied 10 November, 1871.

Plate 100 – Abyssinia. Types of sword blades supplied in the 1920s.

Plate 101 – Arab presentation scimitar and jambiya.

Plate 102 – Left to Right. Two patterns of Prussian and Germanic States; French pattern 1831; Swiss Infantry pattern 1842 and United States Foot Artillery pattern 1833.

Plate 103 – Top left to right; Spanish American war period; Spanish Artillery nco's pattern 1820; Spanish Artillery private's pattern 1902; Argentine Navy cutlass pattern 1890. Centre; Prussian infantry *c.* 1870. Bottom left to right; British 'Dundas' pattern for Artillery drivers; four patterns of Prussian and German last quarter of nineteenth century; British pioneer pattern 1856.

Plate 104 – Japan. Pattern drawings of sword approved in 1872.

Plate105 – Japan. Belt buckle of Naval sword showing device used in the cartouche of the hilt.

Plate 106 – British. Presentation swords made by the Patriotic Fund at Lloyds between 1803 and 1809. Top to bottom. £100 sword; £50 sword and £30 sword.

Plate 107 – Britain. Swords presented to Captain Sir Thomas Staines in 1809 and anovher presented to Captain E. H. Columbine in 1804.

Plate108 – Britain. Presentation sword given by the Honourable East India Company *c.* 1801.

Plate109 – Britain. One of the three types of swords presented by Edward Prince of Wales on his tour of India 1875–6. Only twenty were made of three different types, one of which is shown.

Plate 110 – Detail of the hilt of 109 showing the crest of the Prince of Wales surrounded by the collar of the Order of the Star of India.

Plate 111 – American Bi-Centenary swords 1976. Replica in silver of the sword carried by George Washington; American Independence sword 1976. (Courtesy U.S. Historical Society.)

Plate 112 – Miniature swords. Claymores.

Plate 113– – Miniature swords. Left, rapier. Right French cavalry.

Plate 114 – Miniature swords. Left, three bar light cavalry hilted sword. Right, Guards officer's sword.

Plate 115 – Miniature swords. Left, 1822 Light Cavalry sword. Right, Indian *tulwar.*

Plate 116 – Military style broadsword with decorative hilt and floral and thistle worked panels to guard belonging to the Chief of the Clan Grant.

Plate 117 – Military broadsword of the Breadalbane Fencibles and a dirk of the 100th Highland Regiment *c.* 1760.

Plate 118 – Various silver mounted military dirks post 1881 including at top a piper's dirk of the Cameronians, Scottish Rifles and at the bottom an officer's dirk of the Gordon Highlanders.

Plate 119 – Gold, enamelled and jewelled presentation small sword presented to Major-General Sir David Baird by the field officers under his command in recognition of his victory at

Seringapatam (May 1799) in which the Scots Brigade (94th) took part.

Plate 120 – Officers' dirks pre-1881. Top to bottom; 71st; 92nd; 72nd; 91st and 79th Highlanders.

Plate 121 – Military and civilian dirks eighteenth century.

Plate 122 – Staff Weapons. a) Bill, English sixteenth century. b) Glaive, Venetian *c.* 1620. c) Boer spear sixteenth century. d) Partisan, *c.* 1700. One of the set of the Guard of Augustus II Elector of Saxony and King of Poland. e) Partisan, French *č.* 1660–70. The two escutcheons bear the arms of France and Navarre surrounded by the collar of the Order of St Michel. f) Halberd of the type carried in Britain by Infantry sergeants *c.* 1750–1792. g) Corsèque, Italian early sixteenth century. h) Gisarme, thirteenth century. i) Lochaber axe Scottish seventeenth and eighteenth century. j) Halberd, Italian *c.* 1550–1600. k) Bardiche, Eastern Europe, sixteenth and seventeenth centuries.

Plate 123 – Britain. Lances, top to bottom, 1885 pattern; 1868 pattern; 1860 pattern.

Plate 124 – Britain. Halberd of the Honourable Corps of Gentlemen-at-Arms.

Plate 125 – Britain. Partisan of the Yeomen of the Guard.

Plate 126 – Naval dirks. a) Mexico, *c.* 1910. b) Britain. Presentation curved dirk, *c.* 1805. c) Britain. Cadets dirk pattern 1879. d) Britain. Small straight bladed dirk *c.* 1800. f) Britain. First regulation pattern of dirk introduced in 1856. g) German. Imperial German naval dirk 1871–1918. h) German. Naval dirk 1929–38. i) German. Sidearm used by Midshipmen 1872–90 and Engineer cadets 1890–1918. j) Denmark. The same style with embossed scabbard was copied by the Greek Navy.

Plate 127 – Britain and Nepal. Regulation military *kukri* carried by Gurkha regiments. Note the two small companion implements.

Plate 128 – Britain. Commando knives. Designed by Captains Fairbairn and Sykes in 1940; they were first known as the 'FS' fighting knife. The name was later dropped. Various types and designs of knife are found with differing grips and blades. Various patterns of scabbards are also to be found.

Plate 129 – Hunting knives. Top row left to right. Wolstenholm Bowie knife engraved 'Death to Abolition' American Civil War period; I*XL Bowie knife with German silver hilt and pearl grips *c*. 1850; I*XL Bowie knife with staghorn grip marked on the plate on the grip with the name of the a surgeon who fought for the Union 1861; Very fine example of a Bowie knife with spear pointed blade, German silver hilt and tortoise shell grips, inlaid with mother-of-pearl. Bottom row, left to right. The famous 'California knife' with pearl grips and German silver hilt; Knife designed by Alfred Stevens for Wolstenholm who displayed it at the Great Exhibition 1851; Bowie knife with solid staghorn grip with the 'General Taylor' stamp on the *ricasso.* Bottom. Shakespeare knife manufactured by Wilkinson's and designed by Col. Shakespeare of the Indian Army *c*. 1890.

Plate 130 – Bayonets. British, top Martini-Enfield 1895; left to right; socket bayonets Martini-Henry 1876; Constabulary 1840; Enfield 1853; East India Company version with spring; Lovells spring; Hanoverian catch 1839; East India Company version; Elliot carbine; Land pattern.

Plate 131 – Bayonets. British top to bottom; Baker 1801; Brunswick 1837; Brunswick 1848; Lancaster 1855.

Plate 132 – Bayonets. British, left to right; Enfield 1856/58 bushed for Martini-Henry; Whitworth 1863 with round hole in pommel not usual rectangular one; Enfield 1858; Enfield 1856/58 in steel scabbard as used by the Garrison Artillery and Artillery drivers; Enfield 1865; Enfield 1853 with brass grips for Artillery. The brass grip was soon replaced by that of the other sword bayonets shown.

Plate 133 – Bayonets. British, left to right; Enfield Cutlass bayonet 1859; Jacobs Rifle bayonet 1856; Volunteer pattern sword bayonet *c*. 1860.

Plate 134 – Bayonets. British, left to right; Elcho 1871; Artillery 1875 with saw-back; Irish Constabulary; Artillery 1879.

Plate 135 – Bayonets. British, left to right; Martini-Henry bayonets 1887 Mk 1; 1887 Mk IV; 1887 Mk III; 1856/58 shortened *c.* 1900 for Drill purpose.

Plate 136 – Bayonets. British, left to right; Lee-Metford and Lee Enfield, 1888 Mk I (first version); 1888 MkI (second version); 1888 Mk II; 1888 Mk III; SMLE 1903; 1888 commercial type.

Plate 137 – Bayonets. British, top to bottom; SMLE 1907 with Mk 1 scabbard; 1907 with quillon removed (1916) with Mk II scabbard; P. 13.

Plate 138 – Bayonets. Prussian and German, left to right; Seitengewehr 1871 with brass grips, Mauser rifle; Seitengewehr 1898 with saw back for nco's; Seitengewehr 1898 for 1898 Mauser; Seitengewehr 1898/05 with saw-back; Seitengewehr 1898/05; Seitengewehr 1914 with second type pommel.

Plate 139 – Bayonets. German *Ersatz* types, left to right; 1888/98 all steel hilt; 1888/98 with grooved and shaped hilt; 1888/98 with 'Butcher' bayonet blade with saw back; 1888/98 'Butcher' blade; 1888/98 with shaped flat grips of pressed steel; 1888/98 with cast steel hilt and shaped grips.

Plate 140 – Bayonets. German, left to right; Seitengewehr 1871/84; Seitengewehr 1884/98; Kurzes Seitengewehr with saw back 1898; As previous but with black leather grips; Seitengewehr 1914 with saw back; Seitengewehr 1884/98; Seitengewhr 1884/98 2nd pattern; Trench knife bayonet World War I; Kurzes Seitengewehr 1898 type with leather grips and plated blade and hilt; Trench knife with leather grips shortened from bayonet described previously.

Plate 141 – Bayonets. United States, top to bottom; Springfield 1905; Springfield 1905 dismounted to show parts; Krag Jorgensen 1892; Remington short bayonet 1902; 1873 'Rice' (after Col E. Rice the initiator of the idea) or trowel bayonet, shown with the additional wood grip for use when not fitted to the rifle.

Plate 142 – Bayonets. French, top to bottom; Experimental Daudeteau (Navy) 1895; Gras 1874; Berthier carbine 1892; Berthier carbine 1892 with shortened blade and quillon;

Remington supplied to France during World War I.

Plate 143 – Bayonets. French, top to bottom; Lebel 1886/98/16 (quillon removed in that year): Lebel 1886 with shortened blade; Lebel 1886 with shortened blade and quillon removed; MAS 1936 'ramrod' type bayonet.

Plate 144 – Bayonets. Scandinavia, top to bottom; Sweden, AK4 1965; Denmark, Madsen 1947; Norway, Krag Jørgensen 1894; Krag Jørgensen 1914; Sweden Pattern 1896 for Mauser; Pattern 1914 for 1894/14 Mauser.

Plate 145 – Bayonets. Scandinavia, left to right; Denmark, Krag Jørgensen 1889/98; Krag Jørgensen 1915; Remington 1867; Prussian made socket bayonet 1848 with Khyl's locking spring.

The Principle Edged Weapon Collections outside Great Britain

Austria: Heeresgeschtliches Museum, 1030 Wien, Arsenal, Obj. 1.

Belgium: Musée Royal de L'Armée et d'Histoire Militaire, Pac du Cinquantenaire 3, B-1040 Brussels.
Canada: Royal Ordnance Museum, Toronto.
Denmark: Tøjhusmuseet, 1220 København K, Frederiksholms Kanal 29.
France: Musée de l'Armée, Hotel National des Invalides, Paris. Musée de l'Emperi, Château de l'Emperi, 13- Salon-de-Provence.
Germany: Deutches Klingenmuseum Solingen, 565, Solingen, Grafrath.
Holland: Het Nederlands Leger-en Wapenmuseum 'General Hoefer', Leiden.
Italy: Armeria Reale, Turin.
Norway: Haermuseet, Akershus, Oslo mil, Oslo 1.
Poland: Polish Army Museum, Warsaw.
Museum Nardowe Krakowie, Cracow.
Russia: State Hermitage, Leningrad.
State Historical Museum, Moscow.
Kremlin Armoury.
Spain: Reale Armeria, Madrid.
Museo del Ejercito, Calle Mendez Nunez, 1, Madrid 14.
Museo Naval, Calle Montalban, 2. Madrid 14.
Sweden: Kungl, Armemusaum, S-103 82 Stockholm 7.
United States: Smithsonian Institution, Division of Military History, Washington D.C. 20560.
West Point Museum, US Military Academy, West Point, New York 10996.

The Principle Edged Weapon Collections in Great Britain

London

National Army Museum, Royal Hospital Road, London S.W.3. 4HT.
National Maritime Museum, London S.E.10 9 NF.
HM Tower of London, London E.C.3.
Victoria and Albert Museum, South Kensington, London S.W.7. 2RL.
Wallace Collection, Manchester Square, London W.I.M. 6BN.

Outside London

The Pattern Room, Royal Small Arms Factory, Enfield Lock, Enfield, Middlesex.
Royal Scottish Museum, Edinburgh.
Royal Scottish United Services Museum, Crown Square, The Castle, Edinburgh E.H.1. 2NG.

There are usually a number of military weapons to be found in regimental museums and other types of edged weapons in local museums, but the above mentioned are those with some selection of the various items discussed in this book.

Index

Note: Numbers thus 3=text references; *3*=figure references in text; (3)=colour plate numbers.

Abyssinia, 128, (100).
African weapons, 139.
Argentine. Bayonets, 127.
  Military and naval swords, 70, (87, 88, 89).
Arrows, 10, 11, *12,* (4).
Assyrian swords, 14.
Austria. Bayonets, 112, 113, 114.
  Military and naval swords,
    heavy cavalry, 42.
    infantry officer, 43.
    light cavalry, 42, 43.
    navy and cutlass, 43, 44.
    universal cavalry, 42, 43, 44.

Barong, 128.
Bayonets, general.
  See under country.
Belgium. Bayonets, 110.
  Military and naval swords,
    heavy cavalry, 37.
    infantry private, 38.
    infantry officer, 38.
    light cavalry, 37, 38.
    navy, 38.
Bowie knife, 96–98, (132).
Brazil. Military and naval swords, 70.
Britain. Bayonets, 102–4, 108, (130–137).
  Military and naval swords,
    heavy cavalry, 26, 27, 28, 29, *50,* (29, 32, 45, 46, 47, 60).
    infantry private, 29.
    infantry officer, 29, 30, *50,* (33, 34, 38, 44, 45, 48, 50, 53, 54, 55).
    light cavalry, 27, 29, (35, 56).
    universal troopers, 27, 28. (63, 64, 67, 68).
    Royal Navy, 31, (39, 57, 58, 59).
    cutlass, 32, (59).
    Royal Air Force, 32, 33.
Broadsword, Scottish, 72, 73, 75, 76, (49, 116, 117).
Bronze weapons, 10, 11, 12, (1, 2, 3, 4).
  Manufacture of, 12, 13.

Canada. Bayonets, 125, 126.
Cavalry swords. See under country.
Chile. Military and naval swords, 70.
China. Bayonets, 117, 118.
  Maritime Customs, 51, 52, (99).
  Military and naval swords, 51.
Claymore. See also Broadsword.
Colichemarde blade, 22, 23.
Commando knife, 97, (128).
Cuba. Military and naval swords. 70.

Denmark. Bayonets, 118, 119, (144, 145).
  Military and naval swords, (85, 86, 87, 89).

dragoons, 55, 57.
guard cavalry, 56, 58.
heavy cavalry, 54, 55, 56.
hussars and light cavalry, 56, 57, 58.
infantry private, 58, 59.
infantry officer, 59, 60.
navy, 60, 61, 62, 63.
universal cavalry, 56, 58.
Dha, 129.
Dirk, Scottish, 73–82, (118, 120, 121).
naval, various countries, 89–96.
Double handed swords, 18, (7, 8).

Egyptian swords, 12, 13.

Falchion, 18.
Fencing, the art of, 20, (9, 41, 42).
Fighting knives, 98,(128).
Firangi, 132.
Flamberge, 22.
Flint weapons, 10, *13, 14*.
France. Bayonets, 105–107, (142, 143).
Military and naval swords, (70, 71).
artillery, 34.
heavy cavalry, 33, 34, 35.
imperial and royal guards, 35.
infantry private, 35.
infantry officer, 36.
light cavalry, 34, 35.
navy, 37, *50*.

German influence over design, 26.
Germany. See under Prussia.
Gisarme, 83.
Glaive, 83, (122).
Greek swords, 14.
Guard, development of, 18, 20.
Guatemala. Military and naval swords, 71.

Halberd, 84, (122, 124).
Hand and a half swords, 18.
Hanger, 25, 29, 35, 38, 40, 58, 63, 68, (102, 103).
Holland. Bayonets, 108–109.
Military and naval swords, 38, 39.
Hunting swords, 21, *21,* 22.

India. Bayonets, 117.
Military swords, 53, 54, (52).
Iron age weapons, 14, 15.

Jambiya, 132, *133,* (101).
Japan, Bayonets, 116, 117.
Military and naval swords, 52, 53, (104, 105).
Traditional swords, 129–132.

Kard, 133, *138*.
Khouttar or Katar, 134, *138*.
Kindjahl, 134, *133, 138*.
Kris, 137, *133*.
Kukri, 135, (127).
Kyber knife, 136.

Lance, 84–86, (123).
Linstock, 86.
Lochabar Axe, 87.

Maine gauche, 20, 21, (10).
Makers' marks, *140, 141*.
Mandau, 136.
Mexico, Military and naval swords, 71.
Mortuary sword, 25.

Norway, Bayonets, 121, 122, (144).
Military and naval swords, 64.

Partisan, 29, 87, (122, 125).
Pata, 136, 137.
Pesh Kabz, 137.
Pike, 25, 87.

Poleaxe, 88.
Prussia, Bayonets, (138–140), 109–112.
   Military and naval swords, (72–82).
      heavy cavalry, 39.
      infantry, 40, 41.
      navy, 41, 42, *50*.
      universal cavalry, 40.
      uhlan, 40.

Ranseur, 88.
Rapier, 20–22, (11–15).
Roman swords, 15, 16, (5).
Russia. Bayonets, 114, 115.
   Military and naval swords, (83, 84).
      Asiatic, 46, 47, 48.
      cavalry, 45–49.
      infantry, 48.
      navy, 49, *50*.
      system 1881, 47, 48, 49.

Saxon swords, 16, 17, (6).
Schiavona, *19*, 25, 26.
Scramasax, 16.
Shamshir, 137.
Siam. Bayonets, 116.
   Military and naval swords, (98), 49–51.
Small swords, 22–24, (16–27).
Spontoon, 29, 88.
Stone Age blades, 10, *12*.
Sudan, 137, 138.

Supply of military swords, 26, 27.
Sweden. Bayonets, 119–121, (144).
   Military and naval swords, (86).
      cavalry, 63.
      infantry, 63, 64.
      navy, 64.

Town sword. See Small sword.
Trench knife, 98.
Tuck, 20.
Tulwar, 138, 139.

United States. Bayonets, (41), 122–125.
   Military and naval swords, (90–97).
      cavalry, 65, 66.
      coast guard, 69.
      general officer, 68.
      infantry officer, 68.
      light artillery, 67.
      Marine corps, 69, 70.
      navy, 69.
      revenue service, 69.
      universal army, 68, 69.
      universal cavalry, 67, 69.

Venezuela. Military and naval swords, 71, (87, 89).
Viking swords, 17, (6).

Walking sword. See Small sword.